100 THINGS
LONGHORNS FANS
SHOULD KNOW & DO
BEFORE THEY DIE

Jenna Hays McEachern

TRIUMPH
B O O K S

The Library of Congress has catalogued the previous edition as follows:

Library of Congress Cataloging-in-Publication Data

McEachern, Jenna.
100 things Longhorns fans should know & do before they die / Jenna McEachern.
p. cm.
Includes bibliographical references.
ISBN-13: 978-1-60078-108-7
ISBN-10: 1-60078-108-X
1. Texas Longhorns (Football team) 2. University of Texas at Austin—Football.
3. Football fans—Texas. I. Title. II. Title: One hundred things Longhorns fans should know & do before they die.
GV958.T45U656 2008
796.332'630976431—dc22

2008018873

This book is available in quantity at special discounts for your group or organization. For further information, contact:
Triumph Books LLC
814 North Franklin Street
Chicago, Illinois 60610
(312) 337-0747
www.triumphbooks.com

Printed in U.S.A.
ISBN: 978-1-60078-978-6
Design by Patricia Frey
Photos courtesy of The University of Texas Center for American History, Getty Images, AP Images, and Texas Sports Photography unless otherwise indicated.

To Mother and Daddy, whose integrity and wisdom and love forged the indestructible ties that bind our family together. And to ole No. 6, who embodies the best of what a Longhorn should be.

Contents

Introduction

Before you read this book, be warned: the author is biased. This is not just another book about Longhorn football. It *is* a book of facts and trivia about the Longhorns, yes, but it was written for Longhorns by a Longhorn fan—an unabashedly proud Longhorn who believes that The University of Texas is the finest institution in existence. It is a compilation of facts and lore that I believe supports our claim to be a "University of the first class…the brightest jewel of our greatness as a people and a state." So, if you're an Aggie or a Sooner or an anything-but-a-Longhorn, close the book now, place it back on the shelf, and step away from the bookcase.

As I glance at the bookshelf in my den, I see more than 25 books written about Texas football, in different formats but filled with the same information. The history of Longhorn football has been written and written again by authors more knowledgeable and more skilled than I am; therefore, it is my hope that this book will be a little different. *100 Things Longhorns Fans Should Know & Do Before They Die* isn't a comprehensive history. It isn't heavy on stats or records or play-by-play, yet I hope it contains some facts and stories that perhaps you haven't heard.

While I have attempted to make this book statistically and factually accurate, it is also full of the attitude that Longhorn wannabes like to call "arrogance." Seems Texans—and Longhorns—are as famous for their hubris as they are for their football. Not long ago, a friend from Oklahoma, a gracious Sooner fan, said to me, "It baffles me. I've never seen people so over the top about their state. You Texans have the attitude that no other place even exists." I blushed a bit, or at least I hope that I did, as I said, "I know, I know. But what you mistake for brashness is actually compassion… we just feel a little sorry for folks who weren't born here and who didn't go to The University."

From 1997 through 2004, The University launched a capital campaign that raised $1.63 billion—the most successful campaign at the time for a university without a medical school. To promote the campaign, Texas made a series of videos narrated by the late legendary journalist Walter Cronkite, who attended UT. Each video bragged on some aspect of The University and ended with Cronkite saying in that famous baritone voice, "We're Texas."

That stuck in some folks' craws. So what did UT do next? It followed up with nine new spots, also narrated by Cronkite, which proclaimed, "What Starts Here Changes the World." Yep. We do think rather highly of ourselves. But you know what they say…it ain't bragging if it's true.

Football in the state of Texas and in the Longhorn nation is huge; some claim it's a religion. I don't know about that, but no rational engaged couple would dream of setting a wedding date without first checking UT home football dates. Funeral services are scheduled so as not to conflict with a game.

Ricky Williams, UT's second Heisman Trophy winner and a native Californian, said, "If you want to surf, move to Hawaii. If you like to shop, move to New York. If you like acting and Hollywood, move to California. But if you like college football, move to Texas."

Just like the state itself, just like the Longhorn steer that serves as its mascot, Texas football is big and it's bold, and its proud tradition is a tradition of winning. The University of Texas football team is the second-winningest Division I team in the nation, and that other school has been playing the game longer than Texas has.

Yet as much as I love Texas and believe in its superiority in all things, it's hard to embrace all the changes that have taken place in recent years. I believe UT should represent the best of our state. And when The University does something foolish or beneath its dignity, I'm the first to mention it…but only to family. And since we're all family here….

The football games are almost unrecognizable now. The atmosphere has become a spectacle so distracting, the game itself is almost an afterthought, with 50 cheerleaders, a pom squad dressed in leather chaps and little else, players entering the field in a cloud of smoke, silly digital crowd-participation games on the Godzillatron, and advertisements blaring over the public address system at every resetting of the chains…it's just unseemly.

Back in the good old days—meaning, of course, the days when I roamed the 40 Acres—schools that contrived such a carnival atmosphere at their games seemed desperate for attention, while we, the Longhorns, got attention simply by killing whatever crossed our paths. We were The *by-gosh* University of Texas and we didn't need all that silliness.

Mike Baab, a former Longhorn letterman who played 11 years in the NFL, said in *What It Means to be a Longhorn*, "Back then, Texas was nothing like it is now. Today it's a showplace. It was not like that when we went to school. You were not induced to come to The University by the great facilities; you went to Texas because you wanted to go to Texas. If a little boy could go to Texas, he did…."

So maybe what I've attempted to write is, after all, a history—of the irreplaceable, extraordinary folks who made this program uniquely great, of beloved traditions shoved aside to make room for new ways to attract recruits and new ways to raise money—a history for anyone new to Longhorn football so they might know not just the glitz and the unrivaled facilities of today, but that they might understand and embrace the foundation of our pride.

Today, our facilities and our athletics budget and our income are unmatched in college football. Unlike in years past, Longhorn fans finally think it's cool to show some spirit, and tailgating before games is at an all-time high. Burnt-orange attire has caught on, replacing the fans' former choice of oh-so-sophisticated white. Tens of thousands of fans attend the annual spring game and UT ranks first in merchandise sales among schools in the Collegiate Licensing Company. We have our own television network, by golly. It was and it is great to be a Longhorn.

Trying to extract only 100 things about this illustrious football program was difficult and perplexing. Its history is rich and deep, and limiting the list to 100 things was nigh impossible. I'm sure each Longhorn fan will disagree with some of my choices and will be disappointed at my omissions. I hope I haven't offended; it was great fun researching and writing this celebration of Longhorn football. It is my hope that you will enjoy coming up with your own list of *100 Things Longhorns Fans Should Know & Do Before They Die.*

Hook 'em, Horns,
Jenna Hays McEachern

Acknowledgments

This book was my first solo effort. I had been an editor for many years, but I made an important discovery while writing this book: it's much easier to criticize another's work than it is to create one's own. I am indebted to so many who made this effort easier through their technical support, emotional underpinning, encouragement, and solace.

My deepest gratitude goes to the Longhorn football players who built this great program, who embraced and grew to love the tradition of excellence begun by that very first ball club in 1893.

Were it not for Bill Little, my longtime friend and former pushover boss, I never would have had the opportunity to write this book. He has trusted my abilities far more than I have and has included me in many of his writing projects. But mostly, he's just my loyal friend who knows more about Longhorn sports than any human being alive.

My acquisitions editor, Tom Bast, was such fun to work with and I thank him for his patience and for not demanding the advance back when I missed almost each deadline he'd set.

John Foxworth at Texas Student Publications, Rayda Porter at the Austin Public Library, and Ralph Elder and Mary Ellen Oliver at the Center for American History helped me navigate the maze of identifying and choosing photographs for the book. Joy Lawrence at Texas Sports Photography deserves a big raise for all the "above and beyond" work she did for me. Thanks to Rick Henson and Paul Waits for sharing their wonderful photos.

Tudey Teten, Sibyl Jackson, Gilberto Ocanas, Eleese Lester, Gretchen Evans, Lenora Doerfler, and Laura Kelly have been cheerleaders extraordinaire and have each, in his or her own way, pushed, wheedled, flattered, or shamed me into writing. Britt

Brookshire Buchanan, dear friend and neighbor, served as reader and "suggester."

My brothers, Jack Hays and Jeff Hays, kept me laughing, kept me encouraged, and gave thoughtful suggestions and surprisingly gentle criticism. They are the smartest, wittiest, most loyal friends God ever gave a girl. If I were on a game show, I'd choose them to be my lifelines. The rest of the Hays Mafia did what they do best, encircling me with their confidence and concern and the conviction that I could, indeed, do this thing.

The only thing I wanted more than being a Longhorn cheerleader was to be a mom, and I hit the jackpot with three children of humor and character and pure hearts in Bailey and Hays McEachern and Lester Simmons. My life is enriched by their love.

When I snagged Randy McEachern, I way overmarried. This guy, particularly during the writing of this book, has overlooked more, forgiven more, provided more, loved more, laughed more, and made me laugh more than I have deserved.

And, of course, I thank the Father for saving a wretch like me.

1 Legislated to Be Great

The University of Texas was legislated to be great.

As any Texan worth his Charlie Dunn boots will tell you, Texas is the only state in this country that was ever its own sovereign nation. And when the Texians drafted their Declaration of Independence from Mexico on March 2, 1836, high on their list of grievances was the failure of the Mexican government to "… establish any public system of education.…"

After Texas won its independence, education was a top priority to the founders of the Republic…or so they said, again and again, yet it took Texas 44 years before they managed to open The University of Texas.

In 1838, President of the Republic Mirabeau Lamar urged Congress to establish a system of education, saying, "Cultivated mind is the guardian genius of democracy," a quote The University later borrowed for its motto. The 1839 Congress of the Republic set aside 50 leagues of land to be used for a university and another public college.

Then, in a foreshadowing of the habits of future Texas legislators, nothing happened. For 29 more years.

After Texas became a state in 1845, the legislature allocated more land—some for railroads—and $100,000 in bonds, but with Texas' entry into the Civil War, those plans were shelved and the funds were spent.

The Constitution of 1866 ordered the rapid establishment of a university. Evidently, "rapid" had a different meaning in the 19th century.

TRIVIA
Question

What does Earl Campbell have in common with Davy Crockett, hero of the Texas Revolution and of the Alamo, Stephen F. Austin, colonizer and father of Texas, and Sam Houston, hero of the Battle of San Jacinto, president of the Republic of Texas, and governor of the State of Texas?

Trivia answers on page 255.

Finally, the Constitution of 1876, under which the state of Texas still operates, directed the Legislature to "establish...and provide for the maintenance, support, and direction of *a University of the first class...styled 'The University of Texas.'*"

All true orange-bloods have committed that phrase to memory and taken it to heart.

This Constitution gave Texas an additional million acres of public land for the endowment and support of The University. It also made the Agricultural and Mechanical College, established in 1871, a branch of The University of Texas. Most Longhorns have that part memorized, too.

By 1881, towns around the state were lobbying to be the home of the new university. The location would be determined by a vote of the people, and the campaigning turned decidedly negative.

One Waco newspaper wrote, "Waco is free from distracting scenes and corrupting influences and feverish excitement of the political capital, with its multitudinous temptations to lure the young into the paths of vice." Well, yeah. What more could you want in a college town?

The *Tyler Courier* warned of "drunken legislators, Mexican fandangos, and the Austin mosquitoes...."

Austin was ultimately selected as the site for The University, and in his last message on education to the state legislature, Governor O.M. Roberts declared, "Therefore, I repeat that it cannot be that the people of this state will allow The University of Texas to be anything below first class, as required by the Constitution. Let The University and its branches be more amply endowed, organized, and put in full operation as a first class University…then, after a time, *future generations will proudly point to The University of Texas as the brightest jewel of our greatness as a people and State."*

And so it shall remain.

2 Worship at the Shrine of *Santa Rita*

Don't visit the *Santa Rita* rig on a game day. The oil-drilling rig sits at the corner of San Jacinto and Martin Luther King Boulevard, a main gateway to Darrell K Royal–Texas Memorial Stadium. It's crowded and noisy and busy, not an appropriate atmosphere in which to soak in the magnitude of the rig's impact. It would be like trying to pray in the Alamo Shrine while surrounded by rowdy tourists who don't have enough reverence or sense to remove their gimme caps.

It's easy to ignore the primitive structure with its oil-soaked timbers and to overlook the plaques that bear its condensed history. On game day, not many of the orange-clad revelers streaming toward the stadium will take time to stop, put down their beer cans, and pay attention.

But this crude rig changed everything—*everything*—about Longhorn football, about The University of Texas, about the city of Austin, and about the state of Texas. It affected the fortunes of our education, our commerce, and our culture. It certainly changed our attitudes.

We are who we are today largely because of that simple rig.

The same Constitution of 1876 that established The University—called "the Main University"—and the agricultural and mechanical branch, A&M, gave UT the 50 leagues of land

Poor Relations

Like any poor relatives who come calling on their newly wealthy relations, A&M came visiting with its hand out after the *Santa Rita* well came in. Although the Aggies had been reluctant to recognize the constitutional provision that made A&M a *branch* of The University of Texas, they now came running to claim their part of the "inheritance." In 1931, the Texas legislature authorized a split in the net income from the Permanent University Fund (PUF), with two-thirds going to The University—"the Main University"—and one-third to Texas A&M.

originally granted, but reneged on the gift of land intended for railroads. In exchange, legislators gave The University 1 million acres—and later another million—of wasteland in west Texas, thought to have little or no agricultural or commercial value.

Guess we fooled them.

In 1916, based on a UT geology professor's report touting potential mineral resources on the west Texas land, the Texan Oil and Land Company gathered investors to drill for oil. Drilling partner Frank Pickrell recalled later that the New York group, Catholic women who were worried about their investment, consulted their priest. He advised them to pray to Santa Rita, the patron saint of impossible causes. Santa Rita must have given the go-ahead, because on Pickrell's next New York trip, the ladies handed him their money, along with a red rose that had been blessed by the priest.

"According to their wishes, I climbed to the top of the derrick [and] scattered the rose petals over the derrick and rig," Pickrell said. The hoped-for well was christened the *Santa Rita*. Drilling was slow from 1921 through mid-1923.

Meanwhile, back on campus, The University languished. Texas didn't have an adequate tax base to support the growing University, and the state just wasn't dedicated to higher learning. The campus sprouted decrepit shacks and ramshackle classrooms following

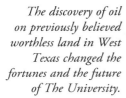
The discovery of oil on previously believed worthless land in West Texas changed the fortunes and the future of The University.

World War I. This "University of the first class" had become an underfunded eyesore. Nevertheless, Ashbel Smith, the president of the Board of Regents, proved to possess the gift of prophecy. When laying the cornerstone of UT's Main Building in November 1922, Smith proclaimed, "Smite the rocks with the rod of knowledge, and fountains of unstinted wealth will gush forth!"

And gush they did.

At 6:00 AM on May 28, 1923, the driller's wife heard a loud hissing noise. When she looked out her door, gas and oil were shooting violently from the well, spraying a black mist for 250 yards over the land that some had called "an oilman's graveyard."

Santa Rita Number One was plugged in 1990, but adjacent lands still pump some 41 million barrels of oil each year.

The Permanent University Fund (PUF), pitifully inadequate prior to the discovery of oil, was resuscitated by the "fountains of unstinted wealth" that gushed forth. The PUF must be invested and cannot be spent. Income from the PUF makes up a large part of the Available University Fund, which is used for operating expenses and permanent improvements. As of 2013, the market value of the PUF was $14.8 billion, not including the value of the land itself.

After the discovery of oil, The University entered a phase of unbridled expansion. It started a major building program, replacing the shacks with magnificent Spanish-renaissance buildings.

So the next time you're on campus marveling at UT's top-notch facilities, take a detour by *Santa Rita Rig Number One*, remove your hat, and take a moment to give thanks.

3 D.X. Bible: The Answer to Prayer

The sign on the welcome-parade float summed up the hopes and the desperation of the Longhorn faithful. It read: "Bible: The Answer to Prayer."

A losing program brings out the worst in Texas fans, and by the time coach Jack Chevigny hit the road in 1936, he had alienated his team—which had grown weary of his insults and his fiery but phony pregame talks—and the fans, who just flat-out won't abide losing. He'd alienated UT power brokers, most importantly wealthy alum and longtime regent Lutcher Stark, who took umbrage at Chevigny's 6–12–1 record during his last two years at Texas.

And, as coaches have had to learn again and again throughout UT's history, to alienate the high school coaches in the state of Texas is to sign one's own death warrant.

The University needed a savior to resurrect the Texas football program, and with Stark leading the charge, it set its sights on Dana Xenophon Bible, the son of a college professor named after an ancient Greek historian. Longhorns were familiar with his work. Bible had won five Southwest Conference championships while at Texas A&M, and when he left to take the coaching job at Nebraska, the UT Athletics Council passed a resolution of regret, calling Bible "an exemplary sportsman both in victory and defeat," and crediting him for restoring civil relations between the two schools.

Nebraska fans were inconsolable when Texas hired him away. UT regents voted unanimously to hire Bible and to pay him the outrageous salary of $15,000 a year to be head coach and athletics director. Some unreasonable types grumbled about Bible making almost twice what UT president H.Y. Benedict made, but the state legislature solved that problem by raising Benedict's salary to $17,500.

Texas got its money's worth. Bible brought intelligence and dignity and a studied approach to the disarray of the football program. He recognized that his first challenge was to unite all the

"Bible wields seemingly effortless but iron-clad discipline over his team, [and] seldom relaxes his dignity on or off the field." Texas Football Magazine, 1941.

Bible Verse

"[The coach] is likely to be a prominent figure in his community, which makes it most important that he live up to his responsibilities as a citizen. He has an obligation to himself to live cleanly, deal fairly, work faithfully at his job, uphold the traditions of clean, hard play and good sportsmanship, and keep his self-respect. He has a tremendous obligation to the game itself."—D.X. Bible, *Championship Football*

various factions of the UT family, so he met with a group of people whose support he felt he needed. Bible opened the meeting with this warning: "Gentlemen, when we leave this room, we'll all be calling the same signals."

Bible recruited few out-of-state players. He believed Texas boys would play with more pride because they were playing for their state's University. And he worked to rebuild a relationship with the Texas high school coaches. Armed with his "Bible Plan," a five-year plan that emphasized education and revolutionized recruiting, he divided the state into regions and assigned an alum, charged with discovering and recruiting promising players, to each region. He assembled a first-rate coaching staff and hired Blair Cherry, the most successful high school coach in Texas, and Bully Gilstrap, a perennial winner at Schreiner Junior College.

The Plan didn't produce immediate results. In Bible's second year, the Horns lost their season opener for the first time in school history.

Texas had lost 10 straight going into its 1938 game against the Aggies and had been tagged "Ali Bible and the Forty Sieves." It seemed inevitable, yet unthinkable, that 1938 would be the year the Aggies would finally win at Memorial Stadium.

But the same Longhorn team that had scored in double digits on only three occasions in '37 and '38 prevailed, 7–6, and protected the Memorial Stadium tradition from the tarnish of an Aggie victory.

The Longhorns had finally righted the ship. Bible called it "the happiest day in all my years of coaching…to me, this appears to be the beginning of happier days for Texas followers."

Amen.

Ten years after inheriting an inconsistent and chaotic program, Bible had shaped the Texas football program into one of national prominence and respect, laying the foundation for the Texas football enjoyed today. The Bible Plan had worked.

Thank heaven for answered prayer.

4 The Coach: Darrell Royal

It boggles the mind to consider what Darrell Royal might have achieved had he not left the game at age 52. Despite his comparatively short tenure, he's still recognized as one of the greatest coaches in the history of college football. And he was ours.

Doug Looney, former senior writer for *Sports Illustrated*, described Royal's legacy beautifully: "The numbers still generate gasps. Rolled into one brilliant package, Darrell Royal was Picasso and Mozart and Einstein and Rockne and Patton and Churchill and John Wayne and Thomas Jefferson; he was also Willie Nelson and a 35-foot sidehill putt for a birdie and a sunset over Maui."

You'd be hard-pressed to find a man less likely to become a true Texas hero. Royal was reared in Oklahoma, a product of the Great Depression and the dismal days of the Dust Bowl, and his youth was marred by tragedies and hardship. Like many Oklahomans, the Royals struggled to find work, and at one point his father moved them to California to chase the dream of feeding a family and getting a little ahead. After young Darrell received a letter from

Darrell Royal's Records

167–47–5 at Texas
184–60–5 overall coaching record
8–7–1 career bowl record
National Championships in 1963, 1969, and 1970
Southwest Conference championships (including shared or tied) in 1959, 1961, 1962, 1963, 1968, 1969, 1970, 1971, 1972, 1973, and 1975
11 top-10 national finishes
Winning percentage of .788
Winningest coach in Southwest Conference history

the high school football coach at Hollis, Oklahoma, he hitchhiked home, lived with his grandmother, and dreamed of playing for the University of Oklahoma.

He made it to OU, became an All-American quarterback in 1949, and is still considered one of the greatest all-around players Oklahoma has ever had. After spending one year each at head coaching jobs in Edmonton (with the Canadian Football League), Mississippi State, and Washington, he got the phone call he'd dreamed of receiving, from coach D.X. Bible and The University of Texas.

Royal wowed the Athletic Council with his preparation; with the help of Bible, Royal learned the name and background of each council member and what each man looked like. He was offered the job that very day.

Royal brought that same preparation, organization, and intensity to the practice fields, the training rooms, and the games. Practices were structured; there was no wasted motion, no standing around. At the blow of a whistle, players changed stations and knew exactly where to go and what to do next. Simplicity, precision, planning, discipline, ferocious play, and integrity were the hallmarks of his program, lessons he learned from Bud Wilkinson at Oklahoma.

Royal inherited a 1957 Longhorn team that had gone 1–9 the previous year, setting the mark for the worst record in UT history. Yet within one year, he had set the program back on course with a 6–4–1 season, a hint of the great things to come.

Texas was so dominant in the Southwest Conference during the 1960s and '70s that one clever writer noted, "Two things in life are certain...death and Texas." In 20 seasons at Texas, Royal led the Horns to 11 SWC titles and 10 Cotton Bowl Classics, including six consecutive appearances from 1968 through 1973.

Then, of course, there were the three National Championships.

During his tenure at Texas, Royal was the winningest coach in the nation. The man never had a losing season. Ever.

Darrell Royal's Awards

Two-time winner of AFCA Coach of the Year Award (1963, 1970) and two-time winner of FWAA Coach of the Year Award, (1961, 1963) one of only four coaches in history to accomplish that feat (others are Joe Paterno, Bear Bryant, and John McKay)

Selected Coach of the Decade (1960s) by nation's sportswriters

Coach of the Year, Touchdown Club of Washington, 1970

President, American Football Coaches' Association, 1975

Texas Sports Hall of Fame, 1976

National Football Foundation College Football Hall of Fame, 1983

Legends of Coaching Award, Downtown Athletic Club, 1991

Oklahoma Sports Hall of Fame, 1992

Horatio Alger Award for lifetime success, 1996

Cotton Bowl Hall of Fame inaugural class, 1998

Four-time Southwesterner of the Year

Five-time SWC Coach of the Year

Bear Bryant Lifetime Achievement Award, 2000 (first-ever recipient)

First-ever recipient of Contribution to College Football Award, 2002

UT Distinguished Service Award, 2006 (fifth person to ever receive award)

Amos Alonzo Stagg Award, 2010

Longhorn Hall of Honor, 1976

Darrell Royal and his players celebrate a 12–7 victory over Mississippi in the 1962 Cotton Bowl, the first bowl victory of Royal's coaching career.

Alfred Jackson, wide receiver on the 1975 and 1977 SWC championship teams, described what it meant to be a Longhorn during that era. "When you walked on the Texas campus and played football for Coach Royal, you just expected to win. You were at The University of Texas. It was never a matter of losing. It was, we're gonna win. It was a feeling of '…this is the best school, we have the best players, the best coach, and we are about winning. It's not something we do on Saturday, it's something we do all the time. And everyone else aspires to be like us.' That feeling transcended everything."

Even more important than the victories was the manner in which Royal conducted his program. Sportswriter Whit Canning wrote in the *Fort Worth Star Telegram* of "…the national image of excellence—and class—that cloaked Royal's teams like the famous burnt-orange jerseys they wore." He demanded that his players be disciplined, well-groomed, and well-behaved. Dedicated students. And good sports.

Every high school and Pop Warner coach since that time has repeated Royal's admonition to his own players: "When you get into that end zone, act like you've been there before."

Through the years, OU made a couple of runs at trying to hire Royal, but he graciously declined to return to his alma mater. He'd long ago become a "dipped and vaccinated Longhorn." Texas was home.

He spent his retirement playing golf almost every day, championing the underdog with his charity work, and enjoying friendships with guitar pickers and his former players.

Alzheimer's eventually gained on him, this former alpha-male, and fogged his once-flawless memory. His hurried stride slowed to a shuffle, and it took longer to call up his trademark "Royalisms". On November 7, 2012, the nation mourned the passing of this great man. We lost him, the face of Texas football, but his name, his victories, and his integrity will forever grace UT's stadium and its program.

5 The Innovator

When his 1960 team failed to score a touchdown in three of their games, Darrell Royal could identify the problem. He just had to figure out a way to get the ball to tailback James Saxton on almost every play.

The seed of the flip-flop offense was planted one day when, according to Lou Maysel's account in *Here Come the Texas Longhorns*, Royal was shooting the bull with a sportswriter and

Longhorn Lore: You Can't Do Any Worse

"Super Bill" Bradley was quarterback in 1968, inaugural year of the wishbone offense, and he was having a tough game against Texas Tech. James Street told the story: "We were struggling, and Coach Royal grabbed me and he looked at me for a minute as if he were having second thoughts about putting me in. Then he looked me straight in the eye and said, 'Hell, you can't do any worse. Get in there.'"

Street went on to win the next 20 games and the 1969 National Championship. Bradley had been starting quarterback for two seasons, but he accepted the change and went on to become a tremendous defensive back and punter. Freddie Steinmark wrote in *I Play to Win*, "Bradley could have quit, but didn't. It was the same with the team. We could have folded right there, but we just worked harder than ever before.... We didn't lose a game for two years. You might say we followed Bradley's example."

commented, "If you could call on [Saxton] 25 times a game... wouldn't he scald some people?" The idea germinated for a while, and eventually Royal decided to put Saxton in the tailback slot all the time: "We decided to just flip-flop the whole thing," allowing the offensive blueprint to flip right or left. This simplified blocking assignments while keeping the strong side always leading for Saxton.

The following four seasons produced some of Royal's best teams. The 1961 team went 10–1, the '62 team was 9–1–1, and in 1963 Texas won the National Championship. In 1964, the Longhorns lost the conference—and the National Championship—by one point, to Arkansas.

In 1968, after three seasons of 6–4, 7–4, and 6–4 records, Royal surveyed his powerful stable of running backs and talked with offensive coordinator Emory Bellard about ways to spread the carries among the backs and give the offense the ability to attack in either direction. Bellard got to work and designed the "wishbone," the most prolific rushing offense in the history of college football.

This offensive breakthrough carried Texas to two national championships and a 30-game winning streak, and it changed the face of college football for more than a decade. The innovation Royal was proudest of, though, didn't make headlines at the time. It did, however, set the standard for every football program in the nation.

Pressed by alums to hire a full-time recruiter, Royal realized that it didn't matter who he recruited if they couldn't stay in school. He didn't need another "get 'em here" coach, he needed a "keep 'em here" coach, so he hired a full-time academic counselor—"brain coach" Lan Hewlett—the first such position in the nation.

It paid off. Of the 48 lettermen on the 1963 National Championship team, 45 graduated. That team's GPA was higher than the GPA of the student body as a whole.

Once again, Royal had put Texas at the forefront of innovation, but this time in the field of academics. Long before the NCAA concerned itself with graduation rates or "progress toward degree," Royal stressed the importance of getting a degree and took measures to help his players in the classroom.

During his 20 years at the helm, without pressure from the NCAA, four out of five men who lettered for Royal went on to receive their degrees.

The 800-Pound Gorilla: DeLoss Dodds

In 2013 *Forbes* magazine ran a column on college football's most valuable teams, and reported that the Longhorns made a profit of $82 million. "It's an ungodly amount of money for a college football team to make in one year," Joseph Zuck wrote.

UT athletics is one of an estimated 23 Division I programs—out of 228—that is entirely self-sufficient; Longhorn football pays for the maintenance of—the *existence* of—18 of UT's 20 athletic programs.

The man who for 32 years oversaw this empire is DeLoss Dodds, the ninth athletics director in UT's history. Hired in 1981, he was the E.F. Hutton of athletics directors. When he talked, people listened.

No one can deny the brilliance of The University's overall athletics program. Few programs in the country have enjoyed more triumphs. In 2002–2003, Texas became the first Division I-A program in NCAA history to accomplish the following in the same academic year: the football program was ranked in the AP Top 10, the men's basketball team advanced to the Final Four, and the baseball team advanced to the College World Series. *Sports Illustrated* named The University of Texas the *number one* overall sports program in the country in 2002.

It takes lots and lots and lots of money to maintain that standing year after year, and since his hiring in 1981, Dodds saw UT's budget grow from $4 million to more than $161.9 million. One of Dodds' most valuable contributions was leading the expansion of the Longhorn Foundation, which has grown to more than 13,000 members; its annual revenue now exceeds $40.3 million. And of course, Dodds was the mastermind behind the creation of the Longhorn Network, a $300 million, 20-year deal with ESPN,

In his 32 years at Texas, he's overseen a most amazing upgrade in facilities, shepherding the makeover of the Erwin Special Events Center; the construction of the climate-controlled Frank Denius Practice Field; the UT basketball practice facility, named for famed heart surgeon Denton Cooley; McCombs Softball Field; and the Mike Myers Track and Soccer Stadium, home of the renowned Texas Relays. Disch-Falk Baseball Field underwent a $26 million facelift, and the north end zone of DKR–Memorial Stadium got a new upper deck and a slew of club spaces, athletic offices, and luxury suites. Tennis, golf, and rowing recently got fancy new facilities.

The pace of activity is dizzying, but necessary if Texas is to have unparalleled facilities to match unparalleled athletic success. As Dodds so famously said, "We don't need to keep up with the Joneses. We are the Joneses."

The good news is that, in keeping with Texas tradition, he believed in doing things the right way. "They want us to win," Dodds said of Longhorn fans and boosters, "but if we win the wrong way, it would be as bad as losing."

Dodds oversaw the birth of the Big XII in 1994, then helped save the Big XII when the Aggies and Missouri fled the conference in 2012. He was widely recognized as *the* guy—the 800-pound gorilla of college athletics.

In September 2013, DeLoss Dodds announced his intention to retire as athletics director of the colossus he helped create. During his tenure, the Longhorns claimed 14 National Championships and 108 conference championships. He was recognized by the Texas Exes with the Distinguished Service Award, the highest honor that can be bestowed on a non-alumnus of The University.

DeLoss Dodd is a member of the Longhorn Hall of Honor.

7 Mack Brown

In 1997, Texas found itself in need of a redeemer, someone to reunite and reenergize the Longhorn faithful. Again.

Texas had gone through three head coaches in the 22 years since Darrell Royal's retirement. Recruiting had suffered, facilities were outdated, and Texas fans were despondent.

The Horns had been on a harrowing roller-coaster ride, peaking during Fred Akers' undefeated regular seasons in 1977 and 1983. The 1990 Southwest Conference championship was sandwiched between two losing seasons. Under John Mackovic, Texas won the last SWC championship in 1995 and the first-ever Big 12 championship in 1996 before plummeting to a miserable 4–7 final season. There had been only six conference championships in those 22 years, and Texas had lost to the Aggies an unfathomable 13 times.

Unaccustomed to losing and put off by the aloof and decidedly un-Texan personality of Mackovic, the Longhorns were desperate to right the ship, to reclaim its rightful place as one of the top programs in the nation. Texas didn't have to win the conference *every* year, but they sure needed to be in contention. The inconsistency was killing UT fans.

Too Cool for School

Texas fans were long known for their "sophisticated" approach to UT football. The stands were rarely full at kickoff, and most fans wouldn't be caught dead wearing burnt orange. That seemed too impassioned, too Aggie-ish.

Former regent Jane Weinert Blumberg, UT class of '37, wrote in *Texas, Our Texas*, "...students were reluctant to express too much enthusiasm because that would not have seemed sophisticated." Forty-something years later, Joe Frantz pleaded in his book *Forty Acre Follies*, "Lord, I wish Texas audiences would arrive on time and remain in their seats until the game is over!"

Mack Brown got it.

As soon as he was hired, he introduced the slogan "Come Early. Be Loud. Stay Late. Wear Burnt Orange with Pride," and repeated it to each new booster group he addressed. The love affair with the fans was instant, and since the fall of 1998 Memorial Stadium—and the Cotton Bowl each October—has taken on a decidedly burnt-orange hue.

Mack Brown was the right person in the right place for the right time. Although not a Texan, he was a southerner, and he rightly idolized Darrell Royal, returning him to center stage of the Longhorn football program. The two became fast friends; Brown invoked Royal's name at every opportunity, and the fans loved him for it.

Royal told Brown that the Texas family was fragmented, as if "somebody dropped a box of BBs and they scattered all over the place." To make this work, Royal said, Brown would "have to get those BBs back in the box."

Mackovic had exiled former lettermen from the weight room and from practices, and it had stung. So during Brown's first year at UT, he invited all former lettermen to a reunion and golf tournament. At the first Mike Campbell Lettermen's Tournament, a member of Brown's newly hired coaching staff was stationed on every tee box to greet the former players. As each foursome reached the 18th green, they were welcomed by Royal and Brown...welcomed home.

Brown's affable, down-to-earth manner endeared him to the high school coaches of Texas, and he publicly bragged about the important role they played in forming future Longhorns. The sentiment was sincere; Brown's dad and granddad had both been high school coaches.

The Texas fans' love affair with Brown was in full bloom. He encouraged fans to "Come Early. Wear Burnt Orange. Be Loud. Stay Late," and they did. He embraced The University, the traditions, and all the things Longhorns held dear. And it didn't hurt that in his first year on the job, the Longhorns went 9–3, beat Oklahoma and the Aggies, and, for only the third time since 1982, won their bowl game.

Brown proved to be a recruitin' machine—one player said Brown could have talked him into eating a catsup popsicle—and

Coach Mack Brown and MVP Vince Young revel in Texas' last-second victory over Michigan in the January 1, 2005, Rose Bowl game.

his recruiting classes ranked among the nation's best, year in and year out. After the 2005, season, he presented the Longhorn nation with its fourth National Championship, and took Texas to another title game after the 2009 season. After quarterback Colt McCoy was knocked out of the game with a shoulder injury, the Horns lost to Alabama for the first time ever.

Neither Brown nor the program seemed to recover from that loss. Things began to fall apart; the team went 5–7 in 2010. There were 17 conference losses in four seasons, three losses to OU in those same four years, two of them humiliating blow-outs. People grumbled about the half-dozen quality quarterbacks we'd let slip through our fingers and about our two conference championships in Brown's 16-year tenure.

After 16 years, it was another coach's turn to re-energize and reunite the fan base; after weeks of "will he or won't he", Mack Brown announced his resignation in December 2013, saying, "It's been a wonderful ride. Now, the program is again being pulled in different directions, and I think the time is right for a change...."

In 2006, Brown was awarded the Paul "Bear" Bryant Award as Coach of the Year. He won the 2008 Bobby Dodd Coach of the Year Award, and after a 13–1 season in 2009, he was named Big 12 Coach of the Year.

Brown left with a record of 158–48, one national championship and a near- miss, and a legacy of winning with integrity.

Mack Brown is in the Longhorn Hall of Honor.

8 We Eat Our Own

Surely no college in America has more demanding fans with greater expectations than The University of Texas. Almost every coach in the 120-year history of UT football, even the great Darrell Royal, has come under the scrutiny of second-guessers and football "experts."

1894: UT's first paid coach, R.D. Wentworth, registered a 6–1 record and outscored Varsity's first six opponents by a score of 191–0. But when Missouri crushed Texas, the fans turned on him like a pack of wolves, claiming Wentworth had bet on Missouri and thrown the football game. Lou Maysel wrote, "The critical

> ## Ride the Coaches
> "Although the alumni have many ways of reaching a football game, they usually ride the coaches." —September 1956 issue of *The Ranger*, UT student publication
>
> "The best thing about the job is that there are 20 million people who care every day what happens with Texas football. The worst thing? That there are 20 million people who care every day what happens with Texas football." —Darrell Royal, on being head coach at The University of Texas

and suspicious nature of fans manifested itself early in the school's football history." Wentworth left under fire and returned to the East Coast to go into business.

And so another Texas tradition was born: disgruntled fans unwilling to accept anything less than a perfect season.

1907–09: A young language professor, W.E. Metzenthin rescued the financially troubled program by accepting no stipend for his coaching duties. His first team finished 6–1–1, but during the 5–4 season in 1908, he was stung by the criticism of fans and he resigned. His successor, Dr. Dexter Draper, stayed only one season before resigning. His 4–3–1 record had him on the hot seat and he determined that pediatrics was less stressful than coaching.

1911–15: Dave Allerdice, All-American halfback at Michigan from 1907 to 1909, was liked and accepted immediately by the Longhorn family. His 33–7 record was remarkable, yet "the critical and suspicious nature" of Texas fans after the 1915 team's nosedive prompted his resignation.

1917–19: Despite the decimation of Texas talent owing to World War I, Bill Juneau managed a 19–7 record. However, Texas suffered its first non-winning season and faced more, thanks to A&M coach D.X. Bible's domination of the Southwest Conference. Juneau resigned under pressure.

1920–22: Berry Whitaker didn't even want the job; after volunteering as an assistant coach, he'd been served notice by athletics director Theo Bellmont that he would be the next head coach. He coached seasons of 9–0, 6–1–1, and 7–2, and after losing to the Aggies in 1922, Whitaker walked to Bellmont's office and resigned. He denied that powerful alum Lutcher Stark had forced him out, saying, "Defeats killed me. I was coming down with ulcers and that kind of thing." He served as UT's intramurals director for more than 40 years.

1923–26: Doc Stewart's interest in the summer camps and the resort he'd invested in—Camp Mystic, Camp Stewart for Boys, and Heart O' the Hills in Hunt, Texas—was his ultimate downfall. A successful coach with a 24–9–3 record, his attention was divided between Austin and the hill country. Finally, in an explosive meeting with Bellmont, Stewart was fired.

1927–33: Even the legendary Clyde Littlefield, revered athlete and respected coach, was not immune to the fickle loyalties of Texas fans. Despite amassing a 44–18–6 record and winning the Southwest Conference, after Littlefield posted a 4–5–2 season— UT's first-ever losing campaign—powerful regent Lutcher Stark pushed for Littlefield's resignation and got it. Littlefield said, "I just made up my mind that if I wanted to live longer, I'd better quit."

1934–36: Brazen self-promoter Jack Chevigny, whose greatest moment came when his '34 team upset Notre Dame in South Bend, is still the only Texas coach with an overall losing record. He resigned just before Stark ran him out of town on a rail.

1947–50: Blair Cherry posted an excellent 32–10–1 record, yet after suffering from insomnia and ulcers, he wrote in the *Saturday Evening Post* that the "over-emphasis on winning" and the critical nature of the media and fans led him to resign.

1951–56: Ed Price was well-loved by his team, but after suffering through the worst season in UT football history at 1–9—and after being hung in effigy three times in one season—Price resigned "for the good of the team."

1977–86: Coach of two teams that went undefeated in the regular season and owner of an 86–31–2 record, Fred Akers was fired after his lone losing season in 10 years. At the time of his firing, Akers was second only to Royal in the number of UT victories.

1987–91: Beloved former Longhorn player and assistant coach David McWilliams was forced out after he followed a 10–1 regular season and SWC championship with his third losing season in five years.

1992–97: John Mackovic managed to offend almost everyone associated with the UT athletics program with his aloof manner and lack of interest in Texas tradition. After Texas' first loss to Rice in 28 years, Mackovic seemed surprised at fans' wrath. "Well, you can't expect to beat Rice every year," was his response. In spite of winning the last-ever Southwest Conference championship and the first Big 12 championship, after losing to UCLA 66–3 and posting a losing record in 1997, he was gone.

1998–2013: Hand-picked by Darrell Royal to redeem the program, Mack Brown energized and united the Longhorn Nation. His friendly, folksy ways endeared him to rich boosters, Texas high school coaches, former lettermen, recruits, and fans. From 2001 through 2009, Brown won 10 or more games each year, bringing home the National Championship after the 2005 season and playing for another in the 2010 BCS Championship Game. After the loss to Alabama for the 2009 National Championship, however, the wheels started coming off Mack's program. He held on to his job after a dismal 5–7 record in 2010, but two Big XII championships in 16 years were not enough. After 17 conference losses in four years, including two blowout losses to OU, the program Brown had united began to splinter, and in December 2013, he was asked to resign.

9 Strong Medicine

After enduring four mediocre seasons and a disorganized mess of a coaching search (one that became public before the current coach had resigned), Longhorn fans believed—hoped—that because "We're Texas," we could have our pick of any coach in the country. There was so much speculation, so much subterfuge surrounding the hiring of Texas' 29th head coach, so many leaks, it became a topic of speculation across the nation. Vegas kept lines on the chances of various coaches being hired. ESPN and Fox Sports' crawlers kept viewers updated with the latest rumors. SI.com even created a 32-coach, winner-take-all bracket similar to the NCAA basketball tournament brackets. More than three tense weeks after Mack Brown resigned, new Texas athletics director Steve Patterson finally decided on...Charlie Strong, the head coach at Louisville.

Oh.

Not exactly the "splash hire" Longhorn fans assumed they'd reel in. One of UT's biggest boosters, offended because he was not consulted in the final decision, publicly insulted the new coach and the decision by saying, "I don't have any doubt that Charlie is a fine coach. I think he would make a great position coach, maybe a coordinator. But I don't believe [he belongs at] what should be one of the three most powerful university programs in the world right now at UT-Austin." A day later, the booster apologized and Strong graciously asked for his help in moving the Texas program forward.

The more Coach Strong talked in the weeks following his hiring, the more excited fans got about the "culture change" expected to take place.

At the press conference introducing him as the 29th head coach in University of Texas history, Charlie Strong got a welcoming hug from Edith Royal, the widow of the legendary Darrell Royal.

His name might not have been well-known, but he has the pedigree. Born in Batesville, Arkansas, a town of about 10,000 people, Strong walked on to the Central Arkansas football team, and soon earned a scholarship as a defensive back. His coaching journey took him from Florida to Texas A&M, to Southern Illinois, back to Florida. He moved to Ole Miss, then Florida, on to Notre Dame, to South Carolina, and back to Florida, where he stayed until he was hired by Louisville in 2009. Along the way, he coached under Steve Spurrier, and served as defensive coordinator for Lou Holtz and Urban Meyer.

In December 2009, the Strong family—Charlie, his wife, Victoria, their son, Tory, and their two daughters, Hailee and Hope—moved to Louisville, where he revitalized the school's football program and the team's academic standing. Louisville was 15–21 in the three years before his arrival. Strong's Cardinals went

TRIVIA
Question

How many Longhorns does it take to screw in a light bulb?

Trivia answers on page 255.

37–15 the next four seasons, were 3–1 in bowl games, and twice won the Big East Conference. He was Big East Coach of the Year in 2010 and 2012.

Every coach claims to emphasize the importance of players completing their education, yet Strong's dedication to the idea seems genuine. In his four years at Louisville, the team's APR score (progress toward degrees) and GSR (graduation rates) jumped significantly. Ninety-three of Strong's 98 players earned their degrees. Strong himself has one undergraduate degree and two master's degrees. "The academic thing is legit," one Louisville athletic department official said. "He is all over those kids about school."

Whether he wins here remains to be seen, but one thing's for sure: no one will accuse Texas of being "soft", as opponents had done in recent years. Within days of being hired, Strong met with the team and allegedly outlined the following expectations:

1. Players will attend all classes and will sit in the front two rows. No texting in class, no headphones in class.
2. If a player misses a class, he runs until it hurts. If he misses two classes, his entire position unit runs. If he misses three, the position coach runs. Position coaches don't like to run.
3. No earrings in the football offices.
4. The team will live together, eat together, hang out together.
5. Players will wear coats and ties to the games.
6. Our focus is on winning and graduating. Anything not pertaining to winning or graduating is a distraction.

Strong is The University's 29th head football coach, and he is the first African American to coach Longhorn football. Texas has long been defensive about its "racist" label, so it was a historic day and a historic hire, as UT administrators and the media stated repeatedly. When asked about the significance of his hiring, Strong said, "…yes, this is a historical day…There's always going to be a first somewhere…. We're going to do what we have to do and we're going to make it better. But I don't want to look at it as 'the first.' I just want to look at it as, 'I'm a coach and that's the way I want to be treated.'"

10 The Oblivious Pioneer: Julius Whittier

In 1958, Oklahoma University's Prentiss Gault became the first black athlete to play football at a major southern university. Jerry Levias integrated the football fields of the Southwest Conference in 1965 at Southern Methodist University, but Texas continued to have all-white football teams long after competing schools were recruiting and signing black players. In fact, the 1969 Longhorn team holds the dubious distinction of being the last all-white national championship team in NCAA history. When Texas won it all the next year, Julius Whittier, Texas football's first black letterman, was on the field.

The SWC was slow to lift the ban on allowing African Americans to play sports, yet even after the conference gave the okay in 1963, The University of Texas regents stubbornly refused to change. Despite UT's lifting of the ban, there was still tacit pressure on head coach Darrell Royal not to rush to integrate the football team.

Royal's first efforts to recruit black players in the mid-1960s were frustrated by various issues. Leon O'Neal, Texas' first black scholarship football player, was on hand to help recruit Whittier, but he left the team before lettering.

Lucky 23

Jim Hart made history in 1899 when he kicked the first field goal in UT history. The 23-yarder helped lift Texas to an 11–0 win over Tulane.

UT placekicker Fred Bednarski also made his mark with a 23-yard field goal. On October 19, 1957, Bednarski became the first soccer-style kicker in NCAA history to kick a field goal. The kick, with Walter Fondren as the holder, came in a 17–0 victory over Arkansas.

Royal had coached black players while at the University of Washington and the Edmonton Eskimos of the Canadian Football League, but recruiters from competing colleges played up the "all-white" image of UT, implying that DKR was a racist. A favorite refrain of coaches trying to sway recruits and their parents was: "They'll never play a black at UT."

None of that mattered to Whittier, a star from an integrated high school in San Antonio. Whittier's parents were acutely aware of UT's racist reputation and were worried by the prospect of Julius walking into a situation where much more than football might be at stake. Yet they left the decision to their son, who chose to "play big-time football 80 miles from home." In *Texas, Our Texas*, Whittier recalled, "Here I was with an opportunity to compete for a spot on a nationally ranked football team. Here was a school with 40,000 students to wander through, meet, and get to know…with an excellent collection of facilities for my academic and athletic careers…with a coach recognized all over the country as one of the most professional and certainly one of the most genuine and successful. Realizing that this was a rare opportunity…I had to accept the challenge of succeeding at Texas."

Whittier told Richard Pennington, author of *Breaking the Ice: The Racial Integration of Southwest Conference Football,* that because he struggled with attention deficit disorder, "I had no time or hard-drive space in my brain to step back and worry over how potentially ominous it was to become a black member of The University of

Texas football team. I was a jock, plain and simple. I didn't care about civil rights or making a mark."

Yet he knew that the only way for Texas football to change would be for black players to sign with Texas, show up, and succeed.

He made a point of working hard on the field and in the classroom, and kept telling himself that as long as he got to play based on his skills, he'd be fine. Whittier lettered two years as an offensive guard before becoming the starting tight end in his senior season.

Whittier swears it was not a difficult time for him. "A few of my colleagues let their tongues slip, but I was comfortable that they didn't mean me any harm," he said. Downplaying the importance his role may have had, he says, "God and The University had the right people in the right places to handle my situation. It turned out to be a small event in the long and luminous life of a great and valuable institution."

False modesty aside, Whittier's willingness to challenge himself and his eventual success blew the doors wide open at UT, changing attitudes on and off the Forty Acres. Because Whittier was brave enough to step on campus, the path was paved for future stars like Roosevelt Leaks, Earl Campbell, and Johnny "Lam" Jones.

Julius Whittier is a member of the Longhorn Hall of Honor.

11 The 1963 Season

Smarting from the championship near-misses of the previous two years, the 1963 team clawed its way to the top, aided by the leadership of quarterback Duke Carlisle, a stingy, ferocious defense, and three captains who willed the team to win.

By the time the Longhorns met Oklahoma in October, the Sooners were ranked number one after having beaten the 1962 national champions Southern Cal, and the Longhorns were in the number two spot. Coach Darrell Royal tweaked the Texas offense and put in the old split-T option just for the Sooners. After Texas shocked OU 28–7, center David McWilliams told Mike Jones in *Dance with Who Brung You,* "It was like they didn't even know how to defense it."

Although OU was considered to be Texas' toughest opponent, the following weeks brought some tough—and close—contests.

Texas beat Arkansas for the sixth time in seven meetings, but Rice—the team that had derailed the Longhorns' national championship run in the '62 season with a 14–14 tie—gave Texas fits again before the Horns sealed the game 10–6. SMU wasn't much easier, but the Horns squeaked by the Mustangs 17–12.

Great Pep Talk Number One

One of the most famous goal-line stands in Texas football history was the setting for one of the most spirited—and now famous—pep talks ever delivered.

In 1962, Texas was undefeated and ranked number one, but number six Arkansas was standing on the Texas 5-yard line with a first down, trying to add to their 3–0 lead.

That's when All-American guard Johnny Treadwell, known for his intensity on and off the field, shouted, "Dammit, get your heads up. We got 'em right where we want 'em! They've run out of room. They can't throw a long pass; they've got to come right at us."

When Arkansas fullback Danny Brabham came right at 'em and attempted to leap over the line, he was sandwiched by Treadwell and Pat Culpepper, who caused a fumble when he put his helmet on the football.

Texas recovered in the end zone for a touchback, then went on to beat the Razorbacks, 7–3. Although the '62 Horns remained undefeated in regular-season play, a tie with Rice knocked them from the national championship race.

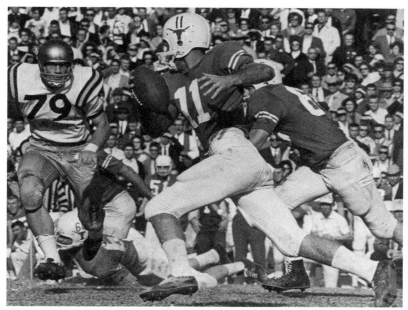

Texas quarterback Duke Carlisle (No. 11) charging forward at the Cotton Bowl on January 1, 1964.

Next up were the Baylor Bears, who were 4–0 in conference play. Baylor had a talented quarterback in Don Trull, but the game turned into a defensive battle. In spite of Texas' offensive dominance in the second and third quarters, the Longhorns were able to score only once. At the end of the third quarter, Tom Stockton took it over from the 1-yard line after Tommy Ford's tough running brought them down the field.

But Baylor wasn't finished; Trull passed the Bears down to the UT 19-yard line with less than a minute left.

Suddenly, defensive coordinator Mike Campbell, acting on a hunch, put quarterback Carlisle in at safety for the first time all season. Trull's favorite receiver, Lawrence Elkins, was wide open in the end zone when Carlisle came from out of nowhere to make the miraculous interception. The game was over. Texas had held on to win 7–0.

Texas shut out TCU, and a week and a half later traveled to Kyle Field on Thanksgiving Day to face the Aggies in a game that was almost cancelled after President John F. Kennedy was assassinated in Dallas on November 22.

Some Texas fans, in retaliation for yet another Aggie kidnapping of Bevo, had stolen into the stadium and used chemicals to write *Bevo* on the grass at Kyle Field. The game was to be broadcast on national television, so the A&M field crew covered the area with dirt and spray-painted it green. When the rains came, the dead grass and green dirt turned the playing surface into a marsh.

UT uber-regent Frank Erwin was furious and tried to commandeer the public address system. When that didn't work, he distributed a written statement in the press box that said, "The condition of the playing field is a disgrace and a reflection on A&M. No university which makes any pretense at having a major athletic program would permit any such condition to exist."

Texas managed to slip and slide past the Aggies, 15–13, to capture its first national championship.

12 The 1964 Cotton Bowl

In 1963, polls named the national champion before bowl games were played, and Texas had been named the champ by virtually everyone. The postseason Cotton Bowl matchup featured number one Texas against number two Navy.

Navy was the darling of the eastern press, and Pittsburgh sportswriter Myron Cope never lived down his pregame comments. "Tune in your television to the Cotton Bowl and you'll laugh yourself silly....Texas is the biggest fraud ever perpetrated

1963 Record
(National Champions, SWC Champions)

Texas	Opponent
21	Tulane 0
49	Texas Tech 7
34	Oklahoma State 7
28	Oklahoma 7
17	Arkansas 13
10	Rice 6
17	SMU 12
7	Baylor 0
17	TCU 0
15	Texas A&M 13
28	Navy (Cotton Bowl) 6

on the football public....Texas plays the kind of football that was fashionable when players wore perforated cowhide helmets....Duke Carlisle executes a handoff like a construction foreman passing a plank to a carpenter....Take a close look at the Texas linemen. They do not look like linemen. They have skinny legs like centipedes or girls and high rear ends."

It was to be a battle between the Texas defense and Navy's Heisman Trophy–winning quarterback Roger Staubach. Staubach was a great passer, but his real strength was his scrambling ability, so Darrell Royal and defensive coordinator Mike Campbell formulated a plan to take away that strength. Campbell's plan was to rush the ends and contain Staubach in the pocket. They worked on the "Staubach chase drill" every day in the three weeks leading up to the Cotton Bowl game.

Texas, everyone presumed, would run the ball. They entered the game ranked seventh in the nation in rushing, Royal's preferred method of moving downfield. Navy was prepared to take away the Longhorns' running game.

Instead, Carlisle came out throwing and tossed a touchdown pass on Texas' first possession. By the time he sat down, he'd surprised the Midshipmen—and writer Myron Cope—with a bowl-record–setting 267 yards of total offense, 213 of which came through the air.

Campbell's game plan and Texas' defense held Staubach to minus-47 yards rushing, completely shutting down his running attack. It was a beautiful thing. Staubach would recall this afternoon in the Cotton Bowl as the worst beating he ever took, comparing Texas' defense to the Pittsburgh Steelers' Steel Curtain.

Texas was the near-unanimous selection of all the major polls, and Royal deservedly won the American Football Coaches Association's Coach of the Year award. The Washington Touchdown Club curiously picked Navy as the national champion and Navy's Rusty Hardin as its Coach of the Year.

The 1969 Season: The Wishbone and Worster

Darrell Royal blames himself for the downturn. After being named the 1963 Coach of the Year, he claims he was off running around the country accepting so many awards and attending so many banquets that he just wasn't around when he needed to be. Recruiting suffered, and so did Texas football. After the first National Championship in 1963 and a 10–1 season in 1964, Longhorn fans endured three four-loss seasons.

Enter the '66 and '67 recruiting classes, containing heralded players such as Ted Koy, James Street, Glen Halsell, and Randy Peschel from the '66 class and Steve Worster, Bobby Wuensch, Bill Atessis, and Cotton Speyrer, who were brought in in 1967.

Longhorn Lore

Darrell Royal was often called the "Barry Goldwater of college football" because of his conservative philosophy and his reluctance to throw the football. One of Royal's oft-quoted observations on football was: "Three things can happen when you pass, and two of them are bad."

During a spring scrimmage one year, a receiver and a defensive back had a colossal collision. Both players were knocked out. Dr. Paul Trickett, the Longhorns' team doctor, was working feverishly over one of the players, whose tongue was blocking his airway. The player was still unconscious and was beginning to turn blue.

According to the memoirs of Jones Ramsey, longtime UT sports information director: "Royal had his head down next to the doctor and kept suggesting different measures. 'Why don't you try this? Can't you do that? Have you tried...?'

"Trickett, without looking away from his patient, barked at Royal, 'Why don't you pass more?'

"Royal got the message, stood up, and left the doctor to his work."

Royal had installed the wishbone offense, designed by then-offensive coordinator Emory Bellard at the beginning of the 1968 season. In the third quarter of the second game of the season, with the Longhorns losing to Texas Tech, Royal replaced two-year starter and team co-captain Bill Bradley with Street. Texas would not lose again until January 1, 1971.

Running the wishbone allowed Texas to do things "that no one else in football was doing...we all started feeling like we were bulletproof," running back Chris Gilbert said in *Dance With Who Brung You*. "By the end of the season we felt that absolutely no one could hang with us." For 30 games, no one did.

The best adjective to describe the 1969 team, other than *undefeated,* is *overpowering.* With Street in command and Koy, Worster, and Jim Bertelsen in the backfield, the Longhorn offense simply ran over everyone.

Against SMU, for the first time in college football history, all four backs rushed for more than 100 yards each. They piled up 611 rushing yards, setting a SWC record. Hayden Fry, coach of the Mustangs, exclaimed, "Texas is the greatest football team that I've ever seen and probably will see." Texas embarrassed TCU, 69–7, and set yet another record for most points scored in an SWC game. After dispatching the Aggies 49–12, the Shootout could commence.

Before the 1969 season began, ABC Sports, needing to fill a December 6 television slot, approached Texas and Arkansas about moving their October 18 game to that date. By the end of November, Arkansas was number two, Texas was number one, and ABC—according to Royal—looked "wiser than a tree full of owls."

It was actually Royal who unintentionally named the game "The Big Shootout." Reporters started talking about the Texas-Arkansas game even before the Horns had faced A&M. Coach Royal told a reporter that he didn't want to talk about Arkansas yet, but if Texas managed to beat A&M, the Arkansas game would be a real shootout. The name stuck.

No regular-season game in the history of football has had such a buildup or such a dramatic ending. Texas had the nation's top-ranked offense and Arkansas led the nation in scoring defense. Arkansas led until late in the fourth quarter, but when it was all over, President Richard M. Nixon was in the Texas locker room presenting the Longhorns with a plaque that named them National Champions in the 100th year of college football.

14 The Big Shootout

The marquee in front of the Fayetteville, Arkansas, church read: "Darrell Royal, cast not thy steers before swine"—to which Royal replied, "I had hoped God would be neutral."

Unlike the state of Texas, Arkansas had only one big-time college, and it seemed every person in the state was a Razorback fan. Leading up to the big game, Arkansas businesses, government offices, and local telephone operators all answered the phones: "Beat Texas. May I help you?"

The Longhorn nation was geared up, too. Thirty-five thousand fans attended the Thursday night pep rally at Memorial Stadium.

The buildup to the game was suffocating. Texas was number one in the nation, 18 games into its 30-game winning streak. Arkansas was number two and had won 15 in a row. The media had been celebrating the 100th anniversary of college football, and this game would be the climax of the centennial. Year in and year out, Arkansas and Texas were intense rivals and usually played one another in close, hard-fought battles. Frank Broyles, Arkansas' head coach, and Royal were good buddies who played golf together in the off-season, but they gave no quarter on the football field.

Best Team Ever

During the wild celebration after the 2005 National Championship game, Texas fans chanted "Best Team Ever," mocking not the worthy warriors of the USC Trojans team, but the media guys whose "Best Team Ever" overkill had helped spur the Longhorns to victory.

Sports Illustrated writer Stewart Mandel quipped that ESPN "spent the better part of Christmas season comparing that Trojan squad to some of the most acclaimed teams of all time, only to find out that they weren't even the best team that season."

The 1969 pep rally before the "Big Shootout" against Arkansas drew almost 35,000 Longhorn fans.

This game really was for all the marbles, and until James Street scored on a busted play, Texas' offense couldn't do anything. Down 14–6, Texas successfully went for two on a counter-option that Royal called before the game started. Royal had anticipated the situation, and while riding the team bus to the stadium he told Street they'd go for two after their first score and told him what play to run.

Arkansas then moved the ball to the UT 7-yard line, but Longhorn Danny Lester intercepted Chuck Dicus' pass and brought it out to the 20. Texas was unable to turn that into points, though, as another drive ended in a fumble, this one on the Arkansas 39. Texas would lose three fumbles before the game was over.

With 4:47 left in the game, Texas had the ball at its own 42, facing fourth-and-three. At the sideline during the timeout, Street was listening to one side of Royal's conversation with the press box. The coaches and Street heard Royal—conservative Darrell

Royal—say, "Pass." When offensive coordinator Emory Bellard tried to argue with him, Royal removed his headset and talked only to Street. Mike Campbell, defensive coordinator, said nothing to Royal, but wheeled around to face his players and shouted, "Defense! Get ready!"

Stunned at the call, Street turned around on his way back to the huddle to make sure he'd heard Royal right. He had. Back in the huddle, Street put a good spin on it. He told the team, "You're not gonna believe this play. But it'll work."

Royal, famous for playing his gut feelings and his hunches, said later, "Every now and then you have to suck it up and pick a number."

It was the "right 53 veer" pass. Steve Worster recalled in *Dance With Who Brung You*, "Chins dropped. Total disbelief…the whole game revolved around that play. I couldn't believe we were throwing the ball, but we weren't doing worth a damn on the ground, so why not?" Because they hadn't worked on the play for the Arkansas game, Street had to explain it in detail.

One Razorback defensive lineman, Terry Don Phillips, was a former teammate of Street's at Longview High. When Street launched the pass to Randy Peschel, Phillips hit the quarterback and knocked him down, so Street was unable to see whether the pass had reached its intended destination. When he realized the pass was complete, Street reached down to help Phillips up and said, "Come on, Bubba. We're way down here now." A few plays later, Jim Bertelsen scored, and Happy Feller's extra point made the score, 15–14.

It was too early to celebrate. There was still 3:58 on the clock, and Arkansas was driving, but a Tom Campbell interception at the Texas 21 killed the drive, saved the day, and sealed the victory.

In the 100th year of college football, the Texas Longhorns were National Champions.

15 I Play to Win

The scoreboard in the south end zone of Darrell K Royal–Texas Memorial Stadium is dedicated to the memory of Freddie Steinmark, a courageous defensive back on the 1968 and '69 Texas football teams who succumbed to cancer. Since Mack Brown's arrival in 1998, it has become a pregame ritual for Longhorn players to stop and touch Steinmark's picture before they take the field to remind them of the courage Steinmark displayed in his fight against cancer.

That little blurb, or something close to it, has been written so many times that it has almost become a cliché. If reading the previous paragraph leaves you unmoved, here's the antidote: read the book.

I Play to Win is the autobiography of Freddie Joe Steinmark. It is not just another sad story about a cancer victim, although it is sad, and Steinmark did die of cancer.

This memoir, written with the help of sportswriting legend Blackie Sherrod, is an intimate rendering of Steinmark's life and of Texas football from a player's unique perspective. The gut-wrenching account of his determination to play in spite of unrelenting pain and of his battle to live shows why he is still revered today.

Steinmark was a two-year starter at defensive back, an intensely competitive overachiever. Just six days after he started against Arkansas in the 1969 "Big Shootout" that propelled UT to its second National Championship, Steinmark's leg was amputated because of a malignant bone tumor.

Less than a month after the amputation, Steinmark, aided by crutches, was standing on the sideline of the Cotton Bowl, cheering as the Longhorns—his teammates—defeated Notre Dame. He

Great Pep Talk Number Two

Texas installed the wishbone offense in the summer of 1968, and at the start of the season the offense was having trouble adjusting to the change. Freddie Steinmark wrote that the defensive players would gather just as practice was dismissed and cheer: "Offense, offense, we can win, if you don't fumble on our 10!"

had rejected offers of a seat in the press box and he refused to sit in a wheelchair. He was an injured player and he would be on the sideline with his team.

Determined to walk across the stage the following January to receive his letter at the Longhorn football banquet, Freddie mastered walking with his prosthesis just five weeks after the operation, a feat which normally takes patients three to six months.

Steinmark didn't just fall into this pile of courage after he was diagnosed with cancer. Coming out of high school, he was an exceptionally talented yet undersized star who believed in his ability to play big-time football, but the only school in the country that initially believed the same was Dartmouth. He had grown up dreaming of playing for Notre Dame, but they would have nothing to do with him. Even the University of Colorado, in his own backyard, paid no attention until after he'd committed to Texas. He had a chip on his shoulder and came to Texas with something to prove.

He wrote, "I had put everything on the line when I had chosen to come to Texas, rather than a lesser school…I gambled everything by coming to Texas. I might have spent my career on the bench. I might never have played a down. Apparently there were some people in Colorado and South Bend who didn't think I could."

"Little Freddie looked more as if he were applying for a student manager's job than a football scholarship at a major university," said Darrell Royal. But the coaches weren't concerned about his size. Steinmark came to Texas, eager to prove that Royal was right to take a chance on him, and as Royal said, "He forced himself to extra effort. He pushed himself into the best condition possible, physically and mentally, because he felt with his lack of size he needed to go full-throttle every step."

Steinmark provides a glimpse of what it was like to be on the inside of the Longhorns' championship drive, but more importantly, his book exposes a rare picture of friendships forged through football and how that team bore the weight of heartbreak with humor and loyalty and love.

I Play to Win should be required reading for every Longhorn who is privileged to touch the picture of Freddie Steinmark and who aspires to grab a little of that courage for himself.

Steinmark is a member of the Longhorn Hall of Honor.

16 The 1970 Cotton Bowl

The hype surrounding the 1964 Cotton Bowl game against Navy had seemed intense, but all of that was just a drop in the bucket compared to the insanity leading up to the 1970 Cotton Bowl.

The New Year's Day game marked the end of the 100th year of college football. After Texas beat Arkansas in the Big Shootout, most polls proclaimed Texas national champs. In a sideshow to the game, some people—most notably Penn State coach Joe Paterno—groused that the national championship should still be up for grabs, even though undefeated Penn State had chosen to play in the Orange Bowl rather than face number one Texas in the Cotton Bowl.

There was great buzz surrounding Notre Dame's talented quarterback, Joe Theismann, who, at the beginning of the season, had

UT quarterback James Street, No. 16, and the Notre Dame defensive line await the ref's measurement on yet another fourth-and-two for the Longhorns.

changed the pronunciation of his last name so that it now rhymed with "Heisman."

And of course, the national press had picked up on the story of Freddie Steinmark. Until mid-December, the two-year starter had been looking forward to playing against Notre Dame. Instead, he would watch the game from the sideline. Shortly after he played in the Big Shootout, doctors had discovered a malignant bone tumor in his leg and had been forced to amputate.

Adding to the frenzy was the fact that Notre Dame had not accepted a postseason bowl bid in 44 years, and now they were challenging the undefeated Longhorns. Texas led the nation in rushing offense and had scored 51 rushing touchdowns. Notre Dame had lost one game and tied another, but they had one of the strongest defenses in the country and they outweighed Texas by almost 20 pounds a man.

And as a climax to the drama, the three surviving members of Notre Dame's famous "Four Horsemen" were on hand for the pregame festivities.

1969 Record
(National Champions, Southwest Conference Champions)

Texas	Opponent
17	California 0
49	Texas Tech 7
56	Navy 17
27	Oklahoma 17
31	Rice 0
45	SMU 14
56	Baylor 14
69	TCU 7
49	Texas A&M 12
15	Arkansas 14
21	Notre Dame (Cotton Bowl) 17

The Dallas Cowboys' playoff game had ruined the field and the continuing rain turned the playing surface into a swamp. He watched anxiously on game day as helicopters hovered over the Cotton Bowl, trying to dry the field. Coach Royal wondered if Texas would be able to move the ball at all, but when a writer asked if Royal would abandon his dependence on the running game, Royal responded with one of his most enduring Royalisms: "No. We're gonna dance with the one who brung us."

Notre Dame managed to get up 10–0 before Longhorn Jim Bertelsen led Texas on a 74-yard touchdown drive. In the fourth quarter, the Horns were trailing 17–14 with just under seven minutes left to play and 76 yards to cover.

Texas produced a 17-play drive, and with 2:26 on the clock, facing fourth-and-two, with the National Championship at stake, Royal once again gambled on a pass. Steinmark recalled in *I Play to Win,* "When Street went back to the huddle, he looked right at Speyrer as he called the play. Then he said something else. He said this could be our last offensive play of the season. We had come too far to see it end with this play."

Street threw the ball low and behind Speyrer, who had to stop, turn around, and dive to catch the ball just before it hit the ground at the 2-yard line. Three plays later, Billy Dale ran it over for the winning touchdown.

With just 38 seconds on the clock, defensive back Tom Campbell intercepted Theismann's pass to save the game, just as he had done against Arkansas three weeks earlier. Campbell held on to the game ball, refusing to hand it over to an official, and gave it to Coach Royal for a locker-room presentation to Freddie Joe Steinmark.

17 The 1970 Season

Texas entered the 1970 football season riding a 20-game winning streak and gunning for another National Championship. But the team was not considered as strong as the 1969 bunch and the pressure was even greater on the players and coaches.

Gone were starters All-American tackle Bob McKay, halfback Ted Koy, linebacker Glen Halsell, defensive backs Mike and Tom Campbell, and safety Freddie Steinmark. Gone, too, was quarterback James Street, the fiery competitor who'd never lost a game he started.

Yet if there was any concern in 1970 about replacing Street, Eddie Phillips soon dispelled those worries.

Texas beat California 56–15 in the season opener and Phillips ran for 129 yards on nine carries. Longhorns collectively let out a sigh of relief. The Horns steamrolled Texas Tech the following week, 35–13. Things were looking good.

Then number 13 UCLA came to call. On a day so hot people suffered heatstroke in the stands, the Bruins' defense shut down

1970 Record
(National Champions, Southwest Conference Champions)

Texas	Opponent
56	California 15
35	Texas Tech 13
20	UCLA 17
41	Oklahoma 21
45	Rice 17
42	SMU 15
21	Baylor 14
58	TCU 0
52	Texas A&M 14
42	Arkansas 7
11	Notre Dame (Cotton Bowl) 24

the wishbone offense, which had managed only a touchdown and two field goals. With 20 seconds left in the game, trailing 17–13, and holding no timeouts, Texas had to have a miracle to pull out a victory and preserve their winning streak.

Phillips barely got a pass off before being buried under defenders, but Santa Rita, patron saint of impossible causes, intervened for Texas once again. The throw was perfect and so was clutch receiver Cotton Speyrer's catch, which he took in for a touchdown and a last-second comeback victory.

Other than a hard-fought 21–14 win over Baylor, which knocked Texas out of the number one spot in favor of Notre Dame, the remaining regular-season opponents posed no threat to the Longhorns. After beating number four Arkansas 42–7 in what had been billed as "The Big Shootout II," Texas was crowned National Champions by the UPI poll, which at that time was still naming the National Champion before the bowl games.

Texas was set to face Notre Dame in the Cotton Bowl for the second year in a row. The Irish were big and powerful and were still smarting from their last-minute loss to the Longhorns the year before.

Notre Dame quarterback Joe Theismann turned in a stellar performance, accounting for 18 of their 24 points. Banged-up Longhorn workhorse Steve Worster, whose injuries prevented him from practicing in the month leading up to the game, was finally contained, gaining only 42 yards. Texas helped the Irish along in their 24–11 victory by giving up five of the 10 fumbles on the day.

Ironically, Eddie Phillips, who ran the wishbone as well as any Texas quarterback had or would, was named outstanding offensive player of the Cotton Bowl. He rushed for 164 yards on 23 carries and passed for 199 yards, but it wasn't enough, and it was no consolation to Phillips, the team, or the fans.

The "Worster Bunch" was gone, leaving a legacy of a 30–2–1 record, three Southwest Conference championships, two National Championships, the 1970 NCAA rushing championship, and the NCAA scoring championship.

The 30-game win streak had ended.

It was time to reload.

18 The 2005 Season

Women were liberated. The Vietnam War ended. The Viking rover landed on Mars. Prince Charles married Diana. Michael Jordan reigned and Michael Jackson moonwalked. ESPN piped 24-hour sports into our living rooms. LPs gave way to eight-track tapes, which gave way to cassettes, which gave way to CDs. Steve Jobs gave us Apples and iPods. Yet still we weren't satisfied.

The Longhorn bench erupts after USC quarterback Matt Leinart's pass fell incomplete, sealing Texas' fourth National Championship.

Throughout the '70s, the '80s, the '90s, and half of the 2000s, the world kept spinning and things kept changing and Longhorns kept hoping and waiting. But on January 5, 2006, all the waiting and frustration fell away.

Texas defeated USC, the team that couldn't be beaten.

ESPN analysts had declared the 2005 USC team to be not just the best team in the country, but perhaps the best team *ever*. During the month-long break before the 2006 Rose Bowl, Longhorns across the country wearied of hearing that Southern Cal was coming to the National Championship game with a 34-game winning streak, two Heisman Trophy winners, and the previous year's championship ring on their fingers. ESPN declared that USC had the best offense in the history of college football, mysteriously ignoring the fact that Texas led the nation in scoring.

The game started off shaky for the Horns. They lost a fumble, then gave up an early touchdown to bruising Trojan running back LenDale White.

Texas finally got a lucky break with their recovery of an ill-advised lateral attempt by Reggie Bush and came away with a field goal, but USC answered by driving to the Texas 25-yard line, where Longhorn safety Michael Griffin intercepted Matt Leinart's pass.

The Longhorns converted the turnover into a touchdown, but missed the extra point. The game continued to be a ferocious defensive battle, and when the warriors went to their locker rooms at halftime, Texas was on top 16–10.

Both teams came out in the second half intent on putting the game away, and what ensued was one of the greatest halves of college football ever played. White scored to make it 17–16, USC. Vince Young's first of three rushing touchdowns and David Pino's point after touchdown put the Horns up 23–17. Then White scored again and the Trojans went ahead 24–23. Texas missed a 31-yard field goal to start the fourth quarter. The tension was almost unbearable, and the fourth quarter had only begun.

USC quarterback Leinart was spectacular in the game, passing for 365 yards and a touchdown. The Trojans drove 80 yards to set up Bush's 26-yard touchdown. Texas fought back to the USC 17,

The spoils of victory: the 2005 National Championship ring.

Great Pep Talk Number Three

It was finished, Coach Mack Brown's second march to the Rose Bowl, but this time it had been for the National Championship. It was finished and the Horns were the victors of one of the most exciting football games ever played.

In the locker room, after the initial celebrating had died down, Brown addressed his team. He didn't talk about the team's performance or their stats. He told them, "Remember that we love you. Be proud of what you have accomplished, and enjoy this moment. Let this be a great thing in your life...but don't let it be the best thing that ever happens in your life. Go on from here, be great husbands and great dads, and make a difference."

but a fumble stymied the drive, and UT settled for a field goal. USC 31, Texas 26.

With just under seven minutes to play, Southern Cal marched down to score, giving the Trojans their biggest lead of the game, 38–26.

Finally, something kicked in...that old Longhorn mojo from the '60s and '70s that left every player and every fan knowing, absolutely, that Texas would win. Perhaps it was something the team felt on a subconscious level...a certainty that Longhorn fans, having come so close after waiting so long, simply could not endure a defeat. Or maybe it was, once again, the Comeback Kids simply refusing to go down. Whatever it was, Young willed that team down the field and scored. After the extra point, Texas was down by five with less than four minutes left.

With two minutes on the clock, USC had possession. It was fourth down. Southern Cal needed just two yards for the first. Trojans coach Pete Carroll called on powerful White to convert. In a game with so many pivotal moments, this was the big one.

The Longhorns—defensive end Brian Robison, tackle Larry Dibbles, cornerback Aaron Ross, and safety Michael Huff—stuffed White and stopped the Trojans less than a foot short of the first-down marker. Texas took possession of the ball at their 44, with just over two minutes left and a lot of turf to cover.

Nine plays later, facing fourth-and-five and with 19 seconds on the clock, Young scored his final touchdown for the Longhorns and made it look easy. A two-point conversion…a complete Leinart pass…an incomplete pass by Leinart…and it was over.

We were the champions, my friend, 41–38, and we were finally satisfied.

19 Frank Medina

"Size matters not. Look at me. Judge me by my size, do you? Hmm? Hmm. And well you should not." —Yoda

How is it that a 4'10" full-blooded Cherokee dressed like the milkman could intimidate hulking defensive tackles and prima-donna quarterbacks into running just one more set of stadium stairs while wearing weight vests and carrying tackling dummies? Why would anyone, especially a 19-year-old college kid, endure humili-ation and intolerable physical pain day after day?

Because Frank Medina told them to.

One of the most feared and most beloved figures in Longhorn football history, Medina was UT's head trainer, a position known today as "strength and conditioning coach," for 32 years. Brought to Texas by D.X. Bible in 1945, Medina kept his job through five coaching changes.

Frank was world-renowned, not just for his well-conditioned teams, but as the head trainer for two U.S. Olympic teams. He trained 16 SWC championship teams and three National Championship teams. His overall record was 261–88–7.

Perhaps the best description of Frank—surprisingly, that's how the players addressed him—came from former defensive back Glenn Blackwood. "This little man…he was a piece of work. It's like Coach Royal was Obi-Wan Kenobi and Frank was Yoda."

When Texas players from that era get together, talk inevitably turns to "Frank stories." Each player seems to have his favorite. Ask any one of them, "So, did you play for Frank?" Then just sit back and enjoy.

Frank didn't call his players by name. He'd trained and taped and scolded and encouraged thousands of young men, and he couldn't possibly remember all their names, so he called them all "Mr. Man" or "Son."

"You think Yoda stops teaching, just because his student does not want to hear? A teacher Yoda is. Yoda teaches like drunkards drink, like killers kill."

His methods were rather unorthodox. Players tell of walking by the steam room and hearing some overweight offensive lineman pounding on the door, locked in and unable to get out. Tom Stolhandske told Bill Little, "If Frank put you in there for X minutes, you were going to stay in there for X minutes…whether or not you passed out."

There's the story of the time Frank loaded up several overweight players in his car, drove them to the outskirts of town, shoved them out of the car, and told them to run the 17 miles back to campus. Glenn Blackwood remembers the "religious relays" where, just to liven things up, Frank would divide the team into different denominations for running drills.

Before football became a year-round enterprise, players often went home for the summer to work or to get classes out of the way at their local community college. Frank's weekly mailings consisted of that week's workout schedule and a letter encouraging the players to keep their bodies and their attitudes in shape for the fall. The letters were full of obscure references and archaic language that few of the players understood. One passage warned against their becoming "well-fed claudicants." Not one knew what that meant, but they all caught Frank's drift: Don't come back to Austin fat and out of shape.

"Try not. Do, or do not. There is no try." —Yoda to Luke Skywalker

In spite of his size, Longhorn trainer Frank Medina (right) was one of the most feared and most respected figures in Texas football history.

Longhorn Lore: Henry's Team

The son of freed slaves, Henry "Doc" Reeves was never without his water bucket or doctor's bag. Reeves served Texas athletes as trainer, masseuse, and medical assistant from 1894 to 1914.

The *Longhorn Magazine* called him "the most famous character connected with football in The University of Texas," and wrote that "he likes the game of football and loves the boys who play it."

In the days when coaches rarely stayed on the job for more than a year, the one constant of UT football was Reeves. Always dressed in a black suit and a black Stetson hat, he was a respected fixture on campus and on the athletic fields. The *Cactus Yearbook* listed two versions of an all-time Texas team; one list was the coach's and the other was "Henry's Team."

When Reeves suffered a stroke at the 1915 A&M game in College Station and lingered for a few months, the heartsick student body took up a collection for his medical costs. An editorial in the *Houston Post* left this lasting image of Reeves: "Doctor Henry can never be forgotten. A picture that will never fade is that of his long, rather ungainly figure flying across the football field with his coattails flapping in the breeze. In one hand he holds the precious pail of water, and in the other the little black valise whose contents have served as first aid to the injured, to many a stricken athlete, laid out on the field of play."

Nothing gets these men laughing more than a good "Frank story"…unless it's a good Mike Campbell story. But underlying the fun-poking and the attempts at imitating Frank's nasal, clipped speech is a powerful admiration and appreciation of what this man pushed them to become. Jerry Sisemore said, "Guys loved him; you always knew where his heart was." Roosevelt Leaks recalled, "When times get hard today, most of us keep going, and that attitude is because of Frank." Wide receiver Alfred Jackson talked of Frank's untiring and relentless pursuit of excellence: "You never realized what your ultimate potential was, but Frank got everything out of you. He made us better."

Frank made them winners.

20 Lutcher Stark

H.J. Lutcher Stark's fingerprints are all over the Forty Acres.

As regent Frank Erwin would do three decades later, Stark influenced the direction and the attitude of The University of Texas in a big way. He had a vision of what this University should be, and like Erwin, he wheedled, pushed, and bullied his vision into reality. He was the prototypical UT power broker, a larger-than-life force of nature and a wealthy visionary who was passionate about the advancement of The University in all areas.

Stark, the son of a wealthy Texas lumber baron, was the first student in UT history to have an automobile on campus. He served as student manager for the squad in 1910 and helped solidify the Longhorn as the mascot in 1913, when he donated wool warm-up blankets emblazoned with the word "Longhorns" to the football team. He was a true friend of The University, giving generously whenever he saw a need and whenever he happened to agree with that need's importance. He was appointed to the Board of Regents in 1919 at age 32, becoming the youngest regent ever. He served on that board for two and a half decades, spending 12 years as chairman.

Stark and his family were great benefactors of Texas. In the 1920s, Stark outfitted the Longhorn Band with its first modern uniforms—white serge tunics with a front panel of orange silk. In 1922 the newly formed Texas Cowboys wore leggings made of oilcloth, since leather was unaffordable. Stark, believing that a University of the first class should have only the best, provided money for the Cowboys to buy leather chaps.

He oversaw the fundraising for and construction of Texas Memorial Stadium and generously pledged to match 10 percent

Eyes
John Lang Sinclair's original manuscript of "The Eyes of Texas" hangs in the UT Alumni Center.

of all funds raised. His family donated the Stark Library and set into motion UT's program of collecting rare books. When The University could afford only 16 bells for the carillon in the belfry of the new Main Building, Stark donated the 17th bell.

He also liked to hire and fire coaches, particularly football coaches. He was rumored to have had a hand in the resignation of Berry Whitaker, although Whitaker denied it. Stark, angered at the cavalier attitude of UT line coach Bill James, threatened to have him fired. When Stark turned his wrath on successful and highly respected coach Clyde Littlefield, Littlefield resigned, saying "I just made up my mind that if I wanted to live longer, I'd better quit." Stark then soured on coach Jack Chevigny and launched a nation-wide search for a coach. He set his sights on D.X. Bible, head coach at Nebraska, gave him a 10-year contract, and pushed through an exorbitant Depression-era salary of $15,000, which was four times the Texas governor's salary.

In Bible, however, Stark met his match. He was accustomed to sitting on the bench at games to make it easier for him to give pep talks or suggest plays, a practice that Bible nipped in the bud. "No team can prosper with two coaches," Bible told Stark, and sent him to the stands.

Lutcher Stark was inducted into the Longhorn Hall of Honor in 1958.

21 Chairman Frank

Frank C. Erwin was UT's most visible, active, and divisive regent since the days of Lutcher Stark in the 1920s and 1930s. From 1966 to 1975 he helped set policy, and he interfered with every area of campus operations. Erwin was a micromanager before the term was ever coined.

No one doubted Erwin's love for The University. He had a vision that Texas would be, in every way, The University of the first class it was intended to be. But like Stark before him, he believed there was only one road to greatness—his road—and if you didn't like the scenery, he'd push you out of the car. There was no compromise in Erwin. *The New York Times* called him "a man who gave little quarter to his foes and received little in return."

While still a student, Erwin met with D.X. Bible to propose forming a booster club to raise money for extras that UT football couldn't pay for. A founding member of the NCAA Rules Committee and a man of legendary integrity, Bible was leery of endorsing any group outside the authority of The University. Bible said, "Frank, I've never seen an alumni group that didn't eventually get a school in trouble with the conference or the NCAA. I won't have it." Erwin thanked him, but told Bible he intended to proceed, with or without his blessing.

Erwin proceeded and succeeded. The Longhorn Club grew into a statewide athletics booster club with branches in every major city.

Erwin was politically connected with President Lyndon Johnson, Texas Governor John Connally, and Lieutenant Governor Ben Barnes, and is credited with single-handedly bringing the LBJ Library and the LBJ School of Public Affairs to The University of Texas.

During his reign as chairman of the Board of Regents from 1966 to 1971, "Chairman Frank" became the students' pet name for Erwin, making unfavorable comparisons to Chairman Mao Zedong of the People's Republic of China. It was a time of student protests, yet Erwin was unbending in his refusal to meet them or even to hear their requests. He refused to leave his office, calling the protestors a bunch of "dirty nuthin's." Erwin threatened to abolish the *Daily Texan's* editorial page for supporting the first Vietnam war protests on campus.

The chain of command meant nothing to Erwin; he *was* the command. He allegedly forced out University president Norm Hackerman and chancellor Harry Ransom; and he fired John Silber, dean of the college of Arts and Sciences, because (some UT sources said) Silber had become too powerful. There was one battle he lost, however, and it infuriated him: after Royal's third 6–4 regular season, (1965–1967), Erwin stood up in front of the Board of Regents and demanded that Royal be fired. It was one of the few of Erwin's power plays that failed.

Yet for every villainous act, there was a heroic one. Erwin went to war to protect the Permanent University Fund from being divided among other state schools. He oversaw the construction of the baseball stadium and the new Texas Swim Center, and the

Longhorn Lore: Bottom of the Fifth

The Wild Bunch, a group of ex-students who sat together at home baseball games in the 1970s and '80s, was notorious for its pranks and its harassment, mostly of opposing players and coaches and umpires.

After Chairman Frank was cited twice for driving while intoxicated, a new ritual was born. Halfway through the fifth inning, the Wild Bunch would stand en masse, raise their cups in a toast, and shout to Erwin, "Hey, Frank! It's the bottom of the fifth." Erwin always rose, faced them, and saluted them with his own cup.

Formidable UT regent Frank Erwin had political ties to President Lyndon Johnson and Texas Governor John Connally.

complex of buildings beyond the interstate. Enrollment soared under Erwin's chairmanship, but so did state appropriations, which increased eightfold while he was in charge.

One of his pet projects was building the SuperDrum, officially named the Frank Erwin Special Events Center, in hopes of building a championship-caliber basketball program. He oversaw construction of the Perry-Castaneda Library, and in a move some suggested was intended to prevent student protests, he built stone planters in the open space in the west mall and surrounded most of the campus with a stone wall.

He most famously oversaw the addition of an upper deck to the west side of Memorial Stadium and the destruction of about 40 cypress and oak trees in a power play so brazen that the story made *The New York Times*. When protestors climbed the trees to prevent their removal, Erwin ordered police officers to drag the people down and arrest them.

Erwin's legacy is checkered, but on balance, UT's athletics program is most assuredly better for having had him on the team. Erwin was named an honorary letterman and is a member of the Longhorn Hall of Honor.

At Frank Erwin's funeral, 2,000 mourners came to the Erwin Special Events Center to pay their respects. UT historian Joe Frantz claimed that half of them were there just to make sure he was really dead.

22 Bloody Mike

Bob Moses, an end on DKR's 1960 and '61 teams, was playing golf several years back with three legendary coaches: John McKay, Chuck Knox, and Colonel Earl "Red" Blaik. The conversation naturally turned to football, and Moses posed this question to the men: "In y'all's opinion, what kind of coach was Mike Campbell?" McKay and Knox agreed that Campbell was the greatest defensive mind of their era.

These days, everyone's a genius, right? That term is tossed around so freely that it's lost its meaning, its impact. But Campbell, defensive coordinator and assistant head coach under Darrell Royal, has been called a genius for so long and by so many, it might as well be his middle name. One definition of genius is "one who possesses exceptional intellectual or creative powers." That describes Campbell on both counts.

Back in 1970, Freddie Steinmark wrote, "Coach Campbell, I must say, is a genius in his way. I've never been associated with a man

Join Texas Exes

Established in 1885, the Texas Exes, or the Longhorn Alumni Association, is more than 100,000 strong and is one of the largest self-governing alumni organizations in the country. Joining Texas Exes has many benefits, not the least of which is that, as a Life Member, you have access to the ticket service program. Beginning three hours before a home game, for the price of face value plus a dollar, the Exes sell tickets that have been turned in by season ticket holders. But they sell them only to Life Members who present their membership cards or key tags.

If you don't have a ticket, just show your Texas Exes membership card to gain entry to the beautiful alumni center across the street from Darrell K Royal–Texas Memorial Stadium, which has televisions galore, drinks, food, and convenient restrooms. It's a great way to watch the game with a few thousand of your closest Longhorn friends.

But you gotta join.

any smarter in meeting all the problems, not just the football problems. He is wise in the ways of the world and he'll explain it all to you in blunt, simple language. He won't allow you to misunderstand.

"We didn't have a defensive playbook full of complicated details. We had a few simple rules which the secondary went over and over until they became second nature."

Royal and Campbell coached together for 22 years. They were of like minds on and off the field and grew into the closest of friends, even brothers. They spent more time with one another during those years than they did with their families.

They shared this understanding and philosophy of football: A confused player cannot be an aggressive player. They stressed fundamentals and simplicity and repetition. Doug English, defensive tackle from 1972 to 1974, said of defense under Campbell, "It wasn't a chess game. You had to whip the guy over you."

But just as a chess master "sees" his opponent's moves several plays in advance, Campbell knew what the opposing offense would do before even they knew it. Before you can be a defensive genius, you must understand the nuances of offense and the tendencies of your opponent. His genius was in his ability to identify what the other team did best and then take that away, making them "beat us left-handed."

Campbell was not a demonstrative man, and his son Tom, a Longhorn defensive back in the late '60s, claimed that "Daddy threw compliments around like they were manhole covers." But his wry sense of humor was well-known. A writer once asked him when a certain overweight lineman, a former blue-chipper, would contribute to the team. Campbell spit a stream of chewing tobacco from his mouth before answering, "When he graduates and joins the Longhorn booster club."

When The University approached Bobby Moses to donate money for a new trophy room, he agreed to let the room to be named in his honor on one condition: The room must also be named for Coach Campbell, "because I wanted to recognize how close together and of one mind that Darrell Royal and Mike Campbell were."

Dan Mauldin, a Longhorn during 1963–64, was visiting practice one day when Jones Ramsey approached him: "Hey, Dan. What are you doing here?" Dan, Phi Beta Kappa at Texas who had seen his share of excellent professors, replied, "Oh, I just like to watch Coach Campbell coach. Of all my professors at The University, he knew his field better than any of the others knew theirs."

If a coach's success can be judged on his players' opinion of him, then no coach has ever been more successful. While on the team, his players called him "Bloody Mike" and lived in fear of being singled out by Campbell in practice. But they loved him fiercely, and today those same men acknowledge with a hint of awe that they were privileged to learn from and play under the best.

23 Earl Campbell

If you think you know a more powerful running back, don't try to tell former quarterback Randy McEachern about it. He swears that the hardest hit he ever took was from Earl Campbell, and that comes from a guy who's been hit by George Cumby, Mike Singletary, and Ross Browner. McEachern was handing off the ball to Earl at practice one day, and when he didn't get out of the way fast enough, Earl flattened him.

After averaging 225 yards rushing per game his senior year in high school, The University of Texas—and every other college in the country—came calling. All that calling and visiting and all that pressure made his mama, Ann Campbell, sick. In the video biography of her son, *The Tyler Rose,* she said, "It just put me in the bed. I could hardly handle thinking about that country boy leaving to go to the city lights…and I *certainly* didn't want him to go to Oklahoma!"

The choice did come down to UT or OU, and he was still confused the night before signing day. So Earl asked God for a sign: "God, if it's your will that I go to Texas, wake me up in the middle of the night to go pee." Earl received his sign, and Texas received God's gift to college football.

Campbell knew what people were saying behind his back. "He'll be back. He'll flunk out of school." But he did not intend to be a rose farmer in Tyler, Texas. He wasn't an A student, not even a B student, and he knew that "of all the people in class, that professor is gonna know when I'm there and when I'm not…I'd sit right on the front row." Darrell Royal compared Earl to a proctor or an alarm clock, saying, "Earl would not miss a class. He'd go through the dorm and knock on the doors. When he went to class he took

Earl Campbell's Statistics and Awards

Freshman Year, 1974
928 yards
162 carries
Six touchdowns
5.7 yards per carry
All–Southwest Conference
SWC Newcomer of the Year

Sophomore Year, 1975
1,118 yards
198 carries
13 touchdowns
5.6 yards per carry
All–Southwest Conference
All-American

Junior Year, 1976
653 yards
138 carries
Three touchdowns
4.7 yards per carry

Senior Year, 1977
1,744 yards
267 carries
19 touchdowns
6.5 yards per carry
All–Southwest Conference
SWC career rushing record
NCAA leading rusher
NCAA all-purpose yardage champion
Longhorns Most Valuable Player
Consensus All-American
Nation's best offensive back
First-ever Davey O'Brien Award for outstanding player in the
Southwest Conference
Heisman Trophy winner
Number one overall NFL draft choice: Houston Oilers

In a prescient move, Earl Campbell seems to strike the Heisman pose on his way to leading the nation in scoring and rushing during the 1977 season.

a crowd with him." Comedian Bob Hope hosted an annual television special to honor the All-America team, and even though Hope offered to send a jet for him, Earl told Hope, "I can't. I have a test."

And always, he heard the echo—"like something on my shoulder"—of people saying, "He'll flunk out of school."

Earl was hurt for much of his junior year, and at the last game of the 1976 season, Earl's coach and great friend and father figure Royal retired from coaching. It was a low point in his college career, but then Texas hired Fred Akers, who warned Campbell he'd better lose 25 pounds because come next fall he'd be running the ball 35 times a game.

Earl got to work. Needing to lose weight, he reported to trainer Frank Medina, but with a secret dream. He wanted Frank to help him win the Heisman Trophy.

Earl remains the standard by which all other runners—at any level—are judged. His exquisite balance, combined with thundering runs and punishing stiff-arms to any who dared try to bring him down, led the 1977 Longhorns to an undefeated regular season.

"We all knew we were playing with Superman," Rick Ingraham, Earl's good friend and one of his offensive linemen at Texas, told *Austin American-Statesman* writer Brad Buchholz. "In that moment, we understood he would be the best player we'd ever step on the field with. He was a man among boys and he earned that Heisman through self-sacrifice."

In 1978, Earl Christian Campbell earned a degree in Speech Communications from The University of Texas.

Campbell is a member of the Texas Sports Hall of Fame and the National Football Foundation College Football Hall of Fame, and was named to *The Sporting News'* list of the 100 Greatest Football Players. Campbell's Longhorn jersey number 20 was retired in 1979. One of three Longhorns inducted into the Pro Football Hall of Fame, Earl is a member of the Longhorn Hall of Honor.

24 Ricky Williams

Ricky Williams is surely the most misunderstood Longhorn, a man of contrasts. He excelled in the toughest of sports, yet he speaks with a small, soft voice and displays an almost childlike honesty. He was revered for his on-the-field prowess, but Texans didn't know

Ricky Williams' Statistics and Awards

Freshman Year, 1995
990 yards rushing
166 attempts
Eight touchdowns
6.0 average
SWC Offensive Freshman of the Year

Sophomore Year, 1996
1,272 yards rushing
205 attempts
12 touchdowns
6.2 average
Consensus All–Big 12

Junior Year, 1997
1,893 yards rushing
279 attempts
25 touchdowns
6.8 average
Consensus All–Big 12
Big 12 Offensive Player of the Year
Consensus All-American
Doak Walker Award

Senior Year, 1998
2,124 yards rushing
361 attempts
27 touchdowns
5.9 average
Consensus All–Big 12
Big 12 Offensive Player of the Year
Consensus All-American
Doak Walker Award
Maxwell Award
Walter Camp Award
AP Player of the Year
Sporting News Player of the Year
Cotton Bowl Offensive MVP
Hula Bowl Offensive MVP
Heisman Trophy Winner

Ricky Williams, Texas' second Heisman Trophy winner, breaks three tackles and the NCAA rushing record in the 1998 A&M game.

what to make of this California boy, who wore a tongue ring and dreads under that helmet.

Not since Earl Campbell had folks seen anything like Ricky's stiff-arm, either, which he'd worked hard to perfect. Or the way he accumulated yardage and broke Earl's single-season rushing record in 1997, putting up 1,893 yards.

By the time Williams finished his junior year, he led the nation in rushing and scoring, had won the Doak Walker Award, and was the darling of Austin and of Longhorn football.

Many felt certain Ricky would bolt for the NFL, but he stunned everyone when he announced, "When I came to Texas three years ago, I set personal and team goals. I also want to get my degree from The University of Texas, and that's why I'm staying another year."

He also had unfinished business; despite leading the nation in rushing and scoring as a junior, he finished fifth in the Heisman voting and was not even invited to the ceremonies.

Ricky was a power runner, like Earl. He had great balance and a great work ethic, like Earl. But where Earl would simply run people over, as if it were too much trouble to alter his course, Ricky ran right by them and made them miss. Quarterback Major Applewhite and Ricky Williams were the keys to the 1998 season and they did not disappoint.

In the game against Iowa State, which Texas won 54–33, Ricky rushed for five touchdowns, a UT-record 350 yards, and set or tied six NCAA records. He also set five UT records that day.

Then, on Halloween night, Texas marched into Lincoln to try to break Nebraska's 47-game home winning streak. Applewhite passed for 269 yards, the Longhorn defense held Nebraska to 311 yards of total offense, and Williams rushed for 150 yards against the vaunted "black shirt" defense. Texas flabbergasted the crowd at Tom Osborne Field and the national television audience by upsetting number seven Nebraska, 20–16.

Going into the Aggie game, Williams needed only 11 yards to break the 22-year-old NCAA rushing yardage record held by Tony Dorsett. The atmosphere was electrifying, and every celebrity you can think of—including Dorsett, who was cheering Ricky on—was standing on the Texas sideline, suddenly looking like Williams' groupies. They didn't have to wait long. With 1:13 left in the first quarter, Williams took the handoff, and breaking three tackles, raced 60 yards to break the record and also score a touchdown.

Williams has won almost every award college football offers. He is the first-ever two-time Doak Walker winner, a Maxwell Award winner, and was the first Longhorn to win the Walter Camp Award, awarded to the nation's top player who exemplifies self-discipline, unselfish team play, desire to excel, mature judgment, and respected leadership. At the end of his Texas career, he owned all or part of 16 NCAA records. A consensus All-American in 1997 and 1998, Williams was a team captain and two-time team MVP. He was named to the "Good Works" Team by the American Football Coaches Association for his efforts on the field and in the community.

He still ranks second on the NCAA's list for career rushing (6,279 yards), and remains in the top 10 for season rushing yardage (ninth), season rushing touchdowns (10th), career rushing touchdowns (third), career scoring (fourth), and all-purpose yardage (eighth, with 7,206 yards). In 1997, he finished fifth in the voting for the Heisman Trophy. The following year, Ricky Williams became UT's second Heisman Trophy winner in a landslide victory. His number 34 jersey was retired by The University in 2000.

Ricky Williams is a member of the Longhorn Hall of Honor.

25 The Academic Heisman

Dallas Griffin graduated—with honors, of course—with degrees in business and finance, and in 2007, he became the first Longhorn ever to win the coveted Draddy Award, the "Academic Heisman."

The Draddy, now named the "William Campbell Trophy," is the centerpiece of the National Football Foundation's scholar-athlete program. Although not well-known outside smart-guy circles, the award recognizes a player as the best in the country for combined academic success, football performance, and exemplary community leadership. One of 15 finalists, Griffin was presented

On Education

"...the coaches themselves must make a consistent effort to convince the public that their aim is honestly education and *not* primarily a desire to win championships. If our aim is not primarily education, then it is both unavailing and hypocritical for us to pose as members of a dignified profession.

"If football is to take its place by the side of the other departments, it must exist primarily to develop an intelligent use of muscle, to regulate the exercise of determination and fight, to teach self-control and sportsmanship, and those finite qualities that are the mark of a flaming and courageous heart. The gridiron...is but the laboratory where the theories and the instruction of the teacher are put to the test.

"The coach must always remember that his program is only one phase of the school's program, and a subsidiary phase at that. The classroom still outranks the stadium." —D.X. Bible, *Championship Football*

with the 24-inch bronze trophy and a $25,000 postgraduate scholarship at the NFF College Hall of Fame's 50th annual awards dinner at the Waldorf-Astoria in New York City.

Griffin, representative of the brains and brawn produced at UT, also received the 2007 Anson Mount Scholar/Athlete Award, honoring the nation's best student-athlete, and was named to *ESPN The Magazine*'s Academic All-America first team.

The four-time Academic All–Big 12 player posted a 3.88 GPA in his double major and somehow also found time to be the starting center for 10 games in 2007 before suffering a season-ending knee injury against Oklahoma State.

Sam Acho, a four-year starter for the Horns, became Texas' second Campbell/Draddy Award winner in 2010. Acho earned a degree in marketing, and at the urging of former Draddy winner Dallas Griffin, added a degree from the honors business school, posting a 3.55 GPA. In 2010, the *Sporting News* named Acho one of the 20 smartest athletes in sports.

Hey, don't act so surprised. Griffin and Acho may be the only Campbell Trophy recipients the Horns have had, but they ain't the only smart guys around.

Tight end Pat Fitzgerald won the Anson Mount Award in 1996. In 1933, quarterback Willson H. "Bull" Elkins became the only UT player to win a Rhodes Scholarship. Texas boasts of 29 academic All-Americans, eight NCAA post-graduate scholarship winners, 11 NFF College Hall of Fame post-graduate scholarship winners, and seven members of the AFCA "Good Works" Team.

26 Celebrate on the Drag

The stars must be properly aligned before a fan can experience this, one of the ultimate experiences for a Longhorn.

The next time Texas wins a National Championship, which shouldn't be too long now, jump in your car and race to Guadalupe Street, known as the Drag. The entire city will erupt; residents will stream out of their driveways and head toward the UT Tower, drawn by some inexplicable force—think of Richard Dreyfus in *Close Encounters of the Third Kind.*

There will be traffic jams—not just on the main thoroughfares, but in the sedate neighborhoods surrounding campus and in the suburbs and in the projects. No matter. Enjoy the ride, or rather the stops. It's as if a pep rally has spread in a 10-mile radius from the newly lit Tower, the epicenter of the celebration. You'll hang out your car window, high-fiving perfect strangers in the car next to yours and you'll become instantaneous—albeit momentary—friends with people driving low-riding Chevys, Escalades, and battered pick-up trucks.

Longhorn Lore

The Longhorns' 652 points scored in 2005 were, at the time, the most scored in a season by any team in NCAA history. That team also set a school record for total offense, with 6,657 yards. The national champs were the fourth team in NCAA history to average more than 50 points and 500 yards per game.

Sad to report, the record didn't last long. The 2008 Sooners team scored 716 and in 2013, that record was blown up by the Florida State Seminoles, who scored 723 points.

The ultimate goal is to drive in front of the Littlefield Fountain to have your photo taken in front of the orange-bathed Tower, where the lit windows form the number "1." Or perhaps the ultimate goal is simply to bask in the elation of the occasion with 10,000 other Texas fans who know at that moment what it's like to be number one.

These spontaneous eruptions of fanhood are not limited to National Championships. None of these events are preplanned, and they are liable to occur anytime Texas wins a big game. After the 1977 Longhorns, ranked number five in the nation, defeated number two Oklahoma to end a six-year drought against the Sooners, the campus emptied and the Drag filled with screaming fans, blocking traffic and frustrating the Austin Police Department. They're accustomed to it by now.

Another occasion for celebration is when a Longhorn is nominated for the Heisman. Grab a table at Dirty's at 29th and Guadalupe; order one of their famous burgers, some tots, and a milkshake; and settle back to watch the Heisman presentation. If our guy wins, as Earl Campbell did in 1977 and Ricky Williams did in 1998, you're perfectly positioned to wander down the Drag and watch the revelry from a safe distance. If our guy is robbed of the hardware, you can always stay at Dirty's, have another pitcher of Shiner, and moan about how the media hates Texas.

27 Vince Young

Pat Forde, a sports columnist for ESPN, wrote that Vince Young had the best legs since Marilyn Monroe. That's certainly the way the story ended, but the beginning was full of suspense.

The signing of Young was a huge coup for Texas. He was *Parade Magazine*'s National High School Player of the Year, and had been pegged by *Sporting News* as the top high school prospect in the country.

Young became a starter for Texas halfway through his freshman year. His scrambling skills were awe-inspiring, but his passing was raw and inconsistent; during his sophomore year in 2004, the fans were howling. Texas had barely beaten Arkansas 22–20 and had lost to OU for the fifth straight time. Vince struggled against the Sooners, completing only eight of 23 pass attempts. Texas' squeaker over Missouri was another tough day, as Vince went three-for-nine and threw two interceptions before he was knocked out of the game in the second quarter. Bill Simmons, writer for ESPN.com, said Young's throwing motion resembled someone trying to fling dog poop off his hand.

Legendary Texas quarterback Bobby Layne once said, "This is a man's game. You have to grow into a man to play it right. A quarterback takes about three years before he knows halfway what's going on. You never really learn this damn thing."

Mack Brown and Greg Davis understood this, and they were willing to wait. They saw Young every day in practice and knew he was just scratching the surface of the boundless store of talent he possessed.

The story goes that Brown pulled Young aside and told him to quit worrying about his throwing motion and making mistakes.

Switzer on Mack Brown

"Good-bye to the I. I threw it out and hired coach Mack Brown from Appalachian State, one of the top young offensive coaches in the country, to join the staff and reeducate us in the art of the triple option. Brown helped Oklahoma develop its best passing attack in years, as he coached quarterbacks Danny Bradley, a first-team All–Big 8 selection, and Troy Aikman, a three-time Super Bowl Champion signal caller with the Dallas Cowboys." —Barry Switzer in his autobiography, *Bootlegger's Boy*, published in 1990

Brown urged Young to just go back to being the player they'd recruited, the one they watched in practice each day.

He took their advice. He began spending more time in the film room, and with each of the Longhorns' next six wins, his confidence grew. Along the way, he grew into the singular leader of the team.

With Young under center, UT became a team you could never count out. The players knew—and the fans came to believe—that regardless of the score, Texas would find a way to come back and win. Vince was the linchpin in the biggest comeback in school history, when Texas rallied from a 35–7 halftime deficit to beat Oklahoma State 56–35.

Teammate David Thomas said in *Longhorn Madness,* "The guy is magnetic. You're just drawn to him. I've seen him morph into the best player in the country." By the end of the season, VY was like the Pied Piper; his teammates would have followed him anywhere.

He led them straight to Los Angeles to Texas' first Rose Bowl appearance and a frenzied 38–37 victory over Michigan. Dusty Mangum's last-second field goal framed him as the hero, but Vince Young was responsible for the other 35 points Texas scored.

At the beginning of the 2005 season, Vince said, "I won't accept what's good right now. I want us to achieve greatness." So they did.

The Longhorns held down the number two position all year as they rolled over their opponents and averaged 50 points per game. In what has been called the greatest bowl game in the history of college football, Young and the Texas Longhorns defeated number one USC, a team that had been touted as possibly the greatest college team—ever.

Young was the first quarterback in UT history to earn consensus first-team All-American honors and is the only quarterback in NCAA history to rush for 1,000 yards and pass for 3,000 in the same season. He was awarded the Maxwell Award, the Davey O'Brien Quarterback Award, and the Manning Award. He wound up his career with 30 wins and two losses as a starter. Young was named to the American Football Coaches Association's "Good Works" Team for service to the community.

In keeping with a promise made to his mother, Young returned to the UT campus each spring and in May 2013, Vince Young earned his degree in Youth and Community Studies.

In December 2013, the Football Writers Association of America chose an All-Century Class, naming just one player from each decade of the Rose Bowl's history. Young, who earned Player of the Game honors in the 2005 and 2006 Rose Bowls, was selected to represent the 2000s. The University retired his number 10 jersey in 2008.

Vince Young finished second in the 2005 Heisman Trophy Award voting.

Colt McCoy

Colt McCoy had a triumphant high school career, leading his team to the AA State Championship Game and being named Associated

Press AA Offensive MVP, but few believed that success at tiny Jim Ned High School in Tuscola, Texas, could translate to success at The University of Texas, where they play big-time football. "There's not even a Dairy Queen in Tuscola," Colt said, "and you don't even have to stop at the stoplight—just drive through. I loved living there. Everyone is so supportive, everyone knows each other, and nobody locks their doors. I couldn't ask to grow up in a better place."

McCoy seemed too good to be true. With his aw-shucks country boy demeanor, he was the boy every daddy would want his daughter to marry. He wasn't shy about proclaiming his Christian faith or attending the Church of Christ every Sunday. His discipline and work ethic set him apart from other high school kids. He was the team's punter, lettered four years in basketball, three in track. Colt was in the National Honor Society, served on the student council, was a class favorite, and was selected Mr. Jim Ned High School. He even gave up carbonated drinks after the 6th grade.

After apprenticing under Vince Young in 2005, the redshirt freshman McCoy led the Horns to a 10–3 season and a win over Iowa in the Alamo Bowl. Along the way he set an NCAA record for freshmen quarterbacks, with 29 touchdowns.

Colt's image as the all-American boy was burnished after he came to the rescue of a man having seizures on the dock of his home. At around 9:00 PM on Memorial Day 2006, Colt and his father, Brad, heard Patina Herrington screaming for help from the other side of the lake. The two men swam 300 yards to the other bank, and as neighbors called 911, Colt raced up a steep incline to flag down emergency rescue crews.

Midway through the 2007 season, however, after losses to Kansas and OU, *Sports Illustrated* named Colt one of the Most Disappointing College Players of the year, noting "five games into this season, McCoy has already thrown more interceptions (9) than he threw all last season (7)."

A two-time All-American, Colt McCoy holds a number of Longhorn records, including most career touchdown passes, most touchdown passes in a season, most career passing yards, most total touchdowns, and most career wins.

Priceless Aggie Moment

Aggie back Herschel Burgess said, "In those days you could fall down, roll around, and get up again; you weren't down until…an official blew his whistle." After Burgess intercepted a Texas pass in the 1928 game, he ran for a few yards and then was tackled. He got up and was handing the ball to the ref, "but a Texas player ran between us and grabbed the ball, and the ref gave Texas possession because he hadn't blown his whistle yet."

Colt responded by catching fire again in 2008, leading the Horns to victory over their first eight opponents. A last-second touchdown by Texas Tech's Michael Crabtree broke Texas' heart and its perfect record. McCoy received consensus All-American honors after leading his teammates to a 12–1 season and a Fiesta Bowl victory over Ohio State.

Things got even better in 2009. The Longhorns were undefeated through the regular season, and number two Texas met number one Alabama in the Rose Bowl for the BCS National Championship. Texas' Rose Bowl dreams turned into a nightmare; fans watched in horror when Colt was knocked out with a shoulder injury on the Longhorns' fifth offensive play of the game. Texas fell to Alabama 37–21.

In his postgame interview, McCoy did not disappoint. His response to having his career end in heartbreak was classic Colt: "I worked and played my whole career to be on this stage, to be given this opportunity. To know that is tough. But at the same time, I am a man of faith. I stand on the rock. I'll never question God for why things happen the way they do."

A two-time consensus All-American in 2008 and '09, Colt won almost every national award available to a quarterback. Among his trophies: AT&T/ABC Sports Player of the Year (2009), two Walter Camp Awards, Manning Award, Maxwell Award, Davey O'Brien Award, and the Unitas Golden Arm Award. He was on the

Academic All–Big 12 team four-times and received a postgraduate scholarship from the NFF College Hall of Fame.

Colt is the only Longhorn to be named team MVP four-times, and he was selected co-captain twice, in 2008 and 2009. His number 12 jersey was retired in 2010.

In 2008, McCoy finished a close second in the Heisman voting, and in 2009, he was third, becoming the first Longhorn to finish among the Heisman's top three vote getters twice.

29 James Saxton

Coach Darrell Royal said James Saxton was the quickest player in America, and he had earned the reputation. Saxton had also earned the nickname "Rabbit" from his teammates, but the rumor that he caught jackrabbits, which can run up to 35 miles an hour, is untrue. He caught cottontails.

Saxton tells the story of mowing alfalfa fields on a ranch in Kaufman, Texas, when he saw rabbits running everywhere. "I got off my tractor and…cut through the circle and caught one…. A guy from the local paper came out to see if I could catch another one, and I did."

Saxton came to Texas in the same class as Jack Collins from Highland Park in Dallas. Both backs were fast, running a 9.9 in the 100, but Saxton was unbelievably quick. Royal said, "He gives you a thrill on a two-yard gain. He's like a balloon full of air. When you turn him loose, there's no telling where he's going."

When Saxton first arrived at Texas, Royal called him a "rural runner" because he covered the whole countryside. Even his

Lifetime Achievement Award...

...goes to Bill Little, former Sports Information Director, for his part in the Longhorns' 1963 victory over the Aggies.

Texas, ranked number one in the country, needed only to beat a struggling 2–7–1 Aggie team to clinch UT's first national championship in football. The game had almost been cancelled because of the assassination of President John Kennedy several days before, and when Texas showed up at Kyle Field, the field conditions were atrocious, thanks to A&M's attempts to cover up the word *Bevo*, burned into the field by UT students with weed killer.

The underdog Aggies had led the entire game, and with 2:34 left, trailing 13–9, Texas saw its national championship hopes die as Tommy Wade's pass to George Sauer fell into the hands of A&M's defensive back Jim Willenborg in the end zone.

Video from the game film shows a man wearing a hat and a trench coat standing behind the goal posts with a clear view of the play. The man waved his arms furiously, signaling an incomplete pass as the defender juggled the ball and fell out of the end zone. The man in the trench coat was directly in the sight line of an official who immediately also signaled that the ball had not been caught. Texas kept the ball, scored the winning touchdown, and was voted 1963 national champs.

The man in the trench coat standing behind the end zone? Bill Little, then–sports editor of the *Daily Texan*, UT's student newspaper. Although Willenborg swore that he caught the ball about a foot inbounds, and A&M coach Hank Foldberg called the play "the greatest injustice to a group of young fellows I've ever seen," Little still insists that the official's call was correct.

teammates commented on it: "Just keep blocking on somebody; he'll be back."

Brought in as a quarterback, Saxton moved to halfback in 1960. Royal's biggest challenge was to get Saxton to quit dancing, dipping, and running side-to-side and just "head upfield." His performance was still magnificent; Saxton led the team in interceptions, and rushing, receiving, and all-purpose yards. During his junior year he started getting the hang of "producing yardage instead of thrills," according to Lou Maysel, in his book *Here Come the Texas Longhorns.*

Royal developed the flip-flop offense, a clever way of getting the ball to tailback Saxton on every play. In this offense, Jack Collins, who'd had an outstanding start at Texas at halfback, was shifted to full-time wingback duties. His unselfishness was praised by both Royal and Saxton. "There are few who would have graciously accepted the move to an unglamorous job...but Jack did it without saying a word," Royal told Maysel.

In *What It Means to Be a Longhorn*, a compilation of oral histories of former Longhorn players, Saxton said, "In 1961, we had one of the most productive offenses in the country. But it wasn't about me, it was about Jack Collins... I had a lot of long runs, and on every one of them...Jack threw the key block. When I think of what Jack sacrificed for me—he should have been an All-American....That's what he did for our team...."

Saxton was one of the most thrilling backs ever to play at Texas, and that 1961 team is considered by some to be Royal's most talented. Saxton was sidelined when he took an errant knee to the head in the TCU game; the resulting 6–0 loss cost the Longhorns the National Championship. Saxton ended the year as the Southwest Conference's rushing leader, with 846 yards on just 107 carries; his 7.9 yards per carry was the best in SWC history at the time.

James Saxton was a unanimous All-American in 1961 and was named the Texas Sports Writers Association Amateur Athlete of the Year. He is a member of the College Football Hall of Fame and was MVP of the Longhorns in 1961. He is a member of the Longhorn Hall of Honor.

James Saxton finished third on the 1961 Heisman Trophy ballot.

30 Roosevelt Leaks

Newspaper editors had fun with Roosevelt "Rosey" Leaks' name. It lent itself to clever headlines, such as "Roosevelt Leaks All Over the Field," after he rushed for 342 yards against SMU in 1973.

But there was nothing funny about the way Leaks played, certainly not to Texas' opponents who were trampled by his punishing runs.

Leaks, like Julius Whittier before him, had taken a great chance in choosing The University of Texas. UT football carried the stigma of being a program that didn't want black players, and it had only a few African Americans on the roster. Leaks, a quiet young man from a small country town, had a promising future as a running back. It would have been easier—safer—for him to turn down Texas and take his talents elsewhere.

When Leaks was named starting fullback, there was grumbling from a few players who questioned whether he should be starting, but, according to Leaks, team leaders Jerry Sisemore and Travis Roach were vocal in their support and things eventually settled down.

All grumbling stopped, however, after Leaks took the field. He was an instant star, and in 1973, Leaks became UT's first black All–Southwest Conference player and the first black All-American. During that year, Leaks was named the SWC's most valuable player and set the conference record for rushing yards, with 1,415. One of the most thrilling highlights of the season came against SMU, where his 342 yards rushing set a single-game rushing record.

But by the time he appeared on the 1973 *Bob Hope Show*, featuring the country's All-American football players, Rosey was wearing a cast. His left knee had been injured against Texas A&M in the last regular-season game of the year. A freak injury in practice

Priceless Aggie Moment

In 1974 at Memorial Stadium, the Aggies lost two fumbles on their first two offensive plays of the game. Within just 54 seconds of the opening kickoff, the Horns led 14–0. On their third offensive play, the Aggies fumbled again, this time yielding only a field goal to the Horns. Final score: 32–3.

the next spring made extensive surgery necessary on his right knee, with a projected six-to-nine-month rehab schedule.

Six months later, after an intensive and courageous attempt to rehab his knee, Roosevelt was back at practice, and although not at full speed, he was declared ready to go for his senior year. Shifted from fullback to right halfback, then back again to fullback, he shared time with freshman phenom Earl Campbell and ended the year with only 409 yards on 96 carries.

Leaks wasn't Texas' first African American player, but he was certainly Texas' first black superstar. In Wilton Sharpe's *Longhorn Madness,* teammate Lonnie Bennett said in 1973, "[Leaks] has provided an image of a black superstar for us. It may not help us in recruiting today, but kids are growing up who now idolize him. In five years it will make a big difference. That's what he's done for blacks here."

Leaks' list of awards is impressive, and though he initially received fame because of his accomplishments in football, his most lasting contribution may be that he inspired generations of African American children to go to college, to come to Texas, and to make a better life for themselves and for their communities.

Leaks was selected a consensus All-American in 1973 and was a co-captain and the team's most valuable player. He is a member of the Texas Sports Hall of Fame, the College Hall of Fame, and the Longhorn Hall of Honor.

Following his junior season, Roosevelt Leaks finished third in the Heisman Trophy voting, the first Longhorn underclassman to be so honored.

31 Steve Worster

Texas football was the perfect storm of talent, offensive scheme, coaching, determination, and lucky breaks in the 1969 season.

James Street was the team's navigator and its mainstay was the "Worster Bunch," acknowledged as the best recruiting class ever to come through the Texas football program. The anchor of that bunch was, of course, Steve Worster, a bruising north-and-south runner from Bridge City, Texas, who was born for the "three yards and a cloud of dust" philosophy of the wishbone offense.

During their time at Texas, Worster and his cohorts would stockpile a record of 30 wins, two losses, and one tie. They would win the Southwest Conference championship three times and capture two National Championships, giving the country memories of some of the best football ever played. Worster was there for the entire 30-game winning streak and was in large part responsible for that streak.

He developed into the most feared running back of his time. In his sophomore year, fans witnessed a preview of things to come when he charged up the middle for a last-minute touchdown to beat the Sooners 26–20. Later that year he averaged 8.5 yards per carry in the Cotton Bowl victory over Tennessee.

During the 1969 championship run, the entire backfield of Worster, Ted Koy, Jim Bertelsen, and James Street rushed for 100 yards apiece against SMU, amassing 611 rushing yards and setting NCAA, SWC, and UT records. After winning the Big Shootout against Arkansas and capturing their second National Championship, the 1970 Cotton Bowl was a game for the ages, and one Longhorn fans will never forget. Worster's 155-yard rushing performance on 20 carries won him Offensive MVP honors for

Longhorn Lore

Paul Simmons, a strong running back on the 1913–15 teams, set a school record when he scored four touchdowns in a single game. That record, although it was tied on several occasions, would stand until Ricky Williams scored five in one game in 1997 and six in one game twice in 1998.

As if his running weren't enough of a threat, Simmons had a trick up his sleeve—he was a talented tumbler. On one of his runs against the hapless Aggies, he performed a flip over the head of the defender who tried to tackle him. His teammate Alva Carlton said in *Here Come the Texas Longhorns*, "It was the darndest thing you ever saw. He had it so well-timed that often his back would hit on the tackler's back. He'd just turn over and keep on running."

The Irish finally stopped Simmons in the Texas–Notre Dame game in 1913. They'd been tipped off about his unorthodox methods, and when Simmons tried the flip play on the Notre Dame defenders, they stood up and grabbed him in midair.

his role in Texas' win over Notre Dame, which ended its 44-year self-imposed bowl game moratorium to play in the Cotton Bowl. Notre Dame's timing stank, however, as Texas ruined the coming-out party by bullying their way downfield to score late in the fourth quarter, securing a victory and UT's 500th win.

Texas was undefeated once again in the 1970 season, but that year's Cotton Bowl matchup with Notre Dame ended differently. A bruised and battered Worster couldn't match his performance of the year before. Texas lost 24–11. Nevertheless, Joe Theismann, quarterback for the Irish in the '70 and '71 Cotton Bowl games, hailed Worster as "a courageous warrior."

Worster was a three-time consensus All–Southwest Conference player and a two-time All-American selection. A co-captain of the 1970 Longhorns, he is a member of the Cotton Bowl Hall of Fame and was inducted into the Longhorn Hall of Honor.

Steve Worster finished fourth in the 1970 Heisman Trophy balloting.

32 Cedric Benson

Cedric Benson was a winner before he ever hit the UT campus. He'd led his Midland-Lee High School team to three consecutive state championships and had racked up 15 touchdowns in those three games.

When Benson reported for football at Texas, he was inevitably compared to Ricky Williams, his high school idol. They had similar builds, both had been taken in the Major League Baseball draft after high school, both were powerful runners, and both wore dreadlocks.

Named Big XII Offensive Freshman of the Year in 2001 Benson became the workhorse of the Longhorn offense; behind his running, Texas was second in the nation for rushing yards per game, averaging 299. In 2003, when number 16 Texas met number 12 Nebraska at Darrell K Royal–Texas Memorial Stadium, Vince Young and Benson became the first Longhorn duo to rush for more than 150 yards each. Benson's contribution toward that victory was 174 yards rushing and three touchdowns.

In 2004, Benson and his teammates celebrated their 11–1 season by beating Michigan in the Rose Bowl on Dusty Mangum's last-second field goal. Benson worked as hard in the classroom as he did off the field and proudly earned a spot on the Big 12 Commissioner's Honor roll. On January 1, 2005, his team voted him co-captain and named him team MVP for the second time.

Longhorn Lore
Two-time consensus All-American linebacker Derrick Johnson finished 12th in the Heisman balloting in 2004, the highest ranked defensive player that year.

By the time Benson left UT after being drafted by the Chicago Bears, he was the sixth-leading rusher in NCAA history and had earned a spot in UT record books as their second-leading rusher, with 5,540 yards.

A winner of the Doak Walker Award and named the Cingular/ABC Sports Player of the Year, this All-American is still on the books as one of the most prolific runners in Texas Longhorn history.

Cedric Benson finished sixth in the Heisman Trophy voting in 2004.

33 Scott Appleton

"Without Scott Appleton," says the Cotton Bowl Hall of Fame website, "Texas may never have won its first National Championship." The Longhorn defense didn't allow Navy a single rushing first down in the 1964 Cotton Bowl and Appleton, accumulating 12 tackles against the Midshipmen, sacked Heisman Trophy winner Roger Staubach twice for losses.

Appleton was the leader of an intimidating defense that allowed opponents only 195 yards per game and only 65 points all season. He was known for his prankish sense of humor off the field, but he took his football seriously.

Time magazine reported that even in practice, "the fanatical Longhorns play for keeps. In a spring scrimmage, the 235-pound All-American interrupted the scrimmage to protest a referee's call. 'Come on,' Appleton yelled at the ref and his teammates. 'Get it right. We're not out here for fun!'"

In 1963, Texas was ranked number two as they filed down the Cotton Bowl tunnel to face number one Oklahoma and its

The Bells of Texas

One of the most charming features of the Texas campus is the serenade that ushers students to class, beautiful music floating down from the top of the UT Tower. Every Monday, Wednesday, and Friday at 12:50 PM, Tom Anderson, UT's carillonneur for the past 60 years, took the Tower elevator to the 27th floor, climbed 85 stairs that wind behind the enormous clock faces to the very top of the Tower of the Main Building, and played songs on the Kniker Carillon, the largest carillon in the state.

The UT Tower had 16 bells when it was built in 1936, with space to add 39 bells. Lutcher Stark, a member of the Board of Regents, donated the 17th bell, but with the bequest of alumna Hedwig Thusnelda Kniker in 1985, The University was able to complete the carillon with a total of 56 bells.

In 2010, a group of students formed the UT Guild of Carillonneurs, determined to preserve the legacy of Tom Anderson and his Tower bells.

The carillonneurs play a variety of tunes, from Bach Minuets to Lady Gaga to "Let Me Call You Sweetheart" on Valentine's Day. Students trudging toward their first day of final exams are treated to "Chopin's Funeral March", and on 105-degree August days, you're likely to hear "Let It Snow." Have a request for the carillonneurs? Email the guild at texascarillon@gmail.com, and they'll do their best to accommodate your request.

The very first song played on the carillon was, fittingly, "The Eyes of Texas". Regardless of what songs are played, each Tower Time ends with "Eyes."

star running back Joe Don Looney. Looney had been running his mouth before the game and had the bad judgment to say, "Appleton's tough, but he ain't met the Big Red yet." Appleton met that challenge, with 18 tackles against the Sooners and a forced fumble that led to a Texas touchdown. When they were finished with the Big Red, the Texas defense and quarterback Duke Carlisle had prevailed 28–7.

UT guard Bobby Gamblin told Looney, who would be dismissed from the Sooner football team the following week: "Hey, Looney, get off the field, you creep. You're killing the grass."

Texas, of course, finished the season undefeated in spite of a handful of tight games, and often it was the Horns' staunch defense that kept them in the game.

Appleton was one of the famed seniors of '63 who compiled an incredible 30–2–1 record over three years' time, narrowly missing the opportunity for three National Championships. A tri-captain of the 1963 Longhorns, he was the only consensus All-American from that National Championship team. In addition to winning the Outland Trophy, he is a member of the Cotton Bowl Hall of Fame and is a member of the Longhorn Hall of Honor.

Scott Appleton, a tackle, finished an incredible fifth in the Heisman Trophy voting in 1963.

34 Bobby Layne

A single chapter can't begin to cover the larger-than-life career and personality of Bobby "the Blonde Bomber" Layne.

He was recruited to play baseball, but when Layne arrived at Texas, baseball coach Billy Disch was gone. Interim baseball coach Blair Cherry, who also happened to be an assistant football coach, persuaded Layne to give football a try.

He was an amazing athlete in the mold of Clyde Littlefield or Bill Bradley, one who could master almost any athletic feat with little effort. Layne was a four-time All-SWC pitcher who never lost a conference game. Over those four years, he was 28–0 in SWC play. Once, while pitching a no-hitter against A&M, he drank 10 beers in the dugout to kill the pain in his foot, which he'd cut open the night before. When asked how he could party all night and then play so well the next day, Layne replied, "I sleep fast."

Longhorn Lore: Almost a Longhorn

Heisman Trophy winner Doak Walker almost became a Longhorn. Walker, an eventual three-time All-American running back, and Bobby Layne were teammates at Highland Park High in Dallas. When World War II broke out, they both joined the Merchant Marines. They were discharged in New Orleans at the same time; after enjoying a football game together they parted ways, Layne believing that Walker would be coming to Texas.

But Rusty Russell, Walker's old high school coach—who was by then a backfield coach at SMU—arranged to travel home to Dallas on the same train with Walker. The following Monday, Layne picked up the newspaper and read that Walker had committed to play for SMU.

Layne's teammate Rooster Andrews always claimed that Walker passed on Texas because his mama told him she didn't want him down in Austin getting in trouble with Bobby.

He did everything fast. Until Vince Young showed up 56 years later, Layne was the winningest quarterback in UT history, with 28 wins. He was the first four-time All–Southwest Conference selection in the school's history, three times as running back (although he took deep snaps from those positions), and once as quarterback, in 1947. He was a consensus All-American in 1947. In addition to leading the team in passing from 1944 to 1947, he was also the Horns' rushing leader in 1944 and 1946.

When the United States entered World War II, Layne interrupted his football career to enlist in the Merchant Marines with his high school buddy Doak Walker, serving in the Atlantic Ocean for nine months.

In the 1946 Cotton Bowl Classic against Missouri, Layne was responsible for all 40 of Texas' points in the 40–27 victory…all 40 points. He passed for two touchdowns, ran for three, caught a pass for another, and kicked four extra points. He completed 11 of 12 attempts for 158 yards, and more than 50 years later, his .917 pass completion percentage is still a Cotton Bowl record.

The Horns' only loss in Layne's senior season came against Walker and SMU. It was as if the two buddies had their own separate competition going on, a game within a game; Walker accounted for 125 of SMU's 199 yards of offense, Layne for 141 of UT's 196. In the 1948 Sugar Bowl against Alabama, Layne was once again named the game's outstanding back.

The talent was there, no doubt about that. But Layne had a tough, competitive streak that drove him. Teammate Peppy Blount, in *Longhorn Madness,* said that Layne would bet on anything. "He'd bet on a raindrop or on two ants crossing a windshield."

Rooster Andrews was Layne's running buddy and roommate and knew him as well as anyone did. "That's what made Bobby go…his competitive spirit. It didn't matter if it was playing washers, horseshoes, tiddly winks, or shuffleboard, he wanted to whip your ass." And he usually did.

Layne was the first Longhorn selected for the National Football Foundation College Hall of Fame. He is a member of the Cotton Bowl Hall of Fame, the Texas Sports Hall of Fame, the Pro Football Hall of Fame, and just about any other Hall of Fame you can think of. In 1995, *Sports Illustrated* named Layne the "Toughest Quarterback Who Ever Lived." The University of Texas retired Layne's number 22 jersey in 2008. Layne is a member of the Longhorn Hall of Honor.

Bobby Layne placed eighth in the Heisman voting in 1946; in 1947, his senior year, he finished sixth.

35 Tommy Nobis

It's almost become a cliché or an addendum to his name: "Tommy Nobis, the greatest defensive player in the history of the Texas Longhorns."

As with most truly great players, it was not just about the talent, although Nobis certainly had that. He was the only sophomore starter on the 1963 National Championship team, and in 1964 and '65, the guy played both ways. Darrell Royal told the *San Antonio Express News,* "If Nobis played just defense, he's going to be out there just half the time. You gotta be crazy having Nobis play less than half the game."

But there were other elements to Nobis—a sense of knowing where the football was, and a love of hitting. According to Lou Maysel's *Here Come the Texas Longhorns,* Nobis was so dedicated to football that he believed "football is like a jealous woman. It needs constant attention." Although he was a blue-chipper out of high school, he worked all the harder to improve.

In the 1964 Cotton Bowl, Scott Appleton and Nobis executed Mike Campbell's defense brilliantly and were able to contain shifty Navy quarterback Roger Staubach, holding him to minus-47 yards rushing. After the whipping, one Navy lineman was asked if he'd like a rematch with Texas. "Not if that Nobis guy is gonna play," he replied.

Coming off the 1963 National Championship, hopes were high for the 1964 team, and they should have won it all again. Nobis made 24 tackles in 28 minutes against Army. The following week, when Texas beat OU 28–7, Nobis got 25 more. After the heartbreaking one-point loss to Arkansas for the conference—and the National—championship, the Horns and Nobis rebounded

To Be a Longhorn

"When you're a Horn, you actually carry a burden. You're supposed to behave, not cause problems, stay out of trouble. You're supposed to put your nose to the grindstone, get your education, and turn out to be something." —Mike Baab, *What It Means to Be a Longhorn*

with a 6–3 victory over Rice and 25 tackles for Nobis. Against SMU, his 21 tackles and an interception turned the tide, resulting in a 7–0 victory. Texas won out in the regular season, then met Alabama and Joe Namath in the Orange Bowl, shutting him down on a famous and disputed goal-line stand to take the win 21–17.

Nobis, whose hair matched the burnt-orange No. 60 jersey he made famous, is the benchmark for Texas linebackers. He ended his career as a four-time Southwest Conference selection—three times at linebacker and once at offensive guard. In 1964 he was named to four All-America teams and in 1965, he was a consensus All-American selection and finished seventh in the Heisman Trophy voting. Winner of the Outland Trophy and the Maxwell Trophy for the nation's outstanding college football player, he was a team captain and a two-time Most Valuable Player for the Longhorns. Nobis averaged 20 tackles per game and is a member of the College Football Hall of Fame, the Texas Sports Hall of Fame, and the Longhorn Hall of Honor. He should be, but is not, a member of the Pro Football Hall of Fame.

Nobis and Texas running back Ricky Williams are the only two Longhorns named to *Sports Illustrated's* All-Century Team. In a nod to Nobis' prowess, astronaut Frank Borman actually called from space just before the NFL draft to "tell Nobis to sign with Houston." Nobis' famed number 60 jersey—used for decades to inspire, motivate, and reward worthy Texas linebackers—was retired in 2008.

Tommy Nobis is in the Longhorn Hall of Honor.

Tommy Nobis, widely regarded as the best Longhorn defensive player ever.

36 Chris Gilbert

It was another of coach Darrell Royal's hunches. When Royal followed his gut, it usually turned out well for the Longhorns, and this time was no different.

Texas was playing Southern Cal at home in 1966, and the Horns were behind. Royal called sophomore Chris Gilbert, who was not expecting to play, off the bench and ran him successfully over and over until, according to Whit Canning in *Texas Longhorns: Where Have You Gone?*, Gilbert finally got so excited that he started hyperventilating and had to be pulled from the game.

Gilbert was fast and quick and could cut on a dime. He had the balance of a cat and was the heart of the backfield in an era that saw the introduction of Royal's famed wishbone offense and the beginning of Texas' 30-game winning streak.

Great Pep Talk Number Four

Texas was behind 7–0 at halftime in the 1967 Texas–OU game in Dallas. They had looked listless the whole first half. In the second half, however, a different team emerged from the locker room. The Horns rallied to beat the Sooners 9–7 for the ninth time in 10 years.

Spectators and reporters left the game, marveling at the turnaround and wondering what inspirational words Royal had spoken to fire up the team. *Fort Worth Star-Telegram* sportswriter Bill Van Fleet said to a fellow writer, "Some Monday morning when I'm hung over and don't want to get up and go to work, I wish Darrell would come up to my room and give me the same talk he made to his team at halftime."

Royal was not a rah-rah type of coach and didn't go for the fiery motivational speeches meant to manipulate players' emotions. He simply told the team, somewhat heatedly, "There's a heckuva fight going on out there. Why don't you join it?"

Texas won seven and lost four in 1966, and in 1967 they went 6–4 and tied for third in the Southwest Conference. Yet in spite of the mediocrity of those seasons, watching Gilbert run was a treat. Gilbert set a Longhorn rushing record in the 1966 Bluebonnet Bowl when, in a 19–0 win over Ole Miss, he rushed for 156 yards on 26 carries.

His 96-yard touchdown against Texas Christian University during his junior year is still in the record books as the longest run from scrimmage by a Texas player.

Gilbert finished his career as the SWC's all-time leading rusher, gaining 3,231 yards, and because freshmen were not then eligible to play varsity ball, he accomplished that feat in just three years. Gilbert became the first running back in the history of the NCAA to rush for 1,000 yards in three straight seasons.

Co-captain of the 1968 Longhorns, Chris was selected the Longhorns' Most Valuable Player three years running, an accomplishment that has never been repeated, and was All–Southwest Conference each of those years. In 1968, Gilbert was named consensus All-American. He is a member of the NFF College Football Hall of Fame and was selected to the All-Southwest team for the 1919–1969 era by the Football Writers Association of America. He is a member of the Longhorn Hall of Honor.

Chris Gilbert placed eighth in voting for the 1968 Heisman Trophy.

37 Kenneth Sims

Defensive guys just aren't supposed to be Heisman candidates.

Although the award allegedly goes to the best college football player of the year, there's some unwritten rule that says it actually goes to the best college player of the year who touches the ball. In the trophy's 79-year history, defensive players have finished in the top five a paltry 23 times. Texas has had three defensive players place in the top 10: Scott Appleton placed fifth in 1963; Tommy Nobis was seventh in 1965; and in 1981, Kenneth Sims, Longhorn defensive tackle, finished eighth.

Sims, from tiny Kosse, Texas, claims that he played scared all the time. "I did not want to go back [home] as a failure." When he arrived on campus, he was sixth on the depth chart, but he didn't stay down there for long. Today, his name is mentioned among the all-time greats of Texas football.

The outgoing and affable Sims was a co-captain of the 1981 Fred Akers' team that went 10–1–1 and upset number three Alabama and Bear Bryant in the Cotton Bowl. Sims was the foundation of that strong defense; he holds school records for quarterback pressures, tackles for a loss, fumble recoveries, and quarterback sacks. His career 15 forced fumbles still tops the UT record books.

A two-time team Most Valuable Player, he was also selected MVP of the Southwest Conference and was the first Longhorn ever to win the Lombardi Trophy, presented to the nation's top lineman. The two-time consensus All-American accounted for 131 tackles in his senior year.

Sims is a member of the Longhorn Hall of Honor.

Kenneth Sims, a defensive tackle and the number one overall choice in the 1982 NFL draft, was eighth on the 1981 Heisman Trophy ballot.

We're Number Two

Through January 2014 The University of Texas is the second-winningest football program in the nation. Michigan, which first played football in 1879, has 910 wins; and Texas, which started its program in 1893, has logged 875 victories. Notre Dame, whose football tradition began in 1887, is a *very* close third, with 874 wins.

38 Jack Crain

The "Nocona Nugget" was as important a player as Texas has ever had. D.X. Bible's first two years had produced a 3–14–1 record, and impatient Longhorn fans were not pleased with the results they were getting from their exorbitantly paid head coach.

Standing 5'7" and weighing just 150 pounds, Jack Crain didn't look the part of a player who could turn the program around. He wasn't even recruited for football; he had come to Austin to play baseball. But he was offered a one-year scholarship and the chance to play for Bible, and he took it.

It's safe to say that Crain's one-year ride was extended after his inaugural season. He shone in the season opener against Florida and led the Horns to a huge upset at Wisconsin, a game that drew national attention to the Texas program.

He was a one-man show against Oklahoma in 1939. Although the Sooners won that day, people began buzzing about Crain's two 71-yard touchdown runs.

In a last-minute, come-from-behind victory over Arkansas, Crain, who had had an 82-yard punt return earlier in the game, caught a short pass and turned it into a 67-yard touchdown run. After catching his breath, and after officials cleared the fans who had streamed onto the field, Crain kicked the extra point to give Texas the 15–14 win.

Texas wrapped up the season with a 5–4 record. The stage was set for a complete reversal of Texas' fortunes, thanks in large part to the amazing talent of little Jack Crain. He was the only Longhorn named to the All-SWC team that year.

Crain was one of those players who did it all. He was an elusive runner who caught passes, returned punts, and kicked extra points.

Great Pep Talk Number Five

The 1939 Longhorns had traveled to Wisconsin and were underdogs to a much larger Wisconsin squad. D.X. Bible's pregame talk appealed to that most basic of Texan virtues: pride in their great state.

"Boys! The Eyes of Texas are upon you. Texans are huddled around their radios from Brownsville to Wichita Falls, from El Paso to Texarkana, in every home, grocery store, drug store, barbershop and hardware store in the state of Texas....Today you are not just representing The University of Texas. Today, you're fighting and playing for the entire state of Texas. This is Texas against Wisconsin!

"Set your jaws! Make up your minds! Let's play a game that will live in the hearts and minds of the people of Texas forever!"

Final score: Texas 17, Wisconsin 7.

As a defensive back, he intercepted seven passes during the 1940 season.

In 1940, Texas victories piled up and so did the honors for Crain. Rice and SMU handed Texas its two losses of the season, but the jewel in the Longhorns' crown was their astonishing upset of the undefeated Aggies.

Bible's 1941 team is widely considered one of the best Texas teams of all time, and Crain helped that campaign by setting rushing and scoring records. His UT career scoring record of 180 points stood for decades, as did his record of 23 touchdowns. A two-time All-SWC selection, Crain was the first Texas player to rush for 1,000 career yards.

Crain is a member of the Texas High School Sports Hall of Fame and is a member of the Longhorn Hall of Honor.

Jack Crain finished 10th in the 1941 Heisman Trophy voting.

39 Nine National Champions

Bear Bryant said, "You only need to win one in a season, then your people can play like they won 'em all." He was talking about the National Championship polls, and if you take the Bear at his word, Texas has won nine.

Much of what follows was taken from Mike Jones' book, *Dance With Who Brung You,* and all Longhorn fans are in his debt for bringing these facts to light.

The Official NCAA Football Record Book lists every college team that has ever been awarded a national title by a major selector. Most folks don't realize that many different polls select a National Champion. Although the Bowl Championship Series (the BCS) dictated the "official" championship games from 1998 to 2014, they are not the only game in town when it comes to naming number one.

The following is a list of the National Championships the Longhorn football team has won, along with the season record, the polls that selected them, and some of the stars from each team. Commit them to memory:

Royal to Mack

"To be the head coach of Texas, you need to smile, you need to like the state of Texas, you need to like the people, you need to stop and talk to them, you need to sign those autographs…you need to know what you're doing on the field, you need to recruit well, and you need to win all your games. Other than that, it's an easy job." — Darrell Royal, explaining to Mack Brown the secret to success at The University of Texas.

1914: 8–0; Billingsley Poll; stars included Gus "Pig" Dittmar, Pete Edmond, Louis Jordan, and Clyde Littlefield

1941: 8–1–1; Berryman Poll, Williamson Poll, Howell Poll, Maxwell Poll; stars included Jack Crain, Noble Doss, Pete Layden, Stanley Mauldin, and Joe Parker

1963: 11–0; all polls but two; stars included Duke Carlisle, Scott Appleton, Tommy Nobis, Tommy Ford, and David McWilliams

1968: 9–1–1; DeVold, Sagarin, Kirlin, Maxwell, and the Matthews System Polls; stars included Chris Gilbert, Bill Bradley, Loyd Wainscott, and James Street

1969: 11–0; just about every poll's pick, although some confused souls chose Penn State; stars included James Street, Steve Worster, Bill Attessis, Tom Campbell, Ted Koy, and Randy Peschel

1970: 10–1; 1ˢᵗ-N-Goal, Royce, Berryman, Football Analysis System, UPI, Montgomery, Washington Touchdown Club, Litkenhous, NFF (MacArthur Bowl); stars included Eddie Phillips, Jim Bertelsen, Cotton Speyrer, Jerry Sisemore, and Bobby Wuensch

1977: 11–1; Berryman Poll, FACT, Sagarin, Self, Nutshell Sports; stars included Earl Campbell, Russell Erxleben, Brad Shearer, Lam Jones, Johnnie Johnson, Alfred Jackson, and Randy McEachern

1981: 10–1–1; National Championship Foundation; stars included Mike Baab, Robert Brewer, Doug Dawson, Tony DeGrate, A.J. "Jam" Jones, Jeff Leiding, Lawrence Sampleton, and Bruce Scholtz

2005: 13–0; unanimous; stars included Vince Young, Will Allen, Justin Blalock, David Thomas, Michael Griffin, Aaron Ross, Jonathan Scott, and Michael Huff

40 The Formidable Longhorn

In the beginning, the Texas football team was called simply "Varsity," which could have referred to any number of college teams across the nation in the late 19ᵗʰ century.

Texas fielded its first football team in 1893, fewer than 10 years after the Chisholm Trail was finally closed by barbed wire and by a Kansas quarantine law. Yet in the trail's brief existence, millions of heads of longhorn cattle were driven north along the Chisholm Trail, part of which ran through Austin as the old Shawnee Trail.

When The University was looking for a mascot, the longhorn steer was the logical symbol. Admired by cowboys for its toughness, its strength, and its determination to survive—and prevail—under the worst of conditions, the longhorn was a prescient choice for the young college. The longhorn and its characteristics have become synonymous with the state of Texas and with The University.

Unlike lions, tigers, or bears, the longhorn is unique among college mascots. There is no symbol in college sports more recognizable than the burnt-orange longhorn silhouette worn on Texas helmets since 1961.

It's been written that "Varsity" became the "Longhorns" after *Daily Texan* sports writer D.A. Frank first referred to the team as "the Longhorns" in 1903. Alex Weisburg, editor of the *Texan*, told his staff to call every University sports team "The Longhorns" and they'd soon have it named. Yet newspaper articles as early as 1900 and 1902 refer to the Texas team as the "Long Horns."

Regardless of when "Longhorns" became Texas' accepted nickname, students and athletes made it official after benefactor

In the late '70s, some peace-loving UT students campaigned to change the mascot from the Longhorn to the armadillo.

and future regent H.J. Lutcher Stark had the word "Longhorns" sewn onto wool warm-up blankets and donated them to the 1913 football team.

Austin's unofficial motto is "Keep Austin Weird," and never was the state capital weirder than in the 1970s. Austin was the Southwest's center of peace, love, and progressive country music. Jim Franklin, a local poster artist, began using the armadillo in his artwork, and when Eddie Wilson opened the Armadillo World Headquarters in an old National Guard armory, the armadillo became a hot commodity.

The Armadillo World Headquarters showcased a variety of musicians and musical styles and was the one venue where hippies, cowboys, and businessmen could convene without getting into philosophical disputes. The Armadillo became the premier music venue in Texas. It helped form the cosmic cowboy music phenomenon, and it spawned a little TV program called *Austin City Limits,* which is still on the air today. The armadillo, previously considered a lowly animal usually found as roadkill, implausibly became a nationwide symbol of harmony, peace, and hippiedom.

In the late '70s, a group of UT students mounted a campaign to change the mascot from the Longhorn to the armadillo. The thundering herd of armadillos…it is our great good fortune that that campaign was unsuccessful.

41 The War Between the States

Darrell Royal called the annual Texas-OU game an "old-fashioned, country, jaw-to-jaw, knucks-down gut check."

Pat Culpepper, co-captain of the 1962 Longhorns, likened smiling to the cameras in pregame introductions to "laughing before you land at Iwo Jima."

Robert Heard, author of *Oklahoma vs. Texas: When Football Becomes War* said, "There is no rivalry to rival this one."

Just reading those quotes makes you want to drive to Dallas tomorrow. It makes your mouth water, makes your heart pump faster, and makes your breathing get shallow.

There…is…no…rivalry…to…rival…this…one.

The first meeting, in 1900, ended up with "Varsity" whipping the University of Oklahoma Territory 28–2. *The Austin American-Statesman* headline read: "Varsity Football Team has a stiff practice game with Oklahoma." That's pretty much the way things went for the first 47 years, with OU sneaking in two handfuls of wins and a couple ties. The series went in fits and starts, with the schools playing at different venues or not playing at all some years. In 1930, the series moved to a neutral site, the Cotton Bowl in Dallas, called Fair Park Stadium at that time. And until about 1948 or so, Texas beat OU on better than a two-to-one basis.

Oklahoma was still reeling from the effects of the Depression and the Dust Bowl. Families were forced to move to California to find work, and when they got there, they faced prejudice and scorn. In John Steinbeck's *Grapes of Wrath*, the author summarized the Okies' plight by having a Texan tell protagonist Tom Joad, "Okie means you're scum." Years of disdain, poverty, hard times,

Great Pep Talk Number 6

The 1914 Longhorns, an enormously talented team, were led by Louis Jordan, a guard from Fredericksburg, Texas. Jordan would later become a second-team selection on Walter Camp's All-America team, the first Longhorn ever to appear on the elite roster.

Oklahoma returned the opening kickoff for a touchdown, marking the first time Texas had been scored on all season. That did not sit well with the usually gentle and gentlemanly Jordan. Teammate Clyde Littlefield recalled in *Here Come the Texas Longhorns*, "He told us in no mincing words, with a few cuss words in German thrown in... 'Nobody leaves this field until we beat the hell out of them.'"

The team followed their captain's orders. Eleven men started the game, and the same 11 men finished it, and they did beat the hell out of OU 32–7.

and losing to the Longhorns had given the state a vast inferiority complex.

Enter George Cross. Oklahoma hired Cross as university president in 1943. In 1945, OU regents suggested that Cross should try to build a good football team, believing it would give Oklahomans a reason to have pride in their state again. After Bud Wilkinson came on board as coach, OU set about doing just that, and the game was on. The Texas-Oklahoma rivalry became one of the most bitter in the country. OU's success was sudden and lasting. It did bring state pride and national attention.

Later, Cross came to believe he'd created a monster. In 1951, a year after OU won its first national championship, Cross was defending a budget request to the state legislature. After an hour-long session in which Cross explained why the university needed this money, one senator interrupted Cross and said, "That's fine. But what kind of football team are we going to have this year?"

Cross snapped back, "I want to build a university the football team could be proud of."

The Texas-OU series tends to run in streaks, and from 1948 through 1957—Darrell Royal's first year at Texas—the Sooners owned the Horns, winning nine out of the 10 contests. Then, starting in 1958, Royal beat his alma mater 11 out of 12 years, after which the pendulum swung the other way, and Texas didn't win for another seven years. Since the AP poll started ranking teams in 1936, 31 of the Texas-OU meetings have pitted two top-20 teams. Nine of those games saw both teams ranked in the top five.

The stakes are even higher now that Texas and OU both play in the Big 12 South. If you don't get by OU in October, chances are you don't win the south zone. As Dan Jenkins wrote in *Sports Illustrated,* "The University of Texas football season begins with the Oklahoma game. Everything before that is just so much throat-clearing."

When the teams meet in October, you can forget about team records or stats or which team has what blue-chippers or what the line is on the game. Texas-OU is a different animal, with the intensity of the entire season squeezed into 60 minutes.

This game, the name of which has been "politically corrected," is not, in fact, a "Red River Rivalry." This is a blood feud, a life-or-death spittin' match, an "old-fashioned, country, knucks-down, jaw-to-jaw, gut check," according to Darrell Royal. This game does not belong in the gentrified arena of Jerryworld. No, this game is so raw and visceral, a stadium like the Cotton Bowl is the only fitting venue. Only the strong survive an afternoon in the Cotton Bowl.

It's a clash of two of the premier programs in the country, meeting at a neutral site where south of the 50-yard line, the crowd is solid crimson; north of the 50 is burnt orange. OU fans hate Texas for being so arrogant; Texas fans claim they're not arrogant, just superior. We think they're cheaters; they think we're whiners. A year's pent-up frustrations spill out and onto the field, drowning out even the marching bands, which play their respective fight songs for the entire 60 minutes.

There is no rivalry to rival this one.

42 Go to OU Weekend

Do whatever it takes. Give 110 percent. Take it to the next level.

We're not talking *playing* football here; we're talking about scoring tickets to OU. In the Longhorn lexicon, "OU" might refer to the University of Oklahoma, but it can also be shorthand for the annual Texas-OU football game in Dallas or the entire OU weekend experience.

No matter. Do whatever you must to attend at least one of these shootouts before you die.

The game's now called the "Red River Rivalry," but "rivalry" is too passive a word for what takes place that weekend in October. "Shootout" was more appropriate, but "hate-fest" is what it really is. One's life as a Longhorn is lived in vain until and unless one experiences the madness that is OU weekend.

This game brings out the best in the teams and the worst in the fans. The weekend is about serious bragging rights, about large groups of fans in crimson or burnt orange, screaming violently at one another about which school or state sucks the worst.

Here are some things you should know before you embark on the pilgrimage:

Helpful Hint #1: Drinking and/or speeding on the drive to Dallas is ill-advised, as IH-35 is lined with police officers caressing their ballpoints and their ticket books, dreaming of exceeding their quotas. Kiwi your car, hang your streamers, stick your Texas flags out the windows, and take your time. As they say, getting there is half the fun. It's like a 192-mile mobile pep rally.

In the good old days before the city of Dallas moved the Friday night melee off of Commerce Street and into the trendy bars of Deep Ellum and Knox-Henderson, the success of the weekend was judged by how many arrests police made. Commerce Street was a free-for-all, with drunk pedestrians weaving in and out of the jammed traffic. The noise of blaring car horns and fans screaming their fight songs at one another added to the frenzy. The revelers, their numbers sometimes swelling to 50,000, occasionally had to dodge TVs, telephones, or end tables flying out of hotel windows. Fistfights broke out everywhere. Barry Switzer, in his autobiography, *Bootlegger's Boy,* said that downtown Dallas on Friday night before the game was a combination Mardi Gras and prison breakout. A good time was had by all, unless you were a proud member of the Dallas Police Department.

Saturday. Game day. Long before the season starts, start praying for a 2:00 PM kickoff. No one, not even those who were sober the night before, wants an 11:00 AM kickoff.

Helpful Hint #2: Leave for the Fairgrounds at least an hour and a half before kickoff. Once inside the State Fair, it's a rite of passage to have a Fletcher's Corny Dog and a beer before the game, even if the kickoff is at 11:00 AM. There's just nothing better, nothing that caps the experience like having a Fletcher's slathered with mustard and chasing it down with a cold beer.

Get to the Cotton Bowl early enough to watch the team buses arrive. The buses creep along with a police escort, and the gladiators on the charters stare blankly out the windows at the sea of fans cheering their own team and cussing the enemy. About five minutes before the buses arrive, the mounted police start moving the crowd back to make way for the convoy.

Helpful Hint #3: Move. You're no match for a 1,000-pound horse, and the officers don't care who gets in the way; their job is to clear the way for the buses and that's what they'll do. Regardless.

State and school pride is always on the line at the annual Red River Shootout against Oklahoma.

Earl's Onlies

As of 2013, 79 men have been awarded the Heisman Trophy. As of 2014, 287 men have been enshrined in the Pro Football Hall of Fame.

Earl Campbell is one of only eight men to have been selected for both honors.

He is also the only player to have tackled Bevo, the 1,200-pound longhorn steer that is UT's mascot. In the 1977 game against the University of Houston, Bevo stood in the corner of the end zone in Rice Stadium, minding his own business. Campbell came barreling into the end zone and hit Bevo in the left flank. "Bevo went down, a cameraman went down, and I did, too," said Campbell. A single tackler could never bring Campbell down; it took a half-ton steer to do that.

Helpful Hint #4: You must have coupons to ride the rides or buy refreshments, and the ticket lines are agonizingly long, especially when you're hankering for a corny dog or a gator bob or a funnel cake. Avoid the lines by preordering tickets at www.bigtex.com. You're welcome.

Helpful Hint #5: If you have even a touch of claustrophobia, don't wait until the last minute to enter the stadium. There's a crush of humanity, a logjam of cute coeds trying to cut in line, drunks spilling beer on your new outfit (see Helpful Hint #6) and stomping on your toes, people ringing cowbells, more fans screaming that the other team sucks. It's slow going at best, so get there early or pack plenty of patience.

Helpful Hint #6: Attending your first OU game is exciting, but resist the temptation to wear your newest fall fashion. The name of this game is comfort. It will either be blazing hot—in which case you'll wish you'd worn flip-flops, shorts, and a T-shirt—or it will be pouring rain, or the Cotton Bowl plumbing will overflow again, leaving you wishing you'd left the Jimmy Choos at home.

Helpful Hint #7: Never tell your friends "I'll meet you at Big Tex." Big Tex is a 52-foot-tall mechanical cowboy wearing size 70 boots. He is the official host of the State Fair and he does his job well, repeating again and again and again, "Howdy, folks. Welcome to the State Fair of Texas." Although he's an easily spotted landmark, if you attempt to meet friends at Big Tex, you'll be joined by about 10,000 other newbies who are also meeting their friends at Big Tex.

Helpful Hint #8: Go ahead, wear burnt orange. When you walk into that stadium and see the south half of the Cotton Bowl in red and the north half all in orange, you'll be proud you were part of it. And remember, if the Horns win, it's the single most significant event of the year. If the Horns lose, heck, it's just a game. We'll get 'em next year.

43 The Southwest Conference

The Southwest Conference seems a distant memory to college football fans of today. Texas now plays in the realm of the Big 12, but during the years from 1915 through 1995, the Southwest Conference boasted some of the nation's best football players and spawned seven National Champions, five Heisman Trophy winners, three Maxwell Awards, five Outland Trophies, and two Doak Walkers award winners, among other national awards.

When Theo Bellmont became UT's first athletics director at the start of the 1913–14 season, he recognized that the football program needed to be regulated, so he removed it from the pool of student organizations and placed it under the jurisdiction of The University's athletics department. Bellmont then began formulating plans for an athletic conference, and he chaired the first organizational meeting in Dallas in May 1914.

The Southwest Intercollegiate Athletic Conference, later the Southwest Conference, was formed that December with founding members Arkansas, Baylor, Rice, Oklahoma, Oklahoma A&M, Texas, Texas A&M, and Southwestern University in Georgetown, Texas. Eventually Oklahoma, Oklahoma A&M, and Southwestern dropped out. Over the years, Texas Christian, Southern Methodist University, Texas Tech, and the University of Houston joined the conference.

The Southwest Conference affiliated with the Cotton Bowl in 1940, and in 1942 the conference directed that the champion team of the SWC must play in the Cotton Bowl.

The Cotton Bowl showcased some of the most exciting stars ever to play the game: Jim Swink, Slingin' Sammy Baugh, Davey O'Brien of TCU; Kyle Rote, Jerry Levias, and Doak Walker of SMU, Dicky Moegle of Rice; John Kimbrough, Dat Ngyuen, and John David Crow of A&M; Lance Alworth of Arkansas; Wilson Whitley and Andre Ware of the University of Houston; Don Trull and Mike Singletary of Baylor. Consider the great coaches who graced those sidelines: Jess Neely. Abe Martin. Dutch Meyer. Gene Stallings. Bill Yeoman. Frank Broyles. Bear Bryant. Lou Holtz. D.X. Bible, Fred Akers, Darrell Royal.

And in this conference that was one of the best in the country, one school dominated the others.

Texas football won 25 conference championships, 19 outright. Texas football brought just shy of 300 All-SWC selections to the table and introduced two Heisman Trophy winners, although Texas joined the Big 12 after Ricky Williams' freshman year. Of the eight National Champions that represented the conference, three of them were produced by Texas.

Toward the end, there were eight teams in Texas, but as Dan Jenkins said, "The [Arkansas] Razorbacks are an only child."

Many factors combined to bring on the demise of the Southwest Conference.

Because the SWC was slow to integrate, many great black athletes either played at historically black universities or left the state to go out west or up north. A lot of talent left, and the conference was weakened.

According to Bill Cunningham in *The Texas Way*, the end began in the early 1980s. TCU, SMU, Baylor, and Rice had become perpetual whipping boys, and their attendance numbers—at their own homes—reflected that trend. In the mid-1980s, as few as 15,000 Rice Owl fans bothered to support the Owls in person. TCU averaged as low as 25,000, and the University of Houston's home attendance gate dropped to as low as 13,346 in 1986.

It didn't help matters when SMU, TCU, Houston, and Texas A&M all went on NCAA probation for recruiting violations; the NCAA's investigation found that SMU's athletics program was "build on a legacy of wrongdoing, deceit, and rules violations." SMU received the NCAA "death penalty" in 1987 and 1988, and their program has never recovered. Without a strong SMU, says Cunningham, the three other strong schools (Arkansas, Texas, and A&M) couldn't carry the conference.

A conference centered in one state simply could not pull the viewing audience needed for lucrative television contracts, and strong schools saw that they were leaving a lot of money on the table. Neither individual teams nor their conferences could survive without television revenue. There was widespread dissatisfaction with the College Football Association's television contract. In 1990, Notre Dame made history by splitting from the CFA.

In June of 1989, Texas was invited to join the Southeastern Conference, but UT wouldn't leave without taking Texas A&M.

TRIVIA
Question

In 1972, his senior year, tight end Julius Whittier led the team in touchdown receptions. As a matter of fact, Whittier caught every single touchdown pass thrown that season. How many touchdown receptions did Whittier have?

Trivia answers on page 255.

Cunningham, president of Texas, and A&M's president Bill Mobley agreed that moving out of the SWC would be a joint decision between the two schools. Those were the days when the leaders of UT and A&M acknowledged that, in spite of their rivalry, the schools were stronger when they stuck together. After studying all options, Texas decided the Big 10 or the PAC 10 was a better fit for the school, while A&M entered into negotiations with the SEC. According to Cunningham, both schools agreed that the Longhorns would go west, A&M would go east, but they would continue to play one another on Thanksgiving Day.

Any new school's entry had to be accepted by all PAC 10 schools, and the president of Stanford decided he didn't want to compete with The University of Texas. The Horns were uninvited to the party. So, in spite of A&M's designs on the SEC, one school would not abandon the other. When Cunningham let Mobley know that UT's invitation had been rescinded, Mobley shut down A&M's discussions with the SEC.

Thus began the decade of disassembling the Southwest Conference. After charter member Arkansas announced it was leaving for the Southeastern Conference in 1990, the Southwestern Conference cratered. Texas—along with A&M, Baylor, and Texas Tech—went searching for a new home. They found it in 1995, when the four schools merged with the Big 8 and a new conference was born: the Big 12.

44 The Cotton Bowl

To the uninitiated, the Cotton Bowl Stadium at Dallas' Fair Park must seem a decrepit relic with its cramped seating and unreliable plumbing. It's not covered, not temperature-regulated, not comfortable, not modern. And today the Cotton Bowl Classic must seem like one more irrelevant bowl game, lacking the glamour of a BCS bowl.

Yet from 1942 until the death of the SWC in 1995, the venerable stadium matched the champion of the Southwest Conference against an at-large opponent in the New Year's Day Cotton Bowl Classic, and the team that played there on more New Year's Days than any other team in the nation was The University of Texas.

The Horns have played in 22 Cotton Bowl games, and they claim 11 former players and coaches in the Cotton Bowl Hall of Fame. No other school comes close.

In the days before there were 35 postseason bowl games, with names like the San Diego County Credit Union Poinsettia Bowl and the Famous Idaho Potato Bowl, before we were subjected to three weeks of mind-numbing, meaningless matchups, the Cotton Bowl was considered a major bowl, along with the Rose Bowl, the Orange Bowl, the Sugar Bowl, and the Sun Bowl.

The Cotton Bowl was the Longhorns' home away from home. If an opposing team met up with Texas in the Cotton Bowl on New Year's Day, they knew Texas had the home-field advantage. For years, UT's home-and-home series with TCU and SMU were played in the Cotton Bowl. Add to that the annual death-match against the Sooners, and there were some years when Texas played four games a year in the Cotton Bowl.

Today there is an ongoing debate about moving the site of the Texas-OU game, and although some folks believe that changing the venue of this game will signal the coming of the Last Days—the author being one of them—there are valid reasons for considering a move.

The plumbing, in spite of upgrades, is unpredictable; at one recent Texas-OU game, the women's restrooms were flooded with four inches of water. Fans needing to use the restroom would stop

Longhorn Lore

Ricky Williams wore three different jersey numbers during his career at Texas. Assigned No. 11 when he arrived, he wanted to change to his old high school number, 34, but that jersey was occupied by a linebacker. The linebacker left the team, but coach John Mackovic did not allow players to change numbers. Williams was stuck with 11.

When Mack Brown took over for Mackovic in 1998, he was happy to give Williams No. 34, and No. 11 went to Major Applewhite.

Williams, a two-time Doak Walker Award winner, became close friends with the legendary Walker. After Walker's death as a result of a snow-skiing accident, the NCAA gave Williams the okay to honor Walker by wearing for one game the jersey Walker made famous—No. 37.

Williams wore Walker's No. 37 in the 1998 game against Oklahoma, which is held in the Cotton Bowl, "The House that Doak Built."

at the door and weigh their decision: just how badly did they need to go? One coed who'd had too much beer at the fairgrounds knew the consequences: "These are my mama's new boots and she's gonna kill me," she wailed as she waded through the water.

Stadium capacity has been increased to 92,100 and it is cramped. The game could go to a home-and-home series; OU's Owen Field at Memorial Stadium holds 83,000, and after DKR–Texas Memorial Stadium's latest renovation, 100,120 Horns would be able to watch the game. But only every other year.

Move the game to the new JerryWorld Stadium at Arlington? The $1.1 billion stadium has a retractable roof and holds up to 105,000 spectators, (25,000 of those will be in standing room only) including the 400 suites. Think of the revenue possibilities!

But aren't some things more important than more dollars? Would you ditch your spouse of 60 years because she no longer looks so hot in a bikini? Would you trade in your '65 Mustang because it doesn't have a built-in GPS? Granted, we can always use the money, but sentiment and tradition and history should count for something.

But we can pop the cork and celebrate; UT and OU agreed recently to extend their Cotton Bowl contract through at least 2020, after the city of Dallas promised to fund new incentives to each school and spend another $25 million to upgrade the stadium, after pumping in $57 million a few months earlier. But the argument's sure to come up again in a few years.

The Cotton Bowl isn't just a relic, an anachronism. It's our history and our heritage, our home away from home. Mike Dean, former Longhorn great who is in the Cotton Bowl Hall of Fame, played in three Cotton Bowl Classics from 1969 to 1971. In describing the stadium, he said, "The two teams are coming out of the tunnel at the same time. It reminded me of two gladiators looking at each other. You see the guy you've studied all week; you see what he looks like without his helmet on. And the moment you stepped out of the darkness, all hell broke loose. It's the only stadium I know that is like that."

45 The Tunnel

"You're wedged so tightly together that your feet are barely touching the ribbed, dirty concrete…you're slowly floating down the ramp suspended among your fellow teammates. You're in the shade of the tunnel now, beneath the stomping, screaming Sooner fans…it's cooler, but you're having trouble catching your breath…." —From former Longhorn place-kicker Billy "Sure" Schott's account of coming down the tunnel, published on orangebloods.com

Most fans will never experience The Tunnel or anything close to it. For the school teacher or the banker or the computer programmer, there will never be 92,000 people screaming for them, imploring them to do their jobs well and groaning loudly if they make a mistake. Most couldn't take the pressure.

But there is not an Oklahoma or Texas football player alive today who can ever forget the sensation of running the gauntlet of The Tunnel: the sound of cleats scraping on concrete, the smell of his own sweat mingled with the diesel fumes from the team buses, the tension of waiting...waiting...waiting in close proximity to the opponent, waiting for the signal to go, waiting for the dam to break so they can take the field.

The Tunnel is the ramp leading from the two locker rooms down onto the floor of the Cotton Bowl. It is the "last mile" of college football—a dark, narrow tunnel leading players toward the daylight, toward the frenzy, toward the moment of truth.

The two teams used to come down the tunnel at the same time and there was the inevitable jostling and taunting until, one by one, the men would grow silent, focusing on the task before them. Former Longhorn coach Fred Akers, who was 5–4–1 against Oklahoma, said, "I don't know how many times we'd get into a

The Golden Hat

The tradition started in 1941 when a genuine felt 10-gallon hat, donated by the State Fair of Texas, was awarded to the winner of the annual Texas-OU game held at the Cotton Bowl in Dallas. Texas beat OU 40–7 and became the first recipient of the hat.

The hat eventually started showing its age, and Cotton Bowl officials realized that a felt hat has a limited shelf life as trophies go. The State Fair had the hat bronzed, and in 1969, the hat was replated in gold.

The Golden Hat goes back each year to the campus of the winning team; the Hat has come home to Austin 60 times and visited Norman 43.

Darrell Royal leads his 1971 Longhorns down the gauntlet of the Cotton Bowl tunnel to face the Sooners.

scrape, with banging, shoving, elbowing…most of the team would have just as soon fight it out in the parking lot, or right there in the tunnel."

Barry Switzer said, "Anyone who could go down the ramp at the Texas-Oklahoma game and not feel extremely excited must be legally dead."

Each player has his own "tunnel memory," a mental snapshot, which evokes the whole of his OU game experience. Ted Koy shared his with Bill Little in *What It Means to Be a Longhorn*. "I'd been there before watching my older brother Ernie. Now I'm coming down the tunnel. I'd heard about it. I'd read about it. I'd seen it. But it was different than anything I expected. You don't hear the crowd, you feel it. You feel like you're standing in front of a giant speaker. I thought, 'What in the heck am I getting myself into?'"

Doug English was a sophomore, starting his first game at defensive tackle against OU. He said, "I remember walking out of the locker room, down the tunnel and onto the field, into that wall of sound… I'd stopped and was looking around, a little stunned. [Coach Pat Patterson] walked up to me, looked all around the Cotton Bowl, and said, 'No place for a timid man, is it?'"

For defensive back Glenn Blackwood, it is this: "I think about walking down that tunnel at the Cotton Bowl, seeing half the stadium in crimson and the other half in orange, in what I believe is the greatest college football game there is. To stand on that field victorious at the end with your horns in the air and the "The Eyes of Texas" playing is one of the things I'll remember for the rest of my life."

46 The Dear Old Texas Aggies

Volumes have been written about Texas' rivalry with A&M—about the history, the Aggie jokes, and the animosity between the two schools. Before the Aggies bolted for the SEC, the Texas–Texas A&M series stood as the third-longest rivalry in Division I football and was the oldest intrastate rivalry among major college football teams. What a great history.

But it's a lopsided history. In spite of the shame of UT's losses to A&M in 2006 and 2007, the 118-game series stands at 76–37–5 in favor of the good guys.

The rivalry started as a class war. Founded as a branch of The University, A&M was to focus on all things agricultural,

Justin Tucker's game-winning 40-yard field goal against A&M in 2011 was the perfect capper to a 118-year rivalry.

mechanical, and military. Texas was to cover the more genteel subjects: classical studies, literature, languages, fine arts. Professionals attended Texas, called the "Main University"; blue-collar types went to A&M. Located in a small and isolated town, A&M was for men only. Somewhere along the line, Aggies became genetically engineered to "whoop" loudly anytime the school or their mascot Reveille or the Twelfth man or College Station or cloning is mentioned at a public gathering.

Of course, those lines have blurred somewhat over time, except for the attitudes. And the whooping. Today, both schools are regulars in the "top large American university" polls. In the introduction to *Aggies & Horns,* U.S. Senator Lloyd Doggett wrote, "It

State Farm Showdown

Not a lot of folks knew about the State Farm Showdown. It was an official competition between Texas and A&M, pitting all varsity men's and women's sports in an annual, year-long competition. The series was created to highlight the competition between the two schools' "nonmajor" sports. Points were awarded to the winner of each head-to-head contest, and each sport in which both schools maintain a team is worth one point. There are a total of 19 possible points, but 10 points are needed to win.

The results so far:

2004–05	Texas: 14.5; A&M: 4.5
2005–06	Texas: 14; A&M: 5
2006–07	Texas: 10.5; A&M: 8.5
2007–08	A&M: 10.5; Texas: 8.5
2008–09	Texas: 9.5; A&M: 9.5
2009–10	Texas: 10; A&M: 9
2010–11	Texas: 9.5; A&M: 9.5
2011–12	Texas: 12; A&M: 7

Total Wins: Texas: 6 (63%); A&M: 2 (37%)

And that's all, folks.

is a rivalry based on what was...a real difference in outlook, with UT representing urban Texas and A&M representing rural Texas at a time when the state was much more evenly divided along those lines... the real differences have faded, but all the trappings have assumed centrality, and the rivalry sustains itself year after year."

Nowhere does the infamous Longhorn arrogance show itself more than when a "teasip," the Aggie's pejorative term for a Longhorn, is in conversation with an Aggie. In his book, *Backyard Brawl*, W.K. Stratton said it best: "UT can be seen as the son Mom always liked best, the one who got the new bike, the better clothes, and a larger allowance and who gloated about it. A&M can be seen as the son with the chip on his shoulder who got the hand-me-downs and leftovers and who stewed about it."

Much of their Aggie War Hymn refers to beating Texas. In fact, the opening line, after the "Hullaboo, caneck, caneck" stuff, says, "Goodbye to Texas University, so long to the orange and white…" They then spend a few minutes swaying back and forth, "sawing Varsity's horns off." It's effective, though: 80,000 Aggies swaying back and forth in Kyle Field with their arms slung over one another's shoulders has quite a dizzying effect.

"Teasips" don't have such a hatred for the Aggies; we regard them as more of a pesky little brother who occasionally got his licks in. When Earl Campbell was asked about Texas' biggest rivals, he said, "When we play OU, it's serious business. But when we play the Aggies, we already know how it's gonna turn out."

Thanksgiving Day 2011 marked the end of the 117-year tradition, as Texas and A&M played one another for the last time. The Aggies were leaving for the SEC and the Horns were staying home in the Big 12.

After more than a century of enduring derision and jokes made at their expense, the agricultural and mechanical branch suffered the ultimate Aggie joke. In their last meeting on the football field, A&M held the lead for much of the game, but just as time expired, Longhorn senior Justin Tucker kicked a 40-yard field goal to give Texas a 27–25 victory.

Game. Set. Match.

47 The Longhorn Network

University athletics director DeLoss Dodds had an idea that just wouldn't leave him alone; he had a vision that The University should have its own television network. Yet, no matter how he worked it, he couldn't see Texas generating enough programming on its own, so sometime in 2007 he called Texas A&M athletics director Bill Byrne and floated the idea of a two-school "Flagship Network."

Dodds didn't hear back from Byrne for more than two years. By then, it was too late.

There were rumblings of conference realignments, of teams ditching the Big 12. UT could have picked its own conference, but Dodds would have had to abandon his dream of forming an exclusive network for The University of Texas. Other conferences precluded schools from having their own channels, but in the face of defections from Nebraska (to the Big 10) and Colorado (Pac 12), and rumors of OU and A&M flirting with the SEC, the Big 12 knew it had to capture Texas. So the Big 12 agreed that the Horns—and its other nine schools—would have the right to form their own channels.

With Texas secured, and A&M and OU still on board, the Big 12 was able to land a 13-year cable deal with Fox Sports for $90 million per year, *on top* of its annual $60 million deal with ESPN/ABC that runs through 2016.

The years from 2000 through 2009 were golden for the Horns. Baseball reached the College World Series in 2000, 2002, 2003, 2004, 2005, 2009, and 2011, winning it all in 2002 and 2005. Women's and men's basketball reached the Final Four in '03. Football won the national championship in 2005, played for another in 2009, beat Michigan in the Rose Bowl following the 2004 season, and Ohio State in the Fiesta Bowl following the 2008 season. Dodds had positioned Texas to be the wealthiest athletic department in the country. We were king of the world.

ESPN recognized this and in January 2011, after Texas had pledged to stay put in the Big 12, they worked out a deal with Dodds that would pay Texas $300 million for 20 years to air the rights to sports like volleyball, softball, Olympic sports, and baseball. It was astounding, an unprecedented deal for an individual school to get

Longhorn Lore: Integration

Here's a little-known fact: The University of Texas was the first Southwest Conference school to integrate its athletics programs.

James Means Jr. of the UT track team was the first black athlete to compete for The University and for the Southwest Conference. Julius Whittier is widely known as the first African American letterman on the Texas football team, and people assume that Jerry Levias of SMU football was the first black SWC conference athlete. But in February 1964, James Means and Oliver Patterson competed in a track meet at A&M, thus becoming the first black UT athletes as well as groundbreakers in the SWC. Patterson subsequently left the track team, but Means stayed and became the first African American athlete to letter in the Southwest Conference. He was a three-year letterman at The University.

While Texas was not a beacon of progressivism, it was the first public university in the South to admit black students. On June 7, 1950—two days after the Supreme Court ruled in favor of desegregation in Sweatt v. Painter—John Saunders Chase enrolled to do grad work in the UT School of Architecture and 50-year-old Horace Lincoln Heath entered the school of engineering. After a successful career in Houston as an architect and community service icon, Chase became the first African American president of the Texas Exes.

that kind of money for third-tier rights. Each Big 12 school and the conference as a whole signed off on the Longhorn Network.

There's been a lot of "he-said-she-said," but Byrne, who was "transitioned" out of the AD role in May 2012, denied Dodds' account and told the *Birmingham News* that he didn't think the Longhorn Network would work anyway.

"Some of you have asked me, 'Isn't it true you had a chance to join Texas in the ESPN venture and would have had a joint channel?'" Byrne wrote to the Aggie faithful in the August 31, 2011, edition of his "Bill Byrne's Weekly Wednesday" column. "Three or four years ago we talked about doing a joint flagship channel. I liked the idea, but our fans should know me better than to think I would pass on a $150 million deal for Texas A&M. That never happened." Of course it didn't; when DeLoss first floated the idea to Byrne, no one could have dreamed that it would end up being a $300 million dollar deal. According to Dodds, Byrne never gave it a chance.

When ESPN unveiled the Longhorn Network's programming schedule, A&M and OU howled in protest. The network planned to televise three Big 12 games and 18 high school games, giving Texas a perceived recruiting advantage. So, even though the schools signed off on the LHN, and the conference as a whole agreed to Texas' agreement with the Longhorn Network, it turned out to be a bigger deal, more pervasive, than anyone had thought. The conference was threatening to explode again. After Big 12 commissioner Dan Beebe placed a hold of some of the network's programming, DeLoss Dodds declared that Texas would not be involved in selecting the games to be broadcast, and it was agreed that high school games would not be shown on the Longhorn Network.

"Nobody seemed concerned with it until it was done," Dodds said. "I find it interesting that it's a problem today....If somebody is surprised by this deal, they haven't been paying attention."

"In the long haul," Dodds said, "us being able to do this gives the ability to A&M...to Oklahoma to be able to do this. We're building a new world."

And, as we all know, "What Starts Here Changes the World."

Longhorn fans' initial excitement and bragging gave way to frustration, as most of the fan base couldn't even subscribe to the network. It launched in August 2011, but it was a full year before AT&T U-verse started carrying the station. In spite of UT's campaign to get viewers to pressure Time Warner into carrying the Longhorn Network, the channel had aired for a full two years before being picked up by Time Warner Cable, the major provider in Texas.

48 The Beginning

The facts related to the beginnings of Texas football are somewhat sketchy. An August 2002 *Texas Monthly* article stated that Texas' first football game was played on December 4, 1883, against the Texas German and English Academy (also called the Bickler School), just two months after The University first opened. Texas lost by two scores to a group of high school kids. Perhaps that's why this game has been largely forgotten.

The next recorded game was an intrasquad scrimmage held in November 1893. The game was interrupted for half an hour after the game ball burst; a student rode his horse downtown to find a replacement. Accounts of this game differed, with the campus literary magazine, *The Texas University,* claiming the game ended in a 6–6 tie, and the *Austin Daily Statesman* reporting a completely different account.

Forty Acres Follies credits yet another football game as being the first—this one against a team from San Antonio and played at the Dam Baseball Park, west of Austin near the Colorado River.

But the day Texas football was truly born was November 30, 1893, when The University of Texas Foot Ball Club accepted a challenge from the Dallas Foot Ball Club, the self-proclaimed champions of Texas. The Dallas team was undefeated for several years and had a reputation for being a rough bunch.

Indeed. Guard Billy Richardson is missing from the Texas Varsity 1893 team picture; he was kicked in the head during the second game against Dallas that season and was in the hospital when the photo was taken.

That Thanksgiving morning when the first match was held, 15 young men arrived by train to challenge the vaunted Dallas

Longhorn Lore

Theo Bellmont was a man of vision. When the former UT law school grad became The University's first athletics director in 1913, he had the opportunity to mold the department to further his vision. One of his first moves was to take the management of UT athletics out of the hands of students and to place it under the authority of The University.

He instituted the student blanket tax, which would help fund the growing athletics program, and beefed up the sports schedules with more prestigious opponents in order to increase the attendance and the gates.

After Texas A&M got rid of coach "Dirty Charlie" Moran in 1914, Bellmont agreed to resume the series with the Aggies. Bellmont was the first to schedule games with Oklahoma, although that wasn't part of the vision; he simply couldn't find any other school to replace Vanderbilt as the annual October opponent.

Bellmont's dream included construction of then–state-of-the-art Memorial Stadium, the famed Texas Relays conceived by Clyde Littlefield, and the establishment of a top-notch intramurals program, still considered one of the nation's best, led by Berry Whitaker. Bellmont founded the "T" Association, the Texas lettermen's organization. The Southwest Conference was his baby; he imagined it, created it, nurtured it.

It is fitting that The University of Texas, whose athletic department was formed by Bellmont, would come to be the dominant force in the Southwest Conference he created.

club. The arrogance that modern-day opponents accuse Texas of displaying has been present from the beginning. Upon their arrival, the Varsity players—most sporting bushy hair in order to protect their heads in the pre-helmet days of football—all bought big cigars and "strutted down Main Street." They were prepared for the rough tactics of the Dallas bunch, and after Dallas made a deliberate attempt to break the leg of one of the Texas players, the boys from Austin took out three members of the Dallas Foot Ball Club. Unable to intimidate the Texas team, Dallas called a truce and requested that the remainder of the game be played "without any rough stuff."

Student-organized and student-coached, the very first University of Texas team marched unafraid into hostile territory that Thanksgiving Day and defeated Dallas by a score of 18–16, causing one Dallas player to moan to a reporter, "Our name is pants and our glory has departed."

Varsity finished its inaugural season undefeated and remained unbeaten through the first six games of 1894, until Missouri came to town and whipped Texas 28–0. Nevertheless, the winning tradition was established and the bar was set impossibly high—where it remains today.

49 The 1890s

The Texas winning tradition has its roots in that very first season. The 1893 team—student-organized, student-coached, and student-managed—compiled a 4–0 record and set the tone for the 115 teams that would follow, building a foundation of winning, of excellence, and as every coach and sportswriter in America loves to say, of "walking with a swagger."

The 1893 team played four games that inaugural season and won all four of them, outscoring their opponents 98–16. No game was more crucial than the very first one, when the Texas Varsity stormed into hostile territory to challenge the Dallas Foot Ball Club, self-proclaimed "champions of Texas." Undefeated for several years and for much of that time unscored on, The Dallas Foot Ball Club was known for its domination of other teams and for the injuries it inflicted on players who dared line up against them.

The Texas team was not intimidated. When the final gun sounded, Texas had won 18–16 and there was a new king of the hill. Later that year, Texas took the starch out of the Dallas team again, beating them 16–0.

Under the leadership of their first paid coach R.D. Wentworth, the 1894 Varsity shut out the first six teams they played, outscoring opponents 191–0. This University team was so dominating that when San Antonio found itself down 57–0, they sought an early end to the game just seven minutes into the second half.

The supremely confident Texas squad traveled to Missouri and to their shock and shame were beaten 28–0, in front of a crowd of 3,000. Many Texas players were so humiliated that they shaved the long hair that had identified them as football players.

A new year brought a new coach and another undefeated team. The 1895 bunch outscored their five opponents 96–0. Led by three-sport star Walter Fisher, who was inducted into the Longhorn Hall of Honor in 1968; fearless halfback Jim Caperton; and quarterback J.S. "Snaky" Jones of Bastrop, they made history

Eastern Press

Yeah, we know that football started in the East. We were about 25 years behind Princeton, Harvard, and Yale. For decades, the Eastern sportswriters and fans pretty much ignored any football played west of the Mississippi. In spite of Texas' growing reputation for being a powerhouse, they pooh-poohed the idea that Texas could play football, sort of like how the SEC feels about the Big 12 today.

In 1903, W.H. Lanigan, sports editor of the *St. Louis Star*, offered this prediction on the future of football in the Southwest: "...the schools are weak financially and numerically...athletics will never have the vogue in a warm climate that they have in the cooler and more invigorating climate of the North...these schools have only limited territory to draw from...these schools are lacking in tradition, both among the faculty and students, which have made athletics so important a part in the history of the Northern university."

The 1895 squad, the only Texas team to be undefeated, untied, and unscored upon.

when they became the first and only team in Texas history to end the season undefeated, untied, and unscored upon.

The last four seasons of the century produced solid winning teams, with a new coach each year and a combined record of 21–7–1. The 1896 team made history by participating in the first-ever collegiate football games played in Mexico. Amid controversy and to the consternation of officials from both schools, the Texas and Missouri teams staged a 10-day exhibition trip, playing games in several cities in Mexico. Missouri in particular was not amused; their coach, Frank Patterson, lost his job, as did the team manager. Mexico never did embrace American football, deeming it "too violent and muscular" a game.

Texas was still playing more "town" teams than college teams, but the 1897 Varsity distinguished itself by beating TCU (then Add-Ran College) for the first time by a score of 18–10.

In the final year of the century, the final year of the infancy of Texas football, the 1899 game with Dallas turned into a bloody free-for-all, leading the Texas faculty to pass a resolution that Texas drop "town" teams from the schedule. Thereafter, Texas' schedules would consist mostly of other colleges.

All in all, it was quite a successful endeavor, this Texas football experiment. By the end of the century, after only seven seasons, Texas had established itself as the dominant team in the state and as an ascendant force in the Southwest.

And we'd begun our mastery over the Aggies, having defeated them three times and outscored them 92–0.

50 Meet Me at Scholz's

Although much has changed about the UT experience and game days over the last century, there's still Scholz's. Built in 1866, Scholz Garten has been welcoming students to its beer garden among the oaks since The University opened in 1883. Not much has changed about the place. On cool evenings there's live music on the patio, and one can still find business deals being cut or legislative compromises being arranged. On blazing hot September Saturdays before and after the game, the place has a carnival atmosphere, jammed with current students and alums alike.

Scholz's was established by German immigrant August Scholz. It has, since the beginning, been a popular place with University students and legislators and is somewhat of a refuge for returning alums. Each generation has had its favorite gathering place, yet as Austin grows and becomes more citified, alums are dismayed with each return trip to Austin to find that one more landmark has been

Longhorn Lore
No, it's not your imagination. There is a private bowling alley, also owned by Saengerrunde, behind the patio at Scholz's. Some nights when the band is on break, you can hear the pins crashing.

razed. Gone are the Perip, Clark Field, the Kappa Sig house on 19th, Taco Flats, Rooster Andrews Sporting Goods, and Jake's. But Scholz's remains and serves as a security blanket for all Longhorns. It is the thread that is woven through the fabric of social life in Austin and the history of The University from the very beginning.

In 1966, the Texas House of Representatives adopted a resolution recognizing Scholz Garten as a "gathering place for Texans of discernment, taste, culture, and erudition, epitomizing the finest tradition of magnificent German heritage in our state." The German Singing Society, Saengerrunde, founded in 1879 and still in existence today, owns Scholz Garten.

Famous Texans from all walks have held court there. According to the *Austin Chronicle*, "notorious gunslinger and one-time City Marshal Ben Thompson celebrated here when he was acquitted of murder charges in San Antonio." Scholz Garten is where the 1893 football team celebrated its first victories. In the 1890s, short-story author O. Henry published his satirical weekly newspaper, *The Rolling Stone*, in Austin. He hung out at Scholz Garten and once wrote, "Newcomers to Texas are warned to beware of the long-haired citizen. He may be only a desperado, but it might be discovered, when too late, that he is a football player."

It is our good fortune that Scholz Garten has been placed on the National Register of Historic Places, ensuring that, unlike so many of Austin's beloved institutions from the past, it will never be demolished and replaced with yet another high rise.

51 Clark Field

Professor John William Mallet was lured to Texas as a member of the first UT faculty with the hope that the Texas weather would improve the health of his sickly son. Mallet, a world-renowned chemist, was selected as UT's first faculty chairman.

Upon his arrival, Mallet discovered that The University building was not ready for classes. When his son's health continued to deteriorate after a year in Texas, Mallet returned to Virginia, but he took with him an indelible impression of the determination and persistence of Texans. "Among the most vivid impressions… is that of the Texas spirit…. It is not very clear how the thing is to be done, but…Texas has said it shall be done and it will be done, somehow."

And so the legend was born, particularly as it applied to The University in its infancy. UT's first ballpark was a vacant lot at Speedway and 24th, where Taylor Hall stands today. It had no name in 1898, but when the owners threatened to evict "Varsity" from using the field, athletics council members borrowed the $1,000 down payment from the bank, and the student body flew into action, raising money for the board fence. The second note of $1,000 was met with donations from faculty members and ex-students.

In 1904, the field was named in honor of much-loved James Clark, an early University jack-of-all-trades. He served as librarian, registrar, bursar, groundskeeper, and even regent. There were few bleachers at Clark Field, mostly just an open lot, until UT students followed the team to the 1907 game with Missouri.

Clark Field's few sets of bleachers accommodated about 500 fans, but important rival games attracted thousands, most of

Longhorn Lore: Early Times

General Robert E. Lee believed that city planners had not sufficiently appreciated or planned for the great possibilities of the future of The University. He suggested that, instead of 40 acres, at least 200 should have been appropriated. And in a prescient moment, he declared, "…the fathers of Texas…were thoughtful and patriotic men, and had made an imperial provision for the education of the youth of the state. If men less wise and less patriotic are not allowed to interfere with the designs of the founders, The University will have a glorious career."
—From the *Waterloo Scrapbook*

whom had to stand four or five people deep along the sideline, according to Jim Nicar's *How to Build a Stadium in Two Weeks*. "To make sure onlookers didn't accidentally intrude onto the playing field, a…barbed-wire fence was erected to keep fans off the gridiron. Those standing in front had the best views, but were in danger of being pushed by the crowd into the barbed wire."

So, in an early case of athletic-facility envy, when Texas players saw the bleachers that Missouri students had erected, it sparked a campaign to build stands at Clark Field. The students were determined that the bleachers would be built in time to host the game against Texas A&M…25 days hence.

The students led the charge, raising $870 themselves and collecting $132 from the Athletics Council. Borrowing the fund-raising method used by Missouri students, Texas students sold "Bleacher Badges," which were white with an orange "T." Coeds living in the women's residence hall created a white satin banner with an orange "T" to be auctioned, with the proceeds going to the building fund.

On November 21, 1907, not three weeks after the Missouri game, construction on the bleachers began. Thanksgiving and the Aggies were only a week away. With faculty consent, student volunteers from the engineering and law schools were excused from class, and just six days after ground was broken, the bleachers were finished.

The impossible had been accomplished. To paraphrase Mallet, it had not been clear how it was to be done, but the students of The University of Texas had said it would be done and it was done, somehow. On Thanksgiving Day, a crowd of 5,000 fans—2,000 of whom had seats—watched the Longhorns defeat the Aggies 11–6.

The Longhorns played their home games at Clark Field until 1924 and during that time, every addition made to the stadium, was accomplished by University students.

52 Great Teams 1900–19

Armed with new "official" school colors of orange and white, a newly formed band that began playing at football games, and yet another new coach, Huston Thompson, the undefeated 1900 squad established itself as the champion of the Southwest by defeating Vanderbilt, Kansas City Medics, Missouri—and in their first meeting ever, Oklahoma. Texas' shut-out record over A&M was extended to five games.

The 1914 team was loaded with talent and their 8–0 record stands as proof. This extraordinary team was captained by guard Louis Jordan who was named a second-team All-American, the first Longhorn ever to receive the honor. Halfback Clyde Littlefield—who would go on to win 12 varsity letters in football, basketball, and track—helped Varsity outscore their challengers 358–21 and shut out five of their eight opponents. Coach Dave Allerdice

Scoring Record

In 1914, standout halfback Len Barrell scored 14 touchdowns and kicked 34 extra points and one field goal, tallying 121 points in a single season for the Longhorns. Barrell held the UT record for points in a season for 83 years, until Ricky Williams broke it in 1997 and again in 1998.

steered this group, which included end Pete Edmond, center Gus "Pig" Dittmar, and halfback Len Barrell, to 20 victories in its last 21 contests from 1913 to 1915.

As testament to the overpowering talent on the 1914 squad, virtually all of the Longhorns were chosen for the all-state teams selected by coaches and sportswriters. Seven members of the 26-man squad have been inducted into the Longhorn Hall of Honor: Len Barrell, K.L. Berry, Alva "Fats" Carlton, Gustav "Pig" Dittmar, Pete Edmond, Louis Jordan, and Clyde Littlefield, as well as coach Dave Allerdice.

The 1918 season saw the Longhorns undefeated once again, although other events that year overshadowed anything that occurred on the athletic fields. The University, and the nation, were preoccupied with the imminent end of World War I, and many of the older students were serving in the military. The deadly Spanish flu epidemic swept through Texas in September of that year and interrupted not only the football season, but also the class schedule for The University. Texas was forced to cancel or postpone all but one of its remaining six games. After the Armistice, however, Texas met also-undefeated A&M and came away with a 7–0 victory and an unblemished season.

53 Show Band of the Southwest

There is no mistaking the Longhorn Band for any of the hundreds of generic marching bands in college football. When LHB takes the field and stretches from sideline to sideline and goal to goal, wearing cowboy hats and distinctively Texan uniforms of burnt orange trimmed with white fringe, the band is unlike any other in the country.

Dr. E.P. Schoch, professor of chemistry, envisioned marching bands as an inspiring addition to football games. In 1900, he and Dr. H.E. Baxter, the first Longhorn Band director, recruited 16 students to form what would decades later grow into "The Show Band of the Southwest." The two men bought the first instruments for $150 at Jackson's Pawn Shop in downtown Austin.

Like the band of today, the original 16 charter members, who wore uniforms of white linen dusters and white caps with black bills, were not just music majors, but were students from varied areas of study. Only 15 percent of today's Longhorn Band members are music majors.

Longhorn Lore: Big Bertha

At 8 feet in diameter, Big Bertha is the largest marching drum in the world; she became the Sweetheart of the Longhorn Band in 1955. Big Bertha was originally built for the University of Chicago more than 90 years ago, but longtime band benefactor D. Harold Byrd purchased Bertha for $1 from Chicago and transported her to her permanent home in Austin.

The All-American Marching Band of Purdue claims that its Big Bass Drum is larger, but as the "exact dimensions of Purdue's drum are a closely guarded secret known only to crew members," the challenge is a moot point.

The Longhorn Band excels not only at halftime, but they're also the most spirited bunch in the stands.

The band has grown in size and in prestige over the years, but it was under the direction of Vincent R. DiNino that the band first allowed women to march, and it was during his 20-year reign that the band grew to its current size and attained the excellence that marks today's Longhorn Band.

"March Grandioso," also introduced to Texas crowds by DiNino in 1955, has become another fight song as *Texas* is spelled out by fans in time with the music. The highlight of halftime is seeing *Texas* spelled out in continuous script as the Longhorn Band plays "March of the Longhorns."

The band is the most spirited group in the stadium, ringing their signature cowbells or starting drum cadences and chants if the crowd gets too quiet. Three hundred–plus clanging cowbells can rattle any opposing fans and team, and the spirit of the band has made a difference in pivotal games throughout the years.

D.X. Bible recognized the influence the band could wield. Arkansas manhandled Texas in 1938, 42–6, and the team had finished with a miserable 1–9 season. At the 1939 Arkansas game, with the Horns trailing 13–7 and less than a minute to play, Bible sent a message to the band to play "The Eyes of Texas." Many fans had already left, certain of UT's demise. But as the band played, Texas went into formation. Jack Crain caught a short pass from halfback R.B. Patrick and turned it into a 67-yard touchdown. After clearing the field of the celebrating fans, Crain then kicked the winning extra point to win 14–13, sealing UT's first SWC opener since 1933.

Bible said later, "That play and that victory changed our outlook—mine, the players', the student body's, and the ex-students'.'" The Horns compiled a 5–4 record that year, marking the first winning season in five years. All-American Mal Kutner, who personally thanked the band, said later that that was the turning point for Texas football.

54 The Eyes of Texas

Colonel Lambdin Prather was a dignified man and a graduate of Washington University where, throughout his four years, he heard Robert E. Lee tell his students, "Gentlemen, the eyes of the South are upon you." When Prather became president of The University of Texas, he borrowed that tradition and always closed any address to the student body by saying, "Students of The University of Texas, the eyes of Texas are upon you."

UT student John Lang Sinclair was given only a few hours to compose a song for the 1903 Texas Minstrel Show. Sinclair, a banjo player, hurriedly composed lyrics based on Prather's famous saying and set it to the tune of "I've Been Working on the Railroad." A quartet dressed in minstrel attire and blackface sang the song and brought the house down. The audience pounded the floor and demanded encore after encore. Soon the students joined in, and the band learned the music and lyrics the next day.

Get It Right

Although many Longhorns think the sixth line of "Eyes" says "Rise up so early in the morn," it was actually written: "At night or early in the morn."

The Eyes of Texas are upon you,
All the livelong day.
The Eyes of Texas are upon you,
You cannot get away.
Do not think you can escape them
At night or early in the morn—
The Eyes of Texas are upon you
'Til Gabriel blows his horn.

The satirical song caught on. Prather was amused by the song, which poked fun at him, and he encouraged the students to sing it. At Prather's funeral in 1905, students sang the chorus as an anthem. "Eyes" was almost immediately adopted as the official alma mater of The University.

"The Eyes of Texas" is played prior to and after all Texas sporting events, and is sung reverentially, with Horns up, of course.

55 Texas Taps

It really is the greatest fight song around. The rousing "Texas Fight," known to the Longhorn Band as "Taps," was written by Colonel Walter S. Hunnicutt with James E. King, then-director of the Marlin High School Band. UT's official fight song is played as the team takes the field, after touchdowns or field goals, and throughout the game to inspire the team. During the OU game, it seems as if it's played for 60 minutes straight.

Longhorn Lore
In spite of what you may hear from UT students singing "Texas Fight," the seventh line of the fight song contains no obscenities.

Hunnicutt wrote in a 1952 letter, "I wrote 'Texas Fight'...in an attempt to counteract the songs and yells of the...Aggies, which were not too complimentary to our student body and some of which tended to ridicule 'Eyes of Texas.'

"The A&M song 'Farmers Fight' was sung to the well-known bugle call 'Taps' in the same slow tempo as...is used by the Army for lights-out...."

After returning from World War I, Hunnicutt attended Texas games and decided an "effective way to strike back at the Aggies was to write...a song in answer to their 'Farmers Fight,' using the same bugle call 'Taps' changed to lively march time and having 'Texas' throughout the song.... 'Texas Fight' or 'Texas Taps' is the result."

Texas Fight, Texas Fight,
And it's goodbye to A&M.
Texas Fight, Texas Fight,
And we'll put over one more win.
Texas Fight, Texas Fight,
For it's Texas that we love best.
HAIL, HAIL, THE GANG'S ALL HERE,
And it's goodbye to all the rest!
(Yell)
Yea, Orange! Yea, White!
Yea, Longhorns! Fight! Fight! Fight!
Texas Fight! Texas Fight!
Yea, Texas, Fight!
Texas Fight, Texas Fight,
Yea, Texas, Fight!

56 PMS 159

It's hard to imagine The University without its trademark burnt orange and white, but Texas fans wore some interesting color combinations before making a final decision.

In 1885, UT baseball fans boarded a train to Georgetown, Texas, to watch the game against Southwestern University. Just before the train pulled out of the station, two coeds decided they all needed to wear colored ribbon to identify themselves as Texas fans. Not willing to disappoint their dates, Venable Proctor and Clarence Miller jumped off the train and rushed to the nearby general store. They breathlessly asked the clerk for three bolts of ribbon, any color. Proctor and Miller barely made it back before the train pulled away, and after getting settled they divvied up the orange and white ribbon, which the students pinned to their lapels.

The colors weren't official, though, and when Texas fielded its first football team eight years later in 1893, the jerseys were gold and white. Two years later, Texas returned to the more masculine orange and white, but the white was difficult to keep clean.

The real outrage occurred when head football coach Dave Edwards decided on his own to change the jerseys to orange and maroon. Most students disliked that combination, but the 1899 *Cactus Yearbook* proclaimed orange and maroon the official colors, while down in Galveston students at the medical school had taken to wearing royal blue as their color. Some students even proposed crimson, for heaven's sake.

The Board of Regents finally held a vote to clear up the confusion, and in 1900, students, faculty, staff, and alums decided upon bright-orange and white as the official colors of The University.

Longhorn Lore: "Dirty Charlie" Moran

Texas A&M coach "Dirty Charlie" Moran, as he was called by Texas fans, was once asked by a faculty member if he was teaching his players how to be good losers. He snapped, "I didn't come here to lose."

On the opening play of the 1911 Texas–Texas A&M game in Houston, UT guard Marion Harold had his leg broken. He was the first of three Longhorn players to suffer broken bones in the game. The reports wired back to The University from the *Daily Texan's* sports correspondent read like this: "A&M rooters throw lemons at Texas team as Kirkpatrick scores TD," and "Puett of UT makes fine end run and gets slugged." That was A&M football under Dirty Charlie.

A fight broke out between opposing fans, and the A&M students, sore at losing 6–0, "…roamed the streets all night looking for anyone who might be suspected of being a Horn," according to *Forty Acres Follies*.

Texas player Arnold Kirkpatrick, who recovered the Aggie fumble and scored the game's lone touchdown, wrote later, "Honesty and fairness have prevailed, professionalism has been sent back to the dirty realms of creation. All Texas is glad, all Texas is intoxicated with the joyous news that pure grit had at last beaten the hired athletes of Charles Moran."

The University suspended the series with the Aggies, allegedly telling A&M officials that Texas would not resume the series as long as Charlie Moran was the coach.

Money talks. Texas A&M's athletic department couldn't afford to lose the $10,000 to $15,000 the annual game brought to the coffers. By the end of 1914, Charlie Moran had left College Station.

The problem was that by the season's end, the football jerseys had faded to an ugly yellow, inviting opponents to refer to the Longhorns as "yellow-bellies."

Head coach and former player Clyde Littlefield decided that enough was enough. In 1928 he ordered jerseys in a darker shade of orange—burnt orange—that wouldn't fade. "Texas Orange" was established by the O'Shea Knitting Mills and became the shade worn by UT teams for more than a decade. But supply shortages during World War II forced Texas back to the old bright-orange and white. Hello, yellow-bellies.

Lots of things changed around the athletics department after Darrell Royal was hired. Facilities were upgraded, practices were better organized, conditioning was tougher, and in 1962, he changed the team color back to Texas Orange. Alums were outraged, and in 1966, students and alums petitioned the regents to return to our "true school colors." After an eight-month study, however, the committee wisely recommended in 1967 that burnt orange was to be the official color of The University of Texas.

So, if you're a new Longhorn recently moved into Texas from the Outer 49, welcome. But be warned: when shopping for your fall wardrobe, accept no substitutes. Nothing screams "rookie" quite like showing up at the game dressed as a Tennessee Vols fan.

57 Bevo

There's an intriguing urban legend about how Bevo got his name.

The first live Longhorn steer was introduced on Thanksgiving Day 1916 at halftime of UT's game against A&M. Perhaps angered that Texas won that game 21–7—or more probably, envious of UT's live mascot, and a mean, ornery one at that—Aggies stole into the corral the following February to brand the steer with the score of the 1915 game, which the Aggies had won 13–0. That much of the story is true.

But legend has it that, in order to disguise the score and the shame of the defacement, UT students changed the *13* to a *B*, the hyphen to an *e*, and inserted a *v*, forming the word *Bevo*. Like many other urban legends, this story is entertaining, particularly to Aggies, but it is false.

In 1916, a 1911 law school graduate named Stephen Pinckney was working in West Texas for the U.S. Attorney General's office, assisting with raids on cattle rustlers. In one raid near the Texas-Mexico border, Pinckney discovered a steer with orange hair, and an idea was hatched. He solicited $1 contributions from 124 alums to buy the steer and transport it by railcar to Austin.

The longhorn arrived just in time for the game against the Aggies, and the frightened animal was dragged onto Clark Field and presented to the UT students at halftime with the score tied 7–7. After the new mascot was presented and a speech was made extolling the virtues of the longhorn, the animal was removed to a stockyard in South Austin, and the Longhorns went on to beat the Aggies 21–7.

The Aggies did, in fact, sneak into the corral and brand the steer, but that occurred months after Ben Dyer, editor of the *Texas Exes Alcalde* magazine, proclaimed in the December 1916 issue of the *Alcalde,* "His name is Bevo. Long may he reign!"

So why Bevo? One theory is that the name *Bevo* was borrowed from Anheuser-Busch, which in 1916 introduced a near-beer called Bevo, a play on *pivo,* the Bohemian term for beer. Good try, but Bevo was not well-known in 1916, so that might be a dead end.

Longhorn Lore: The Baylor Forfeit
Texas was playing Baylor at Waco in 1910 when the Bears had a dispute with the referees and left the field at halftime with the score tied 6–6. Texas won on a forfeit.

Tales from the Texas Longhorns gives this account from the *Cactus Yearbook:* "The squad, accompanied by scores of rooters, went to Waco to meet Baylor. But why waste good white paper on the fiasco? Baylor decided she had a better chance of winning if she turned the game into a debate. No sooner thought than done; the officials demurred and gave the game to Varsity 1–0."

Bevo, a Longhorn steer, symbolizes the toughness, strength, and pride of Texas football.

Another, more plausible theory has to do with popular culture of the day. Beginning in 1904, cartoonist Gus Mager drew a popular comic strip that ran in the Austin papers; it featured monkey-like characters named for their personality traits, with each name ending in "o": Rhymo the Monk, Henpecko the Monk, Groucho the Monk, and the most popular, Sherlocko the Monk. It became a popular fad to add an "o" to names, and it is possible that Bevo is a play on the word *beeves,* the plural for beef.

No matter; the name stuck and Bevo was moved to a ranch outside of Austin, all but forgotten until the end of World War I in November 1919. The unfortunate mascot became too expensive to care for, so he was fattened up and served for supper at the 1920 football banquet. In a gesture of goodwill, the Aggies were invited to the banquet and were presented with the hide that had been branded 13–0.

We're understandably proud of the strength and tenacity of our mascot, but even Bevo was no match for the power of Earl Campbell. On Earl's second touchdown run against Houston in

1977, Campbell broke free, angled for the corner of the end zone. He tried to stop himself, but as he told Jan Reid in an interview for *Texas Monthly*, "Bevo went down, a cameraman went down, and I did, too."

Bevo XIII, whose registered name is Sunrise Express, holds a special place in Longhorn hearts. He was put out to pasture in 2004 after serving The University for 16 years.

His most famous moment came in the 1999 Big 12 championship game. Nebraska had beaten Texas in the Alamodome, and Bevo and his handlers were leaving the stadium when nature called. The Associated Press wrote, "With perfect timing, he left his mark squarely on the Cornhuskers logo."

Bevo XIV, the steer formerly known as Sunrise Studly, is the 14th Longhorn steer to hold the position of UT mascot. He began his tenure on September 4, 2004, and has participated in George W. Bush's second inauguration, the Rose Bowl victory over Michigan, the 2005 National Championship, and of course, the last-second field goal that pierced every Aggie heart, as the Longhorns won the last meeting of their 118-game series.

58 The 1920s

With a quarterback named Icky Elam and a head coach who never applied for or even wanted the job, the 1920 team finished their perfect season 9–0 with a huge upset of D.X. Bible's vaunted A&M team.

After winning the state high school championship two years in a row at Austin High, Berry Whitaker left coaching—or so he thought—to accept the challenge of establishing a men's intramural

Longhorn Lore: A Saxet Pizza

Ike Sewell, a guard on the Texas teams of 1925, 27–28, was a three-year starter and a 1927 All-SWC selection. A native of Wills Point, Texas, Sewell's career took him to Chicago, where he opened a restaurant that served small pies containing meat, cheese, and tomatoes. The restaurant, Pizzeria Uno, was wildly successful, and Sewell became known as the "Father of Chicago Deep Dish Pizza." Sewell was also well-known in Illinois for his philanthropy.

A recipient of the Distinguished American Award from the National Football Foundation Hall of Fame, Sewell never stopped yearning for Texas; his company was named the Saxet Corporation. *Saxet* is *Texas* spelled backwards.

program under UT athletics director Theo Bellmont. After he helped coach the 1919 Texas team, Bellmont called Whitaker and informed him that he'd been appointed head coach for the next year. Whitaker told *Austin American-Statesman* reporter Lou Maysel, "That's the first indication I had of anything going on, and I wasn't too anxious to take it, but I finally agreed."

Good thing he did. Coming into the 1920 A&M game, Texas was undefeated and had outscored their opponents 275–10. A&M had not been scored on in two years, and their season was marred only by a scoreless tie with LSU. The build-up to the game was like nothing the state had ever seen, and the crowd of 20,000—the largest in state history up to that date—was not disappointed. Bible and his Aggies brought their string of 25 shutouts into Clark Field, only to leave with a 7-3 loss and a broken shutout streak. The Longhorns' winning touchdown was set up by a trick play that saw tackle Tom Dennis make a superb one-handed catch. Francis Domingues scored on the next play. The game is considered to be one of the best early Southwest Conference games ever played, and it helped establish the heated rivalry with A&M.

For want of one more opponent in 1923, Texas missed out on being named Southwest Conference champions. The Longhorns had finished the season 8–0–1 behind the thundering runs and wicked stiff-arms of halfback Oscar Eckhardt and the hurry-up offense of coach Doc Stewart. The big game of the year was against powerful Vanderbilt at the Fairgrounds in Dallas. Oscar Eckhardt was again the star, driving down the sideline and "flattening tacklers like dominoes." The Longhorns handed Vanderbilt a 16–0 loss.

At season's end, Texas swept into College Station, where they beat the Aggies at home for the first time since 1915. But when the conference representatives met in Dallas, SMU was voted the SWC champion. SMU was 5–0 in SWC play and Texas was 2–0–1, one conference game short of being eligible for the title.

Texas was invited to play a postseason game with a strong Florida team in Jacksonville, but Southwest Conference rules and the UT faculty prevented the Longhorns from accepting the challenge. Nevertheless, the invitation itself was indication that Texas football had arrived.

59 Memorial Stadium

When it's empty, Darrell K Royal–Texas Memorial Stadium is just concrete and steel and the glass windows of the luxury boxes that ring most of the stadium. But on game day, the place comes alive, and its heartbeat is the thousands of young children who have watched their heroes from the Knothole Section or run onto the field after a game, in hopes of getting a chin strap or a wristband from their favorite player. It's the effort of the weary men on the field who are spent, but manage to line up beside their teammates for just one more play. It is the boundless energy of the cheerleaders and the band playing "Eyes" and the hopes of the fans.

But the soul of Memorial Stadium is born of the memory of every Texan who has served the United States in times of war. The stadium is dedicated to them.

UT students came to the rescue in 1888 when money was needed to fence Clark Field, and it was the students who raised money and built bleachers in time to host the Aggies in 1907.

The idea for a concrete stadium was born in the fall of 1923 when a group of students met with athletics director Theo Bellmont, who shared the dream. A stadium committee was appointed in January 1924, and under the leadership of William McGill, 500 student workers raised $150,000 in six days. As each $10,000 mark was passed, a cannon was fired. Regent Lutcher Stark and other alums and citizens of Austin kicked in $315,000, and excavation of the site began in April 1924. Just seven months later, Memorial Stadium was officially dedicated, and an overflow crowd of 33,000 watched the Horns defeat the Aggies 7–0 for the first of many times in Memorial Stadium.

Memorial Stadium has undergone many facelifts, but back in 1924 it was heralded as "the largest sports facility of its kind in the Southwest." The UT student body resolved that the stadium was to be a statewide war memorial dedicated to all Texans—not just University students—who had fought in World War I. The north end of the stadium held a plaque bearing names of the 5,280 Texans who were killed in World War I, the "War to End All Wars." Sadly, it became necessary to rededicate Memorial Stadium to honor Texas veterans who have served in subsequent foreign conflicts in which Americans have been involved.

In the southeast corner of Memorial Stadium stands a flag-pole, a gift from the citizens of Fredericksburg, Texas. The good people from this small hill-country town donated the flagpole to honor one of its sons, Louis Jordan, a magnificent lineman on the 1911–1914 teams who was the first Longhorn killed in World War I.

Longhorn Lore: Knight in Burnt-Orange Armor

After being discharged from the Army in October 1945, Sergeant Frank Denius was riding an Army troop train back home to Texas. Denius told Whit Canning, author of *Longhorns for Life*, "When we arrived in Texarkana, I got off at the station, looked around, and found a flagpole. I…saluted the flag, then I got down on my hands and knees and kissed the ground. I was finally back home…in Texas."

Denius was the recipient of two Purple Hearts, four Silver Stars for valor in the face of the enemy, and was one of the 10 most decorated soldiers in the European theatre and the D-Day invasion in World War II. He is one of UT's most generous and most loyal fans and has received the esteemed Presidential Citation for lifetime support of The University of Texas.

Denius is devoted to UT football. In 65 years, he has rarely missed a game and he faithfully attends all the team practices. In fact, the enclosed practice facility, "The Bubble" is named for him. Mack Brown once quipped, "He's made more practices than I have."

It is fitting that the Longhorns' special teams are called the "Special Forces" in honor of Denius' service to and love of his country and his Longhorns. In 2012, France awarded Denius the "Chevalier de la Legion d'Honneur"—Knight of the Legion of Honor for his service in WWII. This award, representing "virtue, bravery, and strong commitment to liberation" is the highest honor any individual can receive from the country of France.

Standing sentinel at the south end of the stadium is a stanchion, a remnant of a scoreboard which was dismantled to make way for Godzillatron, at the time the largest high-definition video board in the country. The scoreboard it once supported was dedicated in 1972 to the memory of Freddie Joe Steinmark, an overachieving, undersized defensive back who competed, lived, and died with extraordinary courage.

Although the scoreboard itself no longer exists, every Longhorn football team is still inspired by Steinmark. Since Mack Brown's arrival in 1998, players exiting the dressing room touch Steinmark's picture as a reminder of the tenacity he showed while playing for The University and of the courage he displayed in fighting for his life.

In 1996, Darrell Royal himself was at the root of controversy involving the stadium. The University of Texas Board of Regents moved to rename the stadium "Darrell K Royal–Texas Memorial Stadium" to honor the man who, for more than 40 years, had brought success, recognition, honor, and integrity to The University of Texas and its athletics programs. Royal was speechless when told of the honor, and even though he insisted the tribute to him should never overshadow the true heroes of the stadium—the honored veterans—The University's gesture angered many who believed that the renaming would tarnish the memory of the veterans.

Royal was the one who, some 30 years earlier, actually saved the stadium. Regent Frank Erwin was on a mission to have the stadium moved off-campus to a site north of there, around 45th Street. Royal bowed his neck, saying that if you moved the stadium, people wouldn't even know there was a University here. The stadium stayed put.

In response to concerns and to ensure that the memory of the veterans would always be the focus of the stadium, the athletics department established a Veterans Committee to maintain the integrity of the stadium's original purpose. Chaired by Frank Denius—loyal Longhorn supporter and one of the 10 most decorated soldiers from the European theatre in World War II—the committee oversaw the decommissioning of Memorial Stadium and the removal of the memorial plaques, which were replaced in the Frank Denius Veterans Memorial Plaza, northwest of the stadium. The stadium was recommissioned as a war memorial in 2008.

The most recent expansion allows Darrell K Royal–Texas Memorial Stadium to seat more than 100,119 spectators and offers

144 luxury suites, all of which have been leased. UT is still "the Joneses," the family all others want to keep up with. The stadium remains a place for excitement, for achievement, for excellence. It will always be alive with the sights and sounds of fall and football and with the memory of the heroes who have thrilled Longhorn fans on so many weekends with victories, broken records, and amazing feats.

But it will still be, first and foremost, about those true heroes, men and women who have served our country and provided Americans with the freedom to enjoy those Saturday afternoons.

60 The Trees of Texas

The news was met with wry amusement by Texas fans from the Frank Erwin era: The University of Texas had been awarded the 2007 "Gold Leaf Award for Landscape Beautification" for its efforts to save 16 live oaks that were in the path of the expansion of the north end zone of Royal–Memorial Stadium. The irony…

Thirty-eight years before, in order to make way for an expansion to the west side of Memorial Stadium, Frank Erwin, then-chairman of the Board of Regents, gave approval to bulldoze a stand of 40 giant oaks and cypress trees lining Waller Creek so that the contractor could get his cranes closer to the construction.

Word leaked out that the trees were scheduled to fall, and on October 2, 1969, more than 300 students, faculty members, hippies, and little old ladies caused a halt to the destruction with their protest. Some shinnied up the trees and clung to the branches. A dozen trees had been cleared by the time the Sierra Club obtained a temporary injunction.

Watch *The Tyler Rose*

If you're under the age of 35, and are weary of hearing the old folks talk about the greatness that was Earl Campbell, search around for a copy of *The Tyler Rose*, narrated by Ron Franklin and produced by Grant Guthrie for TVP Home Video.

Pop it in the old VCR, if you still own one, and prepare to be amazed. The 60 minutes of breathtaking highlights—from Earl's days at Tyler–John Tyler High School through his pro football career and acceptance speech at his Pro Football Hall of Fame induction—will serve as proof. There has been no greater running back in the game of football—at any level—than Earl Christian Campbell.

Erwin was incensed. When the bulldozing resumed, Erwin directed the police and state troopers to use fire-engine ladders to dislodge the protestors. He then arranged for the arrest of 21 of the tree-sitters.

The images of Erwin wielding a bullhorn, of destroyed live oaks, and of policemen manhandling the protestors made newspapers across the country. According to Joe Frantz in *Forty Acre Follies,* when Erwin was asked whether University president Norm Hackerman had authorized his action, "he retorted with his usual lack of tact. 'Hell, I can't wait on The University administration. Some things have to be done right now.'" And that's the way things were done back then.

For this most recent stadium expansion, The University has spent more than $700,000 to transplant the 16 trees. According to the *Alcalde* magazine, Pat Clubb, vice president for employee and campus service, said, "We're saving them at all costs." The oaks, some of which weighed as much as 120,000 pounds, will be planted all around campus. In recognition of those efforts, the Texas Community Forestry Awards Program chose UT to receive the 2007 Gold Leaf Award.

Somewhere, James Clark and Dr. William James Battle are smiling. Clark was UT's building and grounds manager from

1885 to 1908. In his spare time, when he wasn't busy serving as proctor, dean of students, registrar, librarian, secretary of the faculty, business manager, bursar, or regent, he propagated trees, which he planted around the UT campus. Battle, a classics professor who also served as acting University president, was the savior of the Battle Oaks, three native Texas live oaks destined for destruction. The University made plans to demolish the trees, one of which predated the Civil War, in order to build a new Biology building. Battle is said to have sat under the branches with his shotgun, daring anyone to come near the trees. The biology building was eventually located in a different spot.

61 Clyde Littlefield

"Littlefield's arrival as a player ushered Texas into the modern football era," wrote Joe Frantz in *Forty Acre Follies*. "Some football historians see the whole Texas story, at least up to the coming of Bible, as divided into pre-and post-Littlefield eras."

Sportswriter Gene Schoor said of Clyde Littlefield, "In the fall of 1912 Clyde Littlefield entered The University of Texas and proceeded to carve out an athletic record in football, basketball, and track that has never been equaled at Texas."

Littlefield could do it all and do all it better than anyone else. At a University that has seen scores of "best-evers," most agree that Littlefield was probably the greatest all-around athlete in UT history.

A four-year letterman in football, basketball, and track, he earned 12 varsity letters. He also pitched a little for Billy Disch's baseball team, and in his minimal at-bats had a batting average of

Longhorn Lore: One Loss

During the 1923–24 academic year, Texas' football team finished 8–0–1, and their basketball team was undefeated with a 23–0 record. The Longhorns lost only one major sports contest the entire year— the baseball team dropped a 2–1 game to Baylor.

1.000. Named to the Helms' All-American Basketball Team, he led both the basketball and the football team in scoring.

Littlefield led the 1914 Longhorn football team to a perfect 8–0 record, and his strong passing arm was the stuff of legend. At that time, a team could pass the ball forward rather than punt, and since he was able to throw three-quarters of the distance of the field accurately, Texas never punted if Littlefield was in the game. In their incredible 92–0 win over Daniel Baker College in 1915, Littlefield ran for three touchdowns; his four touchdown passes in that game set a record that stood for 62 years until it was tied by Randy McEachern against the Aggies in 1977. The 1915 squad outscored their opponents by the jaw-dropping score of 335–69. Venerable sportswriter Grantland Rice called Littlefield "one of the great forward passers of the day."

In 1915, Littlefield led Texas to its first championships of the newly formed Southwest Conference in basketball and in track. Track was his first love and he tied the world record for the 120-yard high hurdles. He lost *one* race in four years of collegiate competition.

Littlefield joined the Texas coaching staff in 1920 as head track coach and assistant football coach. His even-tempered and gentlemanly demeanor made him popular with his players, and that translated into success on the field. After compiling a record of 44–18–6 in seven years of coaching—during which his teams won Southwest Conference titles in 1928 and 1930—he left football altogether but remained as Texas' head track coach. During his 41 years as track coach, his teams won 25 conference championships.

Littlefield had long envisioned hosting a track and field carnival, and on March 27, 1925, four months after Memorial Stadium was completed, the new track was christened with the running of the first Texas Relays. Littlefield nurtured the Relays, and today they are the premier high school and collegiate track event in the country—the Clyde Littlefield Texas Relays.

Clyde Littlefield is a member of the National Track and Field Hall of Fame, the Texas Sports Hall of Fame, and is a member of the Longhorn Hall of Honor.

62 The 1930s

Coach Clyde Littlefield's 1930 Southwest Conference champs had a spectacular backfield, anchored by quarterback Bull Elkins, a three-sport star who earned eight letters in football, basketball, and track. Elkins, UT football's only Rhodes Scholar, was smart enough to share the backfield with Ernie Koy, All-SWC in football and baseball; Dexter Shelley, All-SWC halfback; and Harrison Stafford, the walk-on from Wharton, Texas, who is considered one of the best blocking backs in Southwest Conference history. Koy had attended Blinn College and planned to transfer to A&M, but as he told Lou Maysel, "I went in one door and out the other one and came on home."

A scoreless tie with Centenary and a 6–0 loss to Rice were the only blots on the record. The Longhorns capped their conference championship with a 26–0 Thanksgiving Day shutout of the Aggies in front of a Memorial Stadium crowd of 40,000 fans.

The 1934 home opener against Notre Dame was hands-down the biggest football game Texas had played to that point.

Great Pep Talk Number 7

Jack Chevigny, coach of the Longhorns from 1934 to 1936, played and coached under the famed Knute Rockne. He borrowed not only Notre Dame's offensive formation, but also brought with him some of Rockne's flair in inspiring teams. The UT Athletics Council tried to convince Chevigny to bow out of the Longhorn game against Notre Dame that October, fearing that it would be a debacle, but Chevigny refused, wanting to go ahead and play against his alma mater.

His pregame talk was masterful and emotional. He spoke of Notre Dame traditions, of Rockne's body lying in a nearby grave, and spoke of his mother and of his father who was gravely ill, but who was pulling for the Horns. The team was so moved that in the rush to hit the field, the first player out of the dressing room tripped and fell over a step outside the locker room door.

On the field, their play was inspired. Texas upset the Irish, 7–6, handing Notre Dame its first opening-game defeat in 38 years. After the game, Chevigny's father, miraculously healed, visited the dressing room to congratulate his son and the team.

Longhorn coach Jack Chevigny had played for Knute Rockne, and despite pleas from the UT Athletics Council to cancel the game, Chevigny was confident. Texas handed the Irish their first opening-game defeat since 1896 after Jack Gray recovered a fumble on the opening kickoff, setting the stage for Bohn Hilliard's eight-yard score. Hilliard's point after touchdown made the difference in the 7–6 stunner, which brought Texas football to national prominence.

In 1939, coach D.X. Bible was in the third year of his five-year Bible Plan, and years one and two had yielded a miserable 3–14–1 record. Texas opened the 1939 season with wins over Florida and Wisconsin, but fell to number three Oklahoma 24–12.

The following week Texas was trailing Arkansas 13–7 with less than a minute left to play. Fans were streaming to the exits when Bible sent a message to the Longhorn Band to play "The Eyes of Texas." The band played, the Horns lined up, and after catching a short pass from fullback R.B. Patrick, Jack Crain scored. Fans poured onto the field after Crain's 67-yard touchdown run, but once the field was cleared, Crain kicked the extra point for the 14–13 win. Bible said, "That play and that victory changed our outlook—mine, the players', the student body's, and the ex-students." It was the turning point in early Texas football.

That play changed things for Crain, too. The Nocona Nugget appeared on the fans' and the opponents' radar screen. He was the only Texas player to make the All-SWC team, and his eight touchdowns and 6.8 rushing average helped the Longhorns to a 5–4 finish on the season.

1939 marked the last time D.X. Bible would lose to the Aggies; in fact, the Longhorns would not lose to A&M again until 1950.

63 The Knothole Section

Today there is a waiting list for UT season tickets, a waiting list to join the various stadium clubs, even a waiting list to lease one of the luxury suites that ring three-fourths of DKR–Texas Memorial Stadium. But in the early days of Texas football, particularly in the days during and following the Great Depression, Longhorn games were rarely sold out.

At each home game The University athletics department dedicated two or three sections—1,000 seats per section—in the north end zone for school-age fans and occasionally high school bands. It was a rare opportunity, an opportunity that has disappeared, for low-income kids to see their local heroes in action. It also seemed prudent to put somebody in those seats, even if the tickets were going for just 50 cents each.

My Board's Better Than Your Board

At the time it was installed, the Godzillatron, UT's new video display board, was the largest high-definition video board in the nation. The Aggies' new board, acquired after UT's, is smaller by 3,500 square feet, but A&M athletics director Bill Byrne explained in a column on aggieathletics.com: "If having the largest screen was all we wanted, we could have done that...our big-screen content will be better than on any screen in the country, guaranteed." Well...okay.

Professional sports teams and a NASCAR track now have relegated Texas' video board to the number 10 spot in the world, but UT's remains the largest college-stadium Jumbotron in the USA.

Gordon Bailey, an educator who pitched for UT and maintained a relationship with The University until he died, and Rodney Kidd, state athletics director and eventual executive director of the University Interscholastic League, were in charge of the "Knothole Section." They ran herd over the ushers, usually Boy Scout volunteers, and the wild crowd of kids.

Al Lundstedt, longtime ticket manager and business manager for UT athletics, remembers attending the 1937 Arkansas game as a member of the "Knothole Gang." Mr. Bible was the coach and Arkansas won the game, which was played at night. At that time, Lundstedt remembered, various Austin men's clubs paid the admission price for the Knothole Gang.

Eventually The University began charging kids 50 cents admission. Officials from the UT athletics department delivered Knothole Club membership cards to the public schools. "Even if a kid's financial circumstances wouldn't permit him to attend the actual game," Lundstedt said, "just having that card proving membership in the Knothole Gang gave [kids] great pride in being associated with their Longhorns."

Some parents used the Knothole Club as an inexpensive three-hour babysitter, and many of the Knotholers paid more attention to what was happening in the stands than they did to the action on the field. UT officials separated the rowdy Knothole Section from the regular full-priced seats by placing a chain-link fence on either side of the section.

Knothole ticket prices increased slowly over the decades. Lundstedt says that UT tried to hold on to the Knothole Section for as long as possible, but it became impossible to justify selling 3,000 to 4,000 seats for a few dollars when fans were begging to buy end zone seats at regular price. Success breeds demand and success brings in money, which builds better facilities, which attracts the recruits, which builds more success.

The business of Longhorn football is bigger than ever, and while no one wants to retreat from this pinnacle, there are generations of adults—some former players—who speak wistfully of falling in love with the orange and white while sitting in the north end zone, as proud members of the Knothole Gang.

64 Cowboys and Spurs

Here's how you tell them apart. The Cowboys wear black hats, white shirts, and jeans with leggings. And cowboy boots, of course. The Spurs wear buff-colored hats, burnt-orange shirts, and light pants. And cowboy boots. Still confused? The Cowboys have the firepower, the Spurs have the muscle.

These two service organizations, the Texas Cowboys and the Silver Spurs, are highly visible components of the pageantry of UT football games.

In 1922 head cheerleader Arno "Shorty" Nowotny, later UT dean of students, and Bill McGill, president of the Longhorn Band, envisioned a men's service organization made up of UT students

A 1930 photo of the Texas Cowboys, a campus leadership and service organization founded in 1922.

that would be a leader on campus, promote school spirit, and be a bridge to the Austin community. Nowotny and McGill chose 40 men from all aspects of campus life to be Cowboys and adopt the motto: "Give the best you have to Texas, and the best will come back to you."

The Cowboys became the guardians of Smokey, a cannon built by UT mechanical engineering students in 1954. Smokey rests in the north end zone at football games, and the Cowboys fire the cannon as the Horns take the field and following each score. After a fan complained that the blast caused her to experience temporary deafness, the cannon was altered to accommodate a double-barrel 10-gauge shotgun.

The original Smokey now rests at the bottom of Town Lake, thanks to those charming Aggies and their juvenile antics. The current cannon, Smokey III, is a replica of a Civil War cannon; it stands 6 feet tall and 10 feet long, and weighs about half a ton.

It is a Cowboy tradition to present a black cowboy hat to the opposing coach in a pregame ceremony commemorating that coach's first appearance at DKR–Texas Memorial Stadium.

Down in the south end zone the Silver Spurs tend to Bevo, the 1,200-pound Longhorn steer who is not as friendly as he

Longhorn Lore: Bevo in Earmuffs

A controversy arose in 1989 after an Austin radio disk jockey expressed concern about Smokey's effect on Bevo after seeing the steer jump whenever the cannon was shot. The UT speech and hearing clinic got involved and tried to solve the problem. An Austin-area hearing aid company offered to donate custom-made earplugs, but that would have required making impressions of Bevo's ear canals. There were no volunteers for that job. Besides, no Silver Spur was willing to do bovine earplug duty before and after each game.

There was also a failed plan to have Bevo wear earmuffs or a noise-reducing headset. Aside from the fact that he's too feisty to wear them, Bevo in earmuffs doesn't quite fit the image UT is trying to project.

No solution was forthcoming, so the Spurs and the Cowboys reverted to their usual routine of having Smokey and Bevo in opposite end zones.

may appear. The Spurs, also an honorary service organization, were created in 1937 for the purpose of caring for the school's mascot. Bevo travels in better style than most of the students do; he is transported to games in his own custom trailer. At games he is restrained by handlers holding very, very long leather straps. Can't be too careful around a half-ton animal swinging a 6-foot horn span.

65 The 1940s (The First Half)

The '40s saw the world turned upside-down, but it was a decade of prosperity for the Longhorn football program. It was the era of the "Impossible Catch," the "Immortal 13," *Life Magazine* covers, the "Blond Bomber", and near-total dominance over the Sooners and the Aggies.

Thanksgiving Day 1940 brought the mighty Aggies to Austin en route to Pasadena, California—or so they thought. The defending national champs had won 19 games in a row and were headed toward a repeat championship and an appearance at the Rose Bowl. All they had to do was get by Texas.

D.X. Bible pulled out all the stops in his pregame talk. He handed out copies of the Edgar Guest poem "It Can Be Done," and the team followed along as Bible read the words aloud:

Somebody said that it couldn't be done,
But he with a chuckle replied
That "maybe it couldn't, but he would be one
Who wouldn't say so till he'd tried...."

The inspired Longhorns scored with only a minute gone from the clock. On the third play of that drive Noble Doss got behind A&M's John Kimbrough, turned downfield, and ran like crazy. The pass was perfect, the catch an amazing over-the-head grab. The picture is familiar to all Longhorns: Doss in his leather helmet, eyes closed, clutching the football. The Impossible Catch.

His momentum carried him out of bounds at the 1-yard line and on the next play, Pete Layden plowed over the goal line. After Jack Crain kicked the extra point, the score was 7–0, Texas, and that's where it remained.

In a game Joe Frantz called "57 seconds of offense against 59 minutes of defense," Doss intercepted three passes. The Texas defense was spectacular against the powerful Aggie offense. Nine of the team members played the full 60 minutes, and at the end of the day, only 13 players had seen the field: the Immortal 13.

The 1941 Longhorns broke the Kyle Field hex, but broke Texas fans' hearts as well. Ranked number one in the nation, and

Longhorn Lore: Ma Griff

From 1936 through 1961, Mrs. J.H. "Ma" Griff rode herd over the boys as Moore-Hill Hall housemother; she was one of the few people who could tame the players. The athletic dining hall was her domain. She insisted on having prayer before every meal and she patrolled the tables, daring anyone to act up. The poor soul who dared to throw food or act rowdy would be apprehended. She'd suddenly appear behind them and, grabbing them by the hair, jerk their head back while lecturing them on proper mealtime etiquette. Tom Stolhandske, All-American defensive end in 1952, remembered her carrying a walking stick; if anyone misbehaved, "she'd strike you with her stick."

featured on the cover of *Life* magazine, the unbeatable Longhorns were tied by Baylor in the last seconds. The following week, with Baylor still on their minds, the Horns fell to TCU 14–7, again in the last seconds of the game.

Texas went 8–2 the next year and won the SWC. In 1942 it became mandatory for the conference champion to play in the Cotton Bowl, so number 11 Texas was scheduled to play number five Georgia Tech on New Year's Day. The usual Eastern-press prejudice kicked in and was summed up by International News Service writer Lawton Carver, who wrote, "Texas doesn't belong in the same league with Georgia Tech." The 32,000 fans who, according to the *Cactus Yearbook,* "defied tire rationing to make the game," were treated to a 14–7 victory over Tech in the Horns' first-ever postseason bowl game.

Although Texas fans for decades would hold up the '41 team as the school's best, it was the '42 team that provided Bible's first SWC championship and The University's first since 1930.

66 Traditions

Hook 'Em

The Aggies had had a hand signal for years. It was invented at a pep rally just before A&M played TCU, when a yell leader asked, "What are we going to do to those horned frogs? Gig 'em!"

University of Texas student Henry Pitts decided it would not do for A&M to be leading Texas in any category, even one as seemingly insignificant as the school's hand sign.

At a pep rally before the 1955 TCU game, head cheerleader Harley Clark introduced the Hook 'Em Horns sign to the student body. Clark's friend Pitts had invented the sign, discovering that one could form the head of a Longhorn by extending the index and little fingers while tucking the middle and ring fingers beneath the thumb. He showed it to Clark, and in spite of being told by some of his friends that the sign was "corny," Clark believed the hand sign would catch on with the Longhorn faithful.

Hook 'Em Horns was an enormous hit at the pep rally, and the next day at the game, Clark watched as more and more fans "got their horns up." Today it is probably the second-most recognizable hand sign in the world.

The Torchlight Parade

The Torchlight Parade had its beginnings in 1916 when, on the night before the Thanksgiving Day game with Texas A&M, the Texas Cowboys spirit organization, carrying torches, led students down a parade route to the site of the pep rally. The parades were held sporadically until 1941, when they became a weekly event.

Today, the Torchlight Parade is held before the team leaves for Dallas and the annual battle with Oklahoma. Starting at Kinsolving

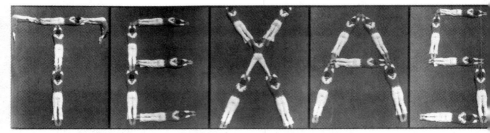

Longhorn cheerleaders use their bodies to spell out "TEXAS" between quarters.

Dormitory, campus leaders bearing torches lead the Longhorn Band and the procession of students south on the Drag (Guadalupe Street), turning on 21st and proceeding up the South Mall to the Main Mall. There, on the steps of the Main Building with the Tower draped in the huge Texas flag, a "Texas-sized" pep rally featuring the Band, the cheerleaders and Pom squad, Smokey the Cannon, and Bevo is held to show support for the team.

Lighting the Tower

When we win, we like to tell the world about it—in a classy way, of course—and we have Carl Eckhardt Jr. to thank for giving Horns the orange tower. Eckhardt was head of the Physical Plant in 1931 and was construction supervisor for the 27-story Main Building Tower. He devised a lighting system for the Tower, integrating

> ### Texas Trivia
> Bill Little, The University's fourth sports information director, holds the all-time record for consecutive games worked by a Division I sports information director. At the 2013 Valero Alamo Bowl in San Antonio, Texas, Little marked the 525th straight game he has worked for UT—every one since the Baylor game on November 7, 1970.
>
> Little suffered a heart attack just before the 1995 Sugar Bowl, threatening to break his streak, but the stubborn and ever-loyal Little convinced doctors that he'd be under more stress staying in the hospital than if he were allowed to attend the game. Streak intact.

orange lighting to announce University achievements. Orange lights first bathed the tower in 1937, and in 1947 Eckhart helped write guidelines for lighting the building.

It used to be fairly easy to figure out why the Tower was orange; a number 1 on all sides highlighted by orange tells us the UT has won a National Championship. The full Tower glowing orange meant we'd beaten the Aggies again, or it was commencement night. When Texas won an athletic contest, the Tower top was lit orange.

Guidelines were revised in 2001, and these days it takes a website to help Longhorns determine why the Tower is lit. Check out www.whyisthetowerorange.com. You'll learn that on December 2, 2013, the Tower was lit in all orange to celebrate Texas' supercomputer team's second consecutive victory in the Student Cluster Competition. It was bathed in all orange in November 2013 in honor of the McCombs Accounting Teams domination in the Beam Abroad Case Competition, and in May 2013, the all-orange Tower honored national championships in three sports clubs: Men's Powerlifting, Texas Rockclimbing, and Texas Quidditch.

67 The 1941 Season

It was the fifth year of coach D.X. Bible's five-year plan and the Longhorns were coming off an 8–2 season that had seen Texas upset the powerhouse Aggies, a four-touchdown favorite, by a score of 7–0. Expectations were sky-high going into the 1941 season.

Hailed by SMU coach Matty Bell as "the greatest team in Southwest Conference history," the 1941 Horns were riding high after handling Colorado, LSU, Oklahoma, and Arkansas with ease. Rice had beaten Texas in six of their last seven meetings, but Jack Crain's 82-yard touchdown return spurred the Horns to a 40–0 shutout of the Owls and sent Texas to the top of the polls, where it was tied with Minnesota.

The next week Texas faced SMU, a team they hadn't beaten in nine years. Heck, they hadn't scored on the Mustangs since 1933. Texas turned the tables by shutting out SMU, solidifying their number one ranking in the AP poll. Texas had outscored their first six opponents by a score of 230–27.

The team's feeling of invincibility was fueled by *Life Magazine's* decision to run an eight-page spread on the Longhorns and to feature the faces of 14 individual Texas players on the cover of the November 17, 1941 issue, which would appear on newsstands after the Baylor game the following week.

The hard-fought SMU victory had taken its toll, however; Pete Layden, Noble Doss, Mal Kutner, and tackle Julian Garrett, along with others, were injured. So the Longhorns, playing with four new starters, faced a fired-up Baylor team and a creative defense installed especially for this game. Texas struggled to a 7–0 lead late in the first half. Doss, a hero in the 1940 A&M game when he made the "Impossible Catch," couldn't produce miracles this year. He dropped a sure touchdown reception, a play which haunted him until the end of his life.

Even so, Texas held onto the lead until, with less than 30 seconds left in the game, Baylor tailback Kit Kittrell lofted a pass over the head of the injured Doss and into the end zone, where Bill Coleman caught it for a touchdown. The game ended in a tie, and the Longhorns were devastated.

The Horns came out flat against TCU the next week and lost 14–7 in the closing seconds of the contest when TCU tailback Emery Nix threw a 19-yard touchdown pass to Van Hall. Doss said, "We were still playing Baylor when TCU was on the field."

Longhorn Lore: The Copycat

In 1940, D.X. Bible and the outmanned Longhorns upset an undefeated A&M team that featured Aggie great John Kimbrough, knocking the Aggies out of the Rose Bowl. To inspire the underdog Longhorns, Bible had read a poem by Edgar Guest entitled "It Can Be Done." No player from that team ever forgot the poem or the effect it had on the Horns that day.

The following year, Texas, undefeated and ranked number one in the nation, intended to dispatch lowly Baylor with ease, then continue on with its winning ways. But Baylor coach Frank Kimbrough, older brother of A&M's John, read to his team the same Edgar Guest poem Bible had used to inspire the Longhorns the year before.

The poem evidently possesses magical powers; Baylor scored in the last seconds of the game to tie Texas, thus marring their perfect season.

Next the Longhorns would travel to College Station, where Texas had not won since 1923. There was talk of a Kyle Field jinx, so some University students visited local psychic and fortune-teller Madame Augusta Hipple for advice on how to break the jinx. Madame Hipple told the students to burn red candles to remove any hex, and that week, dormitory windows all around campus displayed the lit red candles. Texas whipped A&M 23–0 but the Aggies had won the conference.

Texas finished the year by obliterating Oregon 71–7 at Memorial Stadium and ended the season ranked number four in the nation. The team led the country in scoring, averaging 33.8 points per game. It was a year when the eyes of the nation were on the Longhorns and saw the Horns produce their first first-team All-Americans, Chal Daniel and Mal Kutner. Crain set a UT scoring record that held until Earl Campbell came to town. Weldon Hart, writing for the *Austin American Statesman*, said, "When the spry young blades of Texas U, current vintage, are old and gray and come back to the Forty Acres as honored guests, they will still be trying to explain the inexplicable Texas Longhorns of 1941."

Less than 24 hours later, people forgot about football for a while; on December 7, 1941, the Japanese bombed Pearl Harbor.

68 The Little Rose Bowl

Texas, ranked number four in the nation, declined an invitation to play in the Orange Bowl because they had played there the year before. In spite of a loss and a tie, the 1941 team was still considered one of the best in the country.

The Rose Bowl, the "Granddaddy of Them All" even back then, extended an invitation, but the invitation was contingent upon Coach Bible's canceling the last game of the regular season against Oregon. Rose Bowl officials were worried that a Texas loss to Oregon would surely ruin a Texas–Oregon State Rose Bowl matchup.

Noble Doss, an end and defensive back on that 1941 team, told Bill Little in *What It Means to Be a Longhorn:* "Mr. Bible was a man of great character, and he told them he had never canceled a game with an opponent and didn't feel it would be right…he'd guarantee a victory, but he wouldn't cancel the game." Bible also wanted to reward the Longhorn fans by playing one last game at home.

The Rose Bowl rescinded the offer, and Texas trampled Oregon 71–7 in the "Little Rose Bowl Game" in Memorial Stadium, validating Bible's decision and proving that they were still the greatest

---

Get Dirty - Longhorn Lore
The initial *K* in Darrell K Royal's name is just that—an initial, with no period. Royal's dad added the *K* to his name to honor Royal's mother, Katy, who died when he was an infant.

team in the country. The '41 Longhorns finished the season as the highest-scoring team in the nation, totaling 338 points to their opponents' 55.

The "Little Rose Bowl" was played on December 6, 1941. The following day, Japan bombed Pearl Harbor. The Rose Bowl, hosting Oregon State and Duke, was moved from the West Coast to North Carolina.

It would be 63 years before Texas would finally make an appearance at the Rose Bowl.

69 The 1940s (The Second Half)

Rice was the spoiler in 1945. Although Japan had surrendered, bringing about the end of World War II, college football was still in flux at the beginning of the season. Texas had six lettermen returning, but Bobby Layne, UT's quarterback, who had joined the Merchant Marines did not return to the team until six games into the season, just after Texas had missed an extra point against Rice to fall to 1–1 in conference play. Bible commented, "We had a pretty good team by the close of the season."

The Longhorns traveled to College Station, and after diminutive Rooster Andrews, full-time waterboy and part-time place-kicker, faked a conversion kick and passed to his roommate Layne in the flat, the score was 20–10, Longhorns. A highlight of the A&M game came when the Aggies tried the old hidden-ball play. Hub Bechtol told Lou Maysel, "Old [Harlan] Wetz was watching for it and I'll never forget him running over and grabbing that guard who had the ball in the crotch of his legs. He just picked that guard up and shook him loose from the ball like a rag doll...."

Colt McCoy's Stats and Records

Most passing yards, game	470	2009
Most passing yards, season	3,959	2008
Most passing yards, career	13,253	2006–09
Most quarterback victories	45	2006–09
Highest pass efficiency, season	173.8	2008
Highest pass efficiency, career	155.0	2006–09
Most completions, game	41	2008
Most completions, season	332	2008, '09
Most completions, career	1,157	2006–09
Consecutive pass completions	18	2008
Highest completion percentage, game	90.6	2008
Highest completion percentage, season	76.7	2008
Highest completion percentage, career	70.3	2006–09
100-yard rushing/300-yard passing game	175/304	2009
Most touchdown passes, game	6	2006
Most touchdown passes, season	34	2008
Most touchdown passes, career	112	2006–09
Most 400-yard games, career	2	2006–09
(tie: Major Applewhite)		
Most 300-yard games, season	6	2008
Most 300-yard games, career	14	2006–09
Most 200-yard games, season	12	2008
Most 200-yard games, career	38	2006–09
10th in NCAA career passing yards	13,253	
6th in NCAA career total offense	14,824	
2nd in NCAA games won by D-1 quarterback	45	

It was Bible's third and last SWC title, as he had announced his retirement from coaching after the season to focus on his responsibilities as athletics director. Texas beat Missouri in the 1946 Cotton Bowl with a gaudy offensive show. Layne scored 28 points, racking up four touchdowns and four extra points, and passing for two more touchdowns. He finished the game with 11 completions on 12 tries, eight of which were caught by UT's first consensus All-American, Hub Bechtol. When asked for a summary of the game, the Missouri coach simply said, "Too much Layne. Certainly we never ran into one like him before." The 1945 Longhorn squad finished the season 10–1 and ranked number two in the nation, behind Red Blaik's Army team.

The team Bible fielded in 1946, his last team as Texas' head coach, was one of the most talented in University history. Returning lettermen included Layne and Bechtol; ends Dale Schwartzkopf, Peppy Blount, and Max Bumgardner; tackle Harlan Wetz; All-American center Dick Harris; quarterback Jack Halfpenny; halfbacks Byron Gillory, Ralph Ellsworth, Joe Bill Baumgardner, Jimmy Canady, and H.K. Allen…the list goes on and on. The Longhorns had astonished the country with their lopsided victories over Missouri, 42–0; Colorado, 76–0; and Oklahoma A&M, 54–6; but upset losses against Rice and TCU marred their record.

The Horns still led the league in total offense and in passing yardage, and Layne topped the conference charts in scoring, passing, and total yardage.

Texas caught a glimpse of its future when a young Sooner freshman halfback made an impression on Bechtol, who told an Austin writer, "Darrell Royal was by far the best back they had." Bible took notice, too. Eleven years later Bible would hire young Royal to take the reins of the Longhorn football program.

70 Rooster Andrews, All-American Waterboy

The voice on the telephone belied the caller's physical stature. His was a big, gravelly voice, almost shouting, suffused with urgency, as if what he had to say was the most important thing you'd hear all day. "This's Rooster!"

By gosh, he loved The University. He loved football. He loved selling sporting goods. He loved people, and they loved him right back. Darrell Royal always said Rooster had more friends than anybody he knew. He was, according to UT assistant athletics director and former sports information director Bill Little, "the most beloved man ever associated with The University of Texas. Period."

This giant of a man stood 4'11", although Rooster swore that he was 5 feet tall standing on a dime. He and Longhorn All-American Mal Kutner were friends at Dallas' Woodrow Wilson High School. Andrews was headed to A&M in 1941, until Kutner asked Texas coach D.X. Bible if there were any jobs for his friend. Andrews was to leave for College Station on a Wednesday, but on Tuesday evening Kutner called to say that Bible would pay Rooster $16 a month to be assistant manager of the team. Rooster would go on to be the best friend The University ever had.

He enrolled at Texas as "Billy Andrews," but after Jack Crain and Kutner enlisted him for a mission only he could accomplish, he would be known forevermore as "Rooster."

There was to be a cockfight in a small town outside Austin that night, and the football stars' prized rooster, Elmer, was stuck high in

Longhorn Lore: The 1952 Backfield

The entire 1952 offensive backfield—quarterback T Jones and running backs Dick Ochoa, Billy Quinn, and Gib Dawson—made the All–Southwest Conference team, a first in SWC history. That accomplishment has never been duplicated at The University of Texas.

That Longhorn team was the first in UT history to place eight players on the all-conference team. The 9–2 Horns were undefeated in SWC play and went on to beat number eight Tennessee 16–0 in the 1953 Cotton Bowl.

Since that time, Texas has placed eight players on the All-SWC team four times: 1969, 1972, 1979, 1993, and 1995. The Longhorns had nine all-conference players in 1973, 1983, and 1990. The 2005 National Champions had nine players named to the All–Big 12 team.

> ## OU Rough Riders
> In 1905, Texas traveled to Oklahoma City to play the Rough Riders for the sixth time., Oklahoma "won" the game when its fans surged onto the field after a safety put the Rough Riders ahead 2–0.
>
> The fans refused to leave the field, and play was suspended. Somehow, Oklahoma was credited with the win. The *Austin Statesman* recommended that "Texas hereafter refuse to play these small colleges unless it be here or at some place where all arrangements can be made beforehand to eradicate any such foolish performances."

a tree. The other boys were too big to climb up and retrieve Elmer, so they called for Andrews' help. Flashlight in hand, he shimmed up the tree. He located Elmer and grabbed him by the leg, but in the melee of scratching and pecking and clawing, both "Rooster" and the rooster fell from the top of the tree. Crain and Kutner got Elmer; Andrews got a broken arm and a nickname that stuck.

It broke his heart to be turned down by the draft board when many of his teammates were going off to World War II, but he stayed behind and continued as team manager. In 1943, he took on a new role. Rooster proved to be a master at the drop-kick and he lettered in football after kicking two extra points against TCU. Rooster continued to kick extra points over the next two years. On a couple of occasions, he faked the kick and threw to his roommate, famed quarterback Bobby Layne.

No favor—or discount—was too big, especially for the high schools of Texas. Bill Little said it best when he wrote "…when he worked in the sporting goods business, he began to reach countless high schools, their coaches, and their kids. Shoes? See Rooster. Uniforms for the upcoming game that you forgot to order on time? Call Rooster. Budget a little shy? Talk to Rooster. Fact is, he probably gave away more than he made."

During a certain era, Rooster's store on Guadalupe was the only place to be on Saturday morning. It was "information central"; high school and college coaches, the college kids he employed, UT football players, and old Austin buddies congregated in the store and swapped lies and insults and stories for hours.

His love affair with The University spanned almost 70 years. A member of the Longhorn Hall of Honor, Rooster Andrews died at age 84 on January 20, 2008, leaving a 4'11" hole in the heart of the Longhorn family.

71 The 1950s

The Longhorns were the first conference champs of the decade, and only a one-point loss to Oklahoma, on a 23-game winning streak, kept Texas from an undefeated regular season in Blair Cherry's last year as head coach. The 9–2 record of that 1950 team belies how good the team really was.

Behind All-American guard Bud McFadin and All-American defensive end Don Menasco, Texas had stopped the number one SMU Mustangs at Memorial Stadium and held their star running back, Kyle Rote, to minus-three yards on seven carries. The next week, Texas struggled with Baylor until a fourth-quarter punt return by Bobby Dillon went 84 yards for a touchdown to put the Horns ahead 27–20. Texas ended the regular season by spanking the Aggies 17–0, and LSU 21–6. But distracted by the impending loss of their coach—Cherry had made his resignation public the week of the Baylor game—the Longhorns lost to Tennessee in the 1951 Cotton Bowl.

Coach Ed Price's Longhorns won the Southwest Conference in 1952 and finished the year 9–2, their only losses coming to number three Notre Dame and number four Oklahoma. Texas took revenge on Tennessee in the Cotton Bowl, leaning on the

Littlefield's Shutouts

Beginning with the 1928 Texas–Baylor game, Clyde Littlefield's defenses shut out opponents in 14 of their next 16 games.

fierce defense of Harley Sewell and Carlton Massey to beat the Vols 16–0 in the first nationally televised Cotton Bowl.

The Longhorns tied for the SWC championship the following year, but in 1954 and '55, UT's fortunes and their record plummeted. Texas officials decided the 1–9 season of 1956 was as far down as they were willing to go, and Ed Price was fired.

With the hiring of Darrell Royal, the 1957 Longhorns started the march back to the top. Their 6–4–1 record got Texas to the Sugar Bowl, where they met a superior Mississippi team.

The next year's 7–3 was another step in the right direction and featured one of the biggest wins in DKR's career: a 15–14 victory over his alma mater, Oklahoma. Number 16 Texas was a 13-point underdog and had not beaten OU in seven years, but this effort would start the pendulum swinging the other way. Down 14–8 late in the fourth quarter, substitute quarterback Vince Matthews drove the Horns down to the OU 7-yard line, but Royal, playing one of his famed gut feelings, put Bobby Lackey back in the game on third down. Lackey threw a touchdown pass, kicked the extra point, then intercepted an Oklahoma pass to seal the win.

Texas ended the decade as it had started it, by winning a share of the Southwest Conference title. Except for the unsavory loss to number one Syracuse in the Cotton Bowl, the only blemish on the year was a loss to the dreaded TCU Horned Frogs.

72 The "T" Ring

Wearing the burnt orange and white; competing with and against the best athletes in the country; receiving the watches, rings, and bling from bowl games; winning championships...all of these are a source of pride to the young men who play football at The University of Texas. But the experience that a Longhorn cherishes above all others, which represents his membership in an elite fraternity, is the honor of receiving and wearing the coveted "T" ring.

Coach Darrell Royal grew up in a time where a man's integrity and his good name were all he had. In the days following the Depression, a college education was not a given, and Royal never forgot that he was able to realize his dream of being a football coach only because he had received a college degree. He took advantage of the opportunity available to him because of his athletic ability and as a coach he urged his players to do the same.

Although it is a cliché today for a coach to say he emphasizes academics and college degrees over football, Royal was one of the first in the county to put his money where his mouth was.

The "T" ring was started as a personal gift from Royal to his lettermen who graduated; Royal paid for the rings out of his pocket. Each was inscribed on the inside with the player's name and Royal's. The gold ring has a raised orange stone capped with a white *T*. When asked why he paid for the rings himself, Royal commented, "The players need to know it's important to me. I want

A Badge of Honor

"Having played at The University is like a badge of honor. I don't carry a card that says I played at Texas. I just wear that 'T' ring that Coach Royal gave us, and that is identification enough." —Bobby Gurwitz

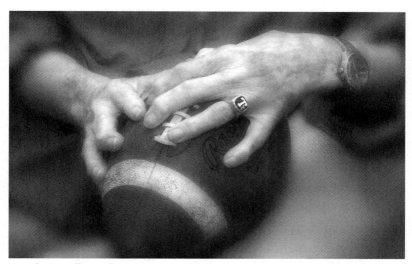

Coach Darrell Royal's "T" Ring. Earning a "T" ring at The University of Texas is a cherished honor for all Longhorn athletes. (Photo by Rick Henson)

those boys to graduate, even if the only reason they do is to make the ole SOB pay for the ring."

Keith Moreland was a football letterman before he went on to become one of UT's baseball greats and then play in the major leagues. He held up his ring as he said, "You can't imagine what it meant to me to get my "T" ring after playing [baseball] 17 years professionally. The first thing I did after I received my sheepskin was to go straight to the athletics department and say, 'I want my "T" ring now.'...I've got a National Championship ring for baseball and a World Series ring, and that 'T' ring is just as important to me as those other two."

Dallas Griffin was the first Longhorn to win the coveted Campbell/Draddy Award, also known as the Academic Heisman. He said, "I'll always remember certain games during my career at Texas, but this ring will remind me of not only those games, but of my time in the classroom, the relationships I've made, and all the hard work that was put in on and off the field. I couldn't be prouder to have it."

Every coach since Royal has continued the tradition, sometimes tweaking the design a bit to reflect his own taste. Some years ago The University established a fund to pay for the rings, but the meaning of the ring remains the same. One must letter, and one must graduate. It is not a treat to be given to supporters or donors or friends of the current coach, like some Cracker Jack prize. One must letter, and one must graduate.

Royal's strategy worked. One player said, "It's a prized part of your UT experience: you come to Texas and you expect to win. You work hard, you play for championships, you finish the course, and you wear the 'T' ring. It's just what you do."

Today, Royal's legacy of insistence upon excellence in the classroom as well as on the field has spread to every sport on campus. Men, women, major sports or minor—if the athlete letters and graduates, he or she will forever carry part of coach Darrell Royal with them.

73 The Longhorn Hall of Honor Banquet

It's the Academy Awards of Longhorn athletics, and the lobby of the Four Seasons Hotel in Austin serves as the red carpet.

Each year, on the evening before the final home football game, The University of Texas inducts athletes into the Longhorn Hall of Honor. Officially called "The Award of Merit and Distinction," the Hall of Honor is the highest honor UT athletics awards.

The Hall of Honor was begun in 1957 with its distinguished inaugural class of Theo Bellmont, first athletics director at UT; William (Uncle Billy) Disch, famed UT baseball coach; Louis Jordan, great lineman and first Texas officer to die in France in

Longhorn Lore: The Varmint Brothers

There was a Varmint brother on the Texas football team for eight years. Don, Charlie, and Diron Talbert, the self-proclaimed "Varmint Brothers", have been politely described as "notorious," "infamous," and "rowdy," but in the late 1950s and the '60s, the Talberts earned a reputation for giving opponents hell on the field and for raising hell off the field.

Coach Bill Ellington was the assistant athletics director under Darrell Royal, and if a player got in trouble with the police, it was Ellington they called. He'd be stern, but would do his best to spare them the wrath of Royal.

One day Ellington was having a face-to-face with a player who kept getting in all kinds of trouble. He told the young man, "Son, if you're here to set a record for troublemaking, you might as well give up that quest right now. Because I'll tell you, you could start today and try your hardest to cause as much trouble as you possibly can, but you would *still* never catch up with the Talberts."

Hill's Café on South Congress used to have an all-you-can-eat buffet, and steak was served on the Sunday buffet. During Don's time at Texas, he and his friends ate so much steak and caused such a ruckus that the proprietor posted a sign on the front door, an early version of the "No shirt, no shoes..." signs seen today.

The sign read, "No Dogs. No Cats. No Talberts."

All three Talberts—Don, Charlie, and Diron—are proud members of the Longhorn Hall of Honor.

World War I; and Dr. Daniel Penick, longtime UT tennis coach. The governing body of the Hall of Honor Council—the guys who do the selecting—is made up exclusively of men who have earned a varsity sports letter at The University. In the ensuing 57 years through 2013, 196 of the 355 inductees have either played or coached football.

The Hall of Honor is not a Hall of Fame: selection to the Hall of Honor isn't based solely on achievements on the field. One can be a four-time All-World, but if he's a ne'er-do-well in his life after UT, forget it. The Hall of Honor Constitution says that "...

the recipient shall possess or shall have possessed in addition to outstanding ability in a sport or sports, other qualifications such as sportsmanship, character, and integrity, and be one who has brought great distinction to The University of Texas."

Several honorees have seen family members join them in the Hall of Honor, but only two families have had three members inducted, and they are both football families: the Koys, with Ernie Sr., Ernie Jr., and Ted; and the notorious Talbert brothers—Charlie was inducted in 2007 to join brothers Don and Diron.

The annual banquet is open to the public, and if rubbing shoulders with legendary Longhorns such as Jerry Sisemore, Tommy Nobis, Earl Campbell, Ricky Williams, and Chris Gilbert is your kind of a thrill, it's worth the price of admission.

74 Vincent R. DiNino

He probably gets tired of being referred to as the "Darrell Royal of the Longhorn Band"; after all, Mr. D. was at Texas a few years before Royal arrived. The comparison does explain a lot, however—particularly when discussing the band with fans who think halftimes are for running up to the Centennial Club to throw down a beer and use the cleaner facilities.

Vincent R. DiNino, director of the Longhorn Band from 1955 to 1975, is one of 39 individuals who have been named honorary "T" men, or football lettermen. There, among the names of major benefactors, successful coaches, and loyal staff members, is the name of a band director. In addition, Mr. D received the highest honor The University athletics department has to award when he was selected to the Longhorn Hall of Honor in 1994 "in recognition of those qualities that brought credit and renown to The University of Texas." A band director? What gives?

He and Royal were alike in so many ways; they were both strict disciplinarians with impossibly high standards and expectations of excellence, not just in their respective areas of education, but in every facet of the student's life. DiNino was a tough and demanding teacher, intent on building excellence in his band and in each of his students. He revolutionized recruiting, reaching out to the high schools of Texas to sell his program and to search for good musicians who were good students. His remarkable memory for names and faces and his perseverance paid off; he inherited a band with

Two Texas icons, Darrell Royal and Vincent R. DiNino, celebrated Longhorn Alumni Band Day in 2005. (Wm. Paul Waits, Houston)

40 members and grew it into a team of 400 before he decided that that size was unmanageable and pared it down to 300.

As Royal did with the football program, DiNino embraced Texas traditions while adding many of his own. Women were first admitted to the marching band during his tenure. He added jazz tunes and show tunes to halftime shows, and introduced tunes that are now considered standards at athletic games, such as "March Grandioso," "March of the Longhorns," and "The Wabash Cannonball." What would halftime be without Big Bertha, the annual performance of the Alumni Band, or the Big Flags Brigade? These were all brought to realization during the DiNino years.

Mr. D. was, like DKR, larger than life and somewhat intimidating. He brought the program to national prominence through his remarkable organization and eye for detail. Scott Harmon, former drum major, wrote: "Mr. D. always favored boldness of action. This was Texas! He encouraged us to be proud and aggressive, to take charge, and then to deliver."

DiNino earned a reputation for being a natty dresser. Talk about boldness of action...the man wore a burnt-orange leather suit to direct the band at one of the many New Year's Day Cotton Bowls.

Great Pep Talk Number Eight

Coach Darrell Royal was famous for folksy quotes, but his players remember that he wasn't big on rah-rah speeches. He had respect for his players' intelligence and didn't try to manipulate their emotions.

In College Station for the 1965 match against the Aggies, Texas was behind 17–0 at halftime. Marvin Kristynik later remembered the "halftime speech" Royal gave: "Coach said he could put all kinds of diagrams on the board, but they wouldn't help us a bit. It was just a matter of whether we wanted to win. Then, just before he went out on the field, he wrote on the blackboard '21–17' and said to us, 'This is what you can do.' And we did." Texas went out and scored three touchdowns to beat A&M by the predicted score of 21–17.

He was an advocate for his pupils and a promoter of the band, insisting that the band's facilities, uniforms, and funding be in line with a University of the first class. He oversaw the improvement of facilities when the band, which had moved around the campus like migrant workers following the crops, finally got its own residence on East 24th Street.

TRIVIA Question

The University of Texas dominated the Southwest Conference in football. How many championships did the Longhorns win?

Trivia answers on page 255.

He ran his band program like Royal ran his football program... or was it the other way around? No matter. They both were gifted at surrounding themselves with the best people possible, then trusting them to do their jobs. No micromanaging, just accountability. The DiNino/Royal era was a golden one in which both programs made the leap to national prominence and excellence.

DiNino was not just a band guy; he was a UT guy, an enthusiastic supporter and friend of the Longhorn football program and of Royal. In tribute to Royal's three national championships, in 1970 DiNino introduced "The Wabash Cannonball," a Royal favorite. Almost 40 years later, it is still a crowd favorite and is played between the third and fourth quarter of every football game.

"Once after a loss on the road when the Texas crowd was sparse, Coach Royal made a commitment that he would never again travel without the Longhorn Band and his friend, the director Vince DiNino," Bill Little said at Coach Royal's memorial service. And so it was. On November 13, 2012, Dr. Vincent R. DiNino, at the spunky age of 93, hopped up the director's ladder while the Longhorn Band and Texas cheerleaders sent Royal off in style with "The Eyes of Texas." Many guests who had been able to hold it together during the moving service finally fell apart as Mr. D paid tribute to his counterpart—his friend—on the occasion of DKR's last road trip.

Vincent DiNino holds the title of Professor Emeritus at The University and lives in Bay City, Texas, close enough to come back each year to direct the Longhorn Alumni Band.

Dr. DiNino is in the Longhorn Hall of Honor.

75 National Awards

Longhorns have been earning national awards and honors since Dana X. Bible won the Amos Alonzo Stagg Award in 1954. Here is just a sampling of some of those many honors:

Heisman Trophy (Est. 1935)
Earl Campbell, 1977
Ricky Wililams, 1998

AT&T/ABC Sports Player Of The Year Award (Est. 2004)
Cedric Benson, 2004
Vince Young, 2005
Colt McCoy, 2009

Butkus Award (Est. 1985)
Derrick Johnson, 2004

Walter Camp Award (Est. 1967)
Ricky Williams, 1998
Colt McCoy, 2008
Colt McCoy, 2009

Lombardi Award (Est. 1970)
Kenneth Sims, 1981
Tony DeGrate, 1984
Brian Orakpo, 2008

Hendricks Award (Est. 2002)
Brian Orakpo, 2008
Jackson Jeffcoat, 2013

Manning Award (Est. 2004)
Vince Young, 2005
Colt McCoy, 2009

Maxwell Award (Est. 1937)
Tommy Nobis, 1965
Ricky Williams, 1998
Vince Young, 2005
Colt McCoy, 2009

Davey O'Brien Award (Est. 1977)
Earl Campbell, 1977
Vince Young, 2005
Colt McCoy, 2009

Outland Trophy (Est. 1946)
Scott Appleton, 1963
Tommy Nobis, 1965
Brad Shearer, 1977

Unitas Golden Arm Award (Est. 1987)
Colt McCoy, 2009

Doak Walker Award (Est. 1990)
Ricky Williams, 1997
Ricky Williams, 1998
Cedric Benson, 2004

Jim Thorpe Award (Est. 1986)
Michael Huff, 2005
Aaron Ross, 2006

76 Four Outta Four

Four National Championships in four years. It coulda happened; it shoulda happened. But, as Darrell Royal was fond of saying, "It all depends on how that oblong ball bounces."

From 1961 through 1964, Royal's Longhorns posted an incredible 41–3–1 record. A total of nine points kept the Longhorns from winning four National Championships in a row.

Behind the new flip-flop offense and All-American halfback James Saxton, whom Royal called their "Roman candle," the 1961 Horns blew out every team they faced except for lowly TCU, which won only three games that season. Texas won the conference and beat Mississippi State in the Cotton Bowl, but the 6–0 loss to the Horned Frogs knocked Texas off the number one pedestal. UT finished the year at number three in the nation.

In 1962, after losing most of their offensive backfield, the defense kept Texas in many of their games. Ranked number one in the nation, a 14–14 tie with Rice cost the Horns a National Championship. They won the SWC and ended the regular season undefeated and ranked at number four.

Determined not to slip up again, tri-captains David McWilliams, Tommy Ford, and Scott Appleton harangued, cajoled, reminded, and finally willed the 1963 team to take advantage of the foundation the '61 and '62 teams had laid. Over the summer the three wrote weekly letters to their teammates, using the pain of their near-misses as a rallying cry. The yardage was hard to come by, but when the season was over, Texas had been crowned the National Champion by UPI and the AP, and the National Football Foundation awarded Texas the MacArthur Bowl.

Professor Royal

After the 1963 season, Oklahoma approached Darrell Royal about returning home, this time as OU's head coach. UT alums went crazy, offering to set up slush funds to keep him, but Royal, making $24,000 at the time, was opposed to receiving a salary "out of line" with that of a top full professor.

Royal was given the job of athletics director at The University of Texas, and instead of a raise, UT chancellor Harry Ransom granted him tenure as a full professor. Many nonfootball types and faculty members were offended and made their opposition known. Even the *Daily Texan* joined the fray, siding with the protestors.

Mickey Herskowitz, sportswriter with the *Houston Post*, came up with a clever solution. He proposed that in the interest of fairness, any department head who won a National Championship should be awarded the title of "Honorary Head Coach."

The 1964 season started as the previous three had, with Texas dominating their first several opponents and beating OU again, marking the seventh win in what would become Royal's eight-year streak over his alma mater. Tommy Nobis, the only sophomore starter on the '63 championship team, was starting both ways, but defense was still his game. Nobis had 28 tackles against Army, and he followed that up by putting 25 on Oklahoma.

This time, it was Arkansas that broke the Horns' hearts. In a back-and-forth game, Texas scored with 1:27 left. Unwilling to settle for a tie, the Horns attempted a two-point conversion, but the pass was incomplete. Texas lost 14–13 and in the process, lost the conference and the National Championship.

"I dream of those games that got away," Royal told Evan Smith on "Texas Monthly Talks" in March 2009. When Smith asked the coach which game he'd like to play over, Royal put his bent index finger up to his lip, looked away, and teared up just a bit. That '64 Arkansas game, he said, "bugs me to this day."

77 The Wishbone

Darrell Royal faced a problem in the spring of 1968. The problem was the embarrassment of riches in the Longhorn backfield.

Those were the carefree days before scholarship limits, the days when it was widely acknowledged that UT's third-stringers could whip any other school's starters.

So Royal's dilemma was this: he had three talented running backs—Steve Worster, Chris Gilbert, and Ted Koy—with only two places to put them. That meant that one of the best players in the country would be sitting on the bench.

So in the spring of 1968, Royal put offensive coordinator Emory Bellard to work coming up with an offense that could utilize all three players. What Bellard devised was a variation of the veer, a triple-option offense, but he added a fullback lined up behind the quarterback. Simply put, the quarterback read the tackles, then either distributed or kept the ball based on what he saw from the defense. Instead of the defense reacting to the offensive play, the play developed according to what the defense committed to.

Over the summer, Bellard grabbed athletics department staff or his son's friends to work out the kinks of the offense in old Gregory Gym, with Bellard playing the role of quarterback. When the team showed up in August for fall practice, he met his quarterbacks—Bill Bradley, James Street, and Eddie Phillips—for breakfast at the Varsity cafeteria. And there, using salt shakers, catsup bottles, the sugar bowl, and water glasses, he laid out a formation using two halfbacks and a fullback who was just a yard behind the quarterback. Phillips said, "All we really had were two plays one way or the other."

Texas came out with three running backs in the read offense, and for a good long while—30 games, in fact—defenses had no

Don't Be Hatin'

Before the Longhorns' game versus Georgia Tech in the 1942 Cotton Bowl, East Coast writers claimed, "Texas doesn't even belong on the same field with the Engineers." That presumably was written before Texas won the game 14–7.

In the 1960 Cotton Bowl versus number one Syracuse, those same writers believed that no team could keep up with strong Syracuse. As one writer said, "Texas and the world has never faced an opponent like this in all football history." Besides, the writer said, Texas players had skinny legs. The Longhorns lost that game 23–14, but in the second half Texas made 198 yards against a team that had held its opponents to an average of 19.3 yards rushing.

When number one Texas was to face number two Navy in the 1964 Cotton Bowl game, Eastern writers howled with laughter. Myron Cope from Pittsburgh made fun of quarterback Duke Carlisle, said Texas linemen looked like girls, and then declared, "Texas is the biggest fraud ever perpetrated on the football public."

Texas 28, Navy 6.

clue what to do. Actually, in the debut of the wishbone, Texas tied Houston and then lost to Texas Tech. But after Royal replaced Bradley with Street in the Tech game, the wishbone powered up.

When sportswriters asked Royal what he called this new offense, he didn't have an answer. Mickey Herskowitz, writer for the *Houston Post,* commented that it "looked like a pulley-bone." And so the wishbone was officially born.

That offense changed college football, and it changed Texas football fortunes. The Longhorns stunned opponents, who couldn't defense the 'bone. Its popularity spread and in a 16-year span, eight wishbone teams won National Championships. Fourteen won national rushing championships. And one by one, other teams fell into line, wanting to jump on the wishbone bandwagon.

That 1968 team lost one and tied one, but starting with the third game of the season, the Longhorns were on a roll rarely seen in college football.

78 World's Tallest Fat Man

Jones Ramsey was, by his own admission, the luckiest man on earth. The self-styled "World's Tallest Fat Man" loved to say that he had worked for two of the greatest college football coaches who ever lived. And although he was the sports information director, the man behind the scenes who did the writing, publicizing, and promoting for Paul "Bear" Bryant and for Darrell Royal, he was every bit as colorful as the two men for whom he worked.

Ramsey learned from Bryant for nine years, and when "Bear" left A&M to return to his beloved Alabama, he urged Royal to hire Ramsey as UT's sports information director. What a winning combination. By the time Ramsey was hired at Texas in 1961, Royal had become more thick-skinned in dealing with the sportswriters and was entertaining them with his "Royalisms."

Jones was more animated—a walking, talking, breathing encyclopedia of trivia and of jokes, which he repeated over and over. But no matter how often they heard the same joke, his audiences still laughed. They couldn't help it. They weren't laughing at the joke anymore, they were laughing at Jones, who was laughing at himself, filling the space with his big personality and with the joy he got from playing host.

He was larger than life, both in stature and in personality; he became, like the coaches he represented, a legend. He was great friends with the sportswriters, greeting them with a "how ya' hittin 'em?" He was at his finest when there was a big game at UT. The writers would come in on Thursday—legends such as Dan Jenkins, Blackie Sherrod, Mickey Herskowitz, and Denne Freeman—and Ramsey's ritual was to take them all to his favorite Tex-Mex

Longhorn Lore: People Run Over

A&M's John David Crow won the Heisman Trophy in 1957, but ranked just fourth in the SWC rushing stats. Sportswriter Mickey Herskowitz pointed this out to Bear Bryant one day, and the coach countered, "That may be true, but if you count the folks he's run over you'll find he leads the nation in that category—People Run Over."

Twenty years later, when Earl Campbell was running toward the Heisman, sports information director Jones Ramsey and assistant SID Bill Little ran a weekly statistical category called "Yards Made by Campbell After First Hit by a Tackler."

This was Ramsey's innovative nod to "People Run Over," in memory of Bryant and Crow 20 years before. Today YAC (yards after contact) is a commonly recorded stat, but The University of Texas was reportedly the first school to track it.

restaurant, Matt's El Rancho. Jones used to say, "If I don't get Matt's food several times a week, I break out in a rash."

Suite 2001 at the nearby Villa Capri hotel served as the postgame party room and press conference. After every home game, Ramsey, Royal, assistant sports information director Bill Little, and the writers gathered at 2001, where the Scotch flowed freely and the outrageous "off-the-record" barbs really were kept off the record.

Ramsey claimed to be the only sports information director in America to have worked with two Heisman Trophy winners at two different schools, A&M's John David Crow and Texas' Earl Campbell.

Jones built a reputation for being professional, punctual, and vocally intolerant of silliness or incompetence. He was well-respected for his professionalism and served as president of the College Sports Information Directors of America. In 1982 he was awarded the Arch Ward Award for service to his profession. He is a member of the CoSIDA Hall of Fame.

Jones Ramsey retired in 1982 and returned to his home in Ponca City, Oklahoma, believing that's where he wanted to live out his last years. But the lure of Austin, UT football, his children, and the beef burritos at Matt's El Rancho drew him back to Austin.

Ramsey, UT's third sports information director and a member of the Longhorn Hall of Honor, died in 2004 from complications of diabetes.

What a hoss.

79 Take a Number

The Texas Longhorns have had 107 players selected as All-Americans, and that does not count players who were selected more than once. Ever wondered which jerseys were worn by the most All-Americans?

No jersey has been so revered—or so feared—as the burnt-orange No. 60. Worn by four consensus All-Americans, it was made famous by Tommy Nobis, who is considered by most historians to be the best defensive player in the 115 years of Longhorn football.

The legend of No. 60 started with Johnny Treadwell, a tough linebacker so intense that his teammates tried to avoid him from Thursday until Sunday because "he was liable to forearm you." Treadwell and his teammate Pat Culpepper were responsible for the immortal goal-line stand against Arkansas in 1962. Treadwell was a unanimous All-American selection in 1962.

Next in line was Tommy Nobis.

No. 60 came to represent the best tooth-jarring defenses UT fielded, as well as its tradition of fielding killer linebackers. The jersey was handed out sparingly, sometimes used as a reward,

Texas Trivia
During the tenure of the NCAA's television broadcasting package, from the mid-1960s through 1983, Texas was the most televised team in college football.

occasionally as incentive to a player perceived as having great potential. There was a lot of history and a lot of pressure associated with wearing No. 60.

Although some stalwart players wore the number in the interim, almost 20 years passed before Jeff Leiding won consensus All-American honors in 1983, wearing the famed No. 60. Britt Hager continued the tradition when he was named All-American in 1990. Now, no other Texas linebacker will have the honor of wearing the jersey, as it was retired in 2008.

Although not as famous, there are other Texas jersey numbers that carry as much history. Here they are, along with the All-Americans who wore them.

No. 10: Retired
Marty Akins, QB: 1975
D.D. Lewis, LB: 2001
James Saxton, RB: 1961
Vince Young, QB: 2005

Peter Gardere, the Sooner Slayer, was not an All-American, but he is the only quarterback in UT history to defeat OU all four years he played. Gardere also wore No. 10.

No. 66:
Chal Daniel, G: 1941
Harley Sewell, G: 1952
Herb Gray, T: 1955
Doug Dawson, G: 1980

Tommy Nobis, a three-year starter, played both ways in 1964 and was named to the offensive and defensive All–Southwest Conference teams.

Johnny Treadwell, No. 60, and Pat Culpepper, No. 31, in one of the most famous goal-line stands in UT history.

Jeff Leiding, the fourth All-American linebacker to wear No. 60, anchored the fearsome 1983 defense.

202

No. 79:

Dick Harris, T: 1947

Terry Tausch, OT: 1981

Ben Adams, OG: 1998

Tony Hills, OT: 2007

No. 77:

Stan Mauldin, T: 1940–42 (second team)

Bill Atessis, DE: 1970

Brad Shearer, DT: 1977 (Outland Trophy Winner)

Kenneth Sims, DT: 1980–81 (Lombardi Trophy Winner)

The winner, however, is jersey **No. 81**. Seven All-Americans have donned No. 81:

Joe Parker, E: 1943

Hub Bechtol, E: 1944–46

Carlton Massey, DE: 1953

Maurice Doke, G: 1959

Shane Dronett, DE: 1991

Pat Fitzgerald, TE: 1995–96

Sam Acho, DE: 2007–10

80 The 1970s

Texas remained strong in the early 1970s. The Horns had won three National Championships in eight years and fans began to believe that was a reasonable expectation. But losses to top 10–ranked Oklahoma between 1971 and 1973, and a fluke loss in the '73 season opener at Miami, kept Texas out of the National Championship picture.

Longhorn Lore

According to Jones Ramsey, former sports information director for both Bear Bryant at A&M and Darrell Royal at The University, the legendary coaches were good friends. In comparing the two coaches, Ramsey used to say, "Darrell was a sweet Bear Bryant." Bryant was the only Southwest Conference coach to contact DKR after he landed the Texas job. Edith Royal still has the Western Union telegram: "Hearty Congratulations. Welcome Aboard. Paul Bryant"

Bryant turned to Royal for help on more than one occasion. When Bryant was at A&M and Royal was coaching at Mississippi State, The Bear solicited Royal's help in teaching the Aggies how to run the split-T offense. Bryant and his assistant, former OU great Jim Owens, traveled to Mississippi State, where Royal showed the coaches a better way to teach the center-to-quarterback exchange.

Years later Bryant credited Royal with saving his coaching career when, after back-to-back seasons of 6–5 and 6–5–1, he secretly visited Royal in the summer of 1971 to learn the wishbone offense from the master. They talked after every game that season to compare how opponents were defending against the wishbone.

Bryant was a good pupil. Alabama finished 11–1 that year and finished the 1972 season in the number two position, only to lose to Texas in the 1973 Cotton Bowl Classic. The Tide was undefeated in the 1973 regular season, their only loss coming in a 24–23 heartbreaker with Notre Dame. Using the wishbone, Alabama claimed shares of the National Championship in 1973, '75, '77, '78, and '79.

Incredibly, the Longhorns lost only one conference game during those three years, and that was to Arkansas in hostile territory. Those teams were on the tail end of six consecutive conference titles and six consecutive Cotton Bowl appearances.

The 1972 loss to Oklahoma was the beginning of suspicions that OU had spied on Texas' practices. The game was a defensive battle until late in the third quarter when OU, up 3–0, had the Horns backed up to their own 25. As Alan Lowry prepared to quick kick, the Sooner defense started shouting "Quick kick! Quick kick!" The kick was blocked into the end zone and recovered for an OU touchdown. Lucious Selmon, who'd recovered the kick, later said that the Sooners had worked all week preparing for the quick kick. He even told reporters that they knew it was coming when Greg Dahlberg went in at center. Darrell Royal had not run the quick kick in four years. The final score was 27–0, snapping a 100-game scoring streak for Texas.

Texas would not lose again that season; they would not even come close until they faced number four Alabama in the Cotton Bowl. Bear Bryant brought offensive tackle John Hannah and star halfback Wilbur Jackson to Dallas. The Tide threatened to run away with the game in the first quarter, but an outstanding defensive effort led by Defensive Player of the Game Randy Braband held Alabama to a 13–3 halftime lead.

Offensive tackles Jerry Sisemore and Travis Roach led the way for quarterback Alan Lowry and running back Roosevelt Leaks. They would not be stopped in the second half. Lowry scored on a three-yard run and Terry Melancon, who had two key interceptions in the game, stole a touchdown pass out of the hands of the Alabama receiver.

Lowry was sick with tonsillitis and fever before the game, but that didn't cloud his thinking or slow him down. He suggested to Royal that they run a bootleg, and after faking handoffs to Leaks and to halfback Tommy Landry, Lowry scooted wide around the left end and hugged the sideline all the way to the end zone. Photos in the next day's papers suggested that Lowry might have hugged a little too tightly. His foot appeared to touch the sideline as he cut back to avoid a tackler, but the refs hadn't noticed.

"I couldn't be prouder of the boys," Royal told Lou Maysel. The team that Royal had said before the season was "average as every day's wash" finished the year 10–1 and number four in the nation.

81 Jerry Sisemore

Coach Bill Ellington called it the most courageous performance he'd ever witnessed.

Texas was battling Baylor in Waco, trying to secure its fifth Southwest Conference championship in a row in 1972. Baylor's defense had shut down the Longhorns' running game and the score was tied 3–3. UT's colossus of an offensive lineman, Jerry Sisemore, had been sidelined with an ankle sprain early in the second quarter, and the senior was watching helplessly as the Horns went nowhere. Finally, he had had enough.

Bill Little, writing for texassports.com, described what happened next. "Sisemore went to trainer Frank Medina, pointed to his ankle, and said, 'Tape it.' One roll of tape and Sisemore tried to run. 'More tape,' he said. Finally, after several sessions of wrapping, he went to the coaches and said, 'I think I can go.'"

Sisemore limped onto the field in the fourth quarter and led the inspired Longhorns on a 70-yard, five-minute drive that culminated in a touchdown, giving Texas a 10–3 lead. The Longhorn defense held, and after Texas got the ball back on their 15, Sisemore took Roosevelt Leaks and the Longhorns down the field for another touchdown, sealing the victory.

For the first three quarters, Texas had managed only four first downs and 128 yards of offense. During the fourth quarter, with team captain Sisemore clearing the way, Leaks ran the ball 22 times for 110 yards. The Horns didn't throw a single pass in the quarter.

At a school that has a tradition of producing great offensive linemen, Sisemore is acknowledged as the gold standard. His 6'4", 250-pound frame belied his quickness and agility. Jones Ramsey remembered that in the 1972 Texas-SMU game, a spotter in the

Texas Trivia

We've all seen the bumper sticker that says, "If God isn't a Longhorn, why is the sunset burnt orange?" Seriously, if God's not a Longhorn, how come 2 million acres of worthless land suddenly spurted out billions of barrels of oil, making Texas the richest public university in all the land?

press box claimed that Sisemore took out five men on one play. The press doubted it, as did Darrell Royal when someone mentioned it to him after the game. But after studying the game film on Sunday, Royal saw that it was fact. Sisemore knocked down two defenders at the line and took care of three more as he escorted quarterback Alan Lowry downfield. He blocked one of the defenders twice on the same play.

The Texas players' egos were bruised when Notre Dame coach Ara Parseghian, among others, believed number four Alabama "took the easy way out" by agreeing to play UT in the Cotton Bowl. 'Bama was leading 13–3 at the half, and once more Sisemore provided inspiration for his teammates with an emotional pep talk—one that Sisemore says he doesn't even remember giving. With Leaks and Lowry working behind the blocking of Sisemore and Travis Roach, and with another great defensive performance, Texas came from behind to beat the Crimson Tide 17–13.

Jerry Sisemore was a sophomore starter on Texas' 1970 National Championship team. A two-time All-SWC selection and two-time consensus All-American, he was a finalist for the Lombardi Award. He is a member of the Cotton Bowl Hall of Fame, the College Football Hall of Fame, and the Longhorn Hall of Honor.

82 The Spy Game

As if the Texas-OU series weren't bitter enough, the events surrounding the 1976 game blew things right out of the water.

Between 1957 and 1970, Darrell Royal's teams dominated his alma mater, winning 12 out of 14 contests. But the wind shifted in 1971, and Royal would not beat Oklahoma again.

In 1970, a brash young assistant coach named Barry Switzer convinced head coach Chuck Fairbanks to switch—the week of the Texas game—to the wishbone offense. They lost to Texas that year, but for the next five years OU ran the wishbone to perfection and beat Royal with the very offense he and assistant coach Emory Bellard had created.

The outgoing Switzer related well to kids; he was known as a "players' coach," and he brought his winning personality—and some said bucketfuls of money—south of the river and started winning Texas recruits with ease. But OU's image wasn't helped much when they were put on NCAA probation for an assistant coach's involvement in changing the transcripts of two recruits.

Texas had installed a quick kick play the week of the 1972 OU game. To run the play, Texas substituted the regular center for one who was a better long snapper. That was the only change, the only indication that the quick kick was coming. Texas had not run the quick kick for four years, so unless you'd witnessed the play during one of Texas' closed practices, the substitution shouldn't have raised any red flags.

Yet when Texas sent the new center into the game, the Sooner defense started yelling, "Quick kick! Quick kick!" They knew exactly what was coming. Oklahoma blocked the kick and went on to win the game 27–0. When Lucious Selmon told a reporter after the game

The expressions on the faces of Barry Switzer and Darrell Royal, shown here with President Gerald Ford, center, convey the bitter controversy that surrounded the 1976 Texas-OU game.

that they'd worked on the play all week and knew what to look for, Royal was pretty sure OU had pulled some funny business.

Fast-forward to 1976. Convinced that Oklahoma had spied on his practices, convinced that they paid players, and feuding openly with Switzer over proposed NCAA changes in recruiting rules, Royal wanted badly to beat the Sooners. According to ESPN.com columnist Robert Heard, Royal and defensive coordinator Mike Campbell worked a little every day, starting before the season began, on a defensive scheme for that game.

Not long before the 1976 Oklahoma game, word filtered back to Royal that OU had, in fact, spied on Texas practices. Lonnie Williams, a former coach and friend of OU's defensive coordinator Larry Lacewell, allegedly admitted to a Texas alum that he sneaked into Memorial Stadium, took notes on the Longhorns' practice, and reported back to Lacewell.

Royal was livid. He publicly accused Switzer of spying and even offered to give Switzer, Lacewell, and Williams $10,000 each if they could pass a lie-detector test. Switzer snorted derisively and refused.

Admissions and Retractions

In Barry Switzer's 1990 autobiography, *Bootlegger's Boy*, he admitted: "It did happen…although I didn't know it at first. Darrell was right to accuse us of that. It was my fault because I was the head coach… and when I found out about it, I denied that it had happened…it was a bad, embarrassing deal that should never have happened. I wish I'd said that at the time."

Yet 30 years after the accusations were leveled, Switzer denied that it happened. In an October 2006 article written by *Dallas Morning News* reporter Barry Horn, Switzer said, "My staff did not spy on Texas, and I say that emphatically." When the paragraph from his book was read back to him, he said, "I was trying to admit in the book that Darrell was really right to make him feel better. I really didn't care."

Larry Lacewell maintains that the spying took place. He told Horn in that same article, "We were young and ignorant and foolish…some overzealous young guys doing things they shouldn't have done. If I had to do it again today, I wouldn't do it, particularly against Coach Royal….Oklahoma-Texas is too great a rivalry to mess with."

Lonnie Williams remains silent, saying that he considers this ancient history. And to the end of his days, Darrell Royal graciously declined to speak publicly of the whole mess, saying, "There's no sense picking old scabs or digging up old bones."

All this was being played out in the press the week of the game. Switzer denied the spying charges and tried to paint Royal as a paranoid old fool. Royal called them "sorry bastards," thinking his remarks were off the record. When game time finally rolled around, the two walked to midfield for the coin toss with President Gerald Ford walking between them. Not a word was exchanged between the two coaches.

Campbell's defense was brilliant; Texas kicker Russell Erxleben had scored the only points of the game on two field goals. With six minutes left to play, Texas had the ball on its own 36, but an OU defender stripped the ball from the Longhorn running back and OU recovered on UT's 37-yard line.

It took OU 10 plays, but they finally scored. A high snap derailed the extra-point attempt, and the game ended in a tie, with each team believing it should have won.

The cheating and overly aggressive recruiting tactics of other schools, resentment at having to pander to demanding 18-year-old kids, a failure to beat Oklahoma, the first non-winning season of his career…the combination wearied Royal and at the season's end, one of the greatest minds and one of the most respected men in the game retired at age 52.

The years of frustrating losses to OU teams loaded with Texans and the suspicions of cheating and spying spewed from the Longhorn fans in a rage directed at Oklahoma and their coach. Impossible as it seemed, the rivalry grew even more bitter.

83 The 1977 Season

"I don't think this can be viewed as anything but a rebuilding year," head coach Fred Akers told the press.

The Longhorns' new head coach was switching to a new offense, the veer. The offensive line was questionable, the quarterbacks were inexperienced, and Earl Campbell and halfback Johnny "Ham" Jones had injuries.

Akers had hired a new defensive staff as well, and defensive coordinator Leon Fuller was tweaking the defense for the upcoming year. The defense had lost seven regulars and would have to look to youngsters to fill in.

Texas fans didn't want to hear about rebuilding. They wanted victories and conference championships, and they wanted Oklahoma's head on a platter. The 5–5–1 season of the previous

Brad Shearer and George James carry coach Fred Akers off the field after clinching the 1977 Southwest Conference championship by crushing the Aggies 57–28.

year still left an acrid aftertaste, and it had been six long, humiliating, agonizing years since Texas had won the Red River Shootout.

So when Texas, starting 10 sophomores, snowballed Boston College 44–0 in the season opener, everyone—Akers included—was surprised. The Horns, unranked in the preseason, moved to the number 18 spot.

The 68–0 whipping of Virginia got people's attention. Campbell gained 156 yards on 19 carries and sat down before the first half was over. Now they were number nine.

Akers introduced his team to the concepts of deep relaxation and visualization, psychological tools that stressed self-motivation and individual accountability. On October 1, the Longhorns visualized themselves a big ole 72–15 win over Rice. Russell Erxleben set an NCAA Division I record with a 67-yard field goal and Campbell ran for 131 yards in only 13 carries. Texas moved to number five, and Oklahoma was up next at number two.

Longhorn Lore
Kicker Russell Erxleben became the first Longhorn player in history to score in four different games against the Sooners. In the 1975–1978 OU games, he scored 22 points, six field goals, and four points after touchdowns.

Texas fans were squirming in their seats, eager for a shot at the Sooners, certain—absolutely certain—that this year would belong to the Longhorns. And it would, but it would cost them dearly.

The sellout crowd, the burnt-orange half of it, watched in horror as first Mark McBath, the starting quarterback, was helped to the locker room with a broken ankle and then talented backup Jon Aune left the field with a wrecked knee. No one—not the radio announcers, not the fans, not the stunned offense, not even third-string quarterback Randy McEachern himself—knew who was going in. The announcers couldn't pronounce his name, and he'd been so far down the charts in the preseason that his bio wasn't even in the Longhorn media guide. But once McEachern got rid of the jitters, he moved the team 80 yards in six plays for the only touchdown of the game, a 24-yard run by Campbell made possible by a block from freshman Steve Hall of Broken Arrow, Oklahoma.

The heroes were many in the 13–6 win. Erxleben had field goals of 64 and 58 yards and his punting was spectacular. Johnnie Johnson and Brad Shearer stuffed Thomas Lott on a fourth-and-one near the goal line to preserve Texas' lead. After the Horns went three-and-out, Erxleben boomed a 69-yard punt from out of the Texas end zone. Campbell and the Sooner defense punished one another the entire game, but Campbell ended that glorious afternoon with 124 yards on 23 carries.

Thirty minutes after the game, the south end zone was deserted, but no one on the north half of the Cotton Bowl would leave. The Longhorn faithful had been starving for this, and they weren't leaving until they were full. When the team plane arrived at the Austin airport, among the throng of people were students sporting T-shirts that read, "Randy is Dandy."

Arkansas was no easier, especially for McEachern. Against OU, he had been an unknown with nothing to lose. One week later, he was a hero under huge pressure to perform. He did not disappoint, directing a passing drive in the fourth quarter that included an impossible snag by Alfred Jackson and a pass to Campbell in the flat that he took to the Arkansas 1-yard line. Campbell ran for 188 yards behind an offensive line that "commanded the line of scrimmage," according to Akers. Another superlative effort by the defense helped put Texas on top 13–9.

Texas hit number one after they beat SMU and held onto that spot as they rolled over Texas Tech, Houston, TCU, and Baylor. The A&M game turned into an offensive highlight film as Texas won 57–28, producing the most points ever scored by the Horns against the Aggies. McEachern passed for 172 yards and threw four touchdown passes—two to Jackson, one to "Lam" Jones, and one to Campbell for the only touchdown catch of his career—to tie a school record set by Clyde Littlefield in 1915. Campbell rushed for 222 yards and matched a school record with his four touchdowns.

But key injuries, six turnovers, and a subpar showing let the National Championship slip through the Longhorns' fingers as they lost to Notre Dame 38–10 in the Cotton Bowl.

Texas ended the season 11–1, as champions of the Southwest Conference and slayers of the Sooners. Longhorn fans won't forget the year when a Heisman Trophy winner, an Outland Trophy winner, an Olympic gold medalist, the Coach of the Year, and Cinderella shared the field.

Not bad for a rebuilding year.

84 The 1981 Season

The Longhorns of 1981 ripped through their first three games before meeting Oklahoma. In spite of Texas' four fumbles, OU was simply no match; everything was clicking for Texas and after defeating the Sooners, they moved into the number one spot.

And then they went to Arkansas. The team that had clicked a week before turned into a clunker as the burnt orange fell apart in almost every way imaginable. The Longhorns came home smarting from the 42–11 humiliation they'd suffered, but they got back on the winning track against a tough SMU team.

Against Houston in the Astrodome, Texas was down 14–0 by the time Robert Brewer replaced starting quarterback Rick McIvor at the half. The game ended in a tie, but not before Brewer, a former walk-on, had won the starting job. Texas won their next three games easily, ending the regular season with a 21–13 win over the Aggies.

Alabama was ranked third in the country when the Horns faced them in the 1982 Cotton Bowl. Texas struggled the first three quarters and was down 10–0. Facing a third-and-10 at the Alabama 30 with just over 10 minutes to play, coach Fred Akers called a quarterback draw. As Akers said later, "Robert's never seen that much grass." Not known for his speed, Brewer was just fast enough on his 30-yard touchdown run to give Texas the momentum.

Terry Orr scored his first touchdown of the season with two minutes left, and when William Graham intercepted at the Texas

Priceless Aggie Moment
A&M's yearbook was called *The Longhorn* from 1903 until 1949, when a student vote decided the new name would be *The Aggieland.*

1-yard line, the deal was done. Texas had beaten a Bear Bryant team for the eighth time in 10 tries. Brewer, the former walk-on quarterback, was named Cotton Bowl MVP, and Texas finished number two in the nation.

85 The 1983 Season

As he had in his "rebuilding year" of 1977, Fred Akers took his 1983 Longhorns through the regular season without dropping a game, and they were headed to the Cotton Bowl, this time to take on Georgia.

The 1983 team's amazing collection of talent yielded four All-Americans: offensive guard Doug Dawson, linebacker Jeff Leiding, and defensive backs Mossy Cade and Jerry Gray. The defense was strong and stingy, leading the NCAA with an average 212 yards per game, and place-kicker Jeff Ward was money, hitting 15 of 16 through the regular season.

It was also a year of a stalled-out offense and quarterback by committee. In 1981, Robert Brewer had won the starting job from Rick McIvor, and Brewer remained the starter throughout his senior season of 1982. When Brewer hurt his hand before the 1982 Sun Bowl, Todd Dodge filled in as starter.

But the next year, Brewer had graduated and Akers passed over both McIvor and Dodge when choosing a starter for the opener against number one Auburn; he went with inexperienced backup Rob Moerschell. Texas beat Auburn and the great Bo Jackson 20–7 in Memorial Stadium, so Moerschell kept his job.

After dispensing with North Texas and Rice, it was time for Dallas and the Sooners. Texas, at number two in the country, had no

Longhorn Lore: NFL History
The University of Texas set an NFL record in 1984 with 17 draft picks, more than any other school in the draft's 77-year history. The supplemental draft added one more, bringing the total number of Horns drafted in one year to 18.

Texas has had at least one player selected in a record 76 consecutive drafts.

trouble with Oklahoma, and an outstanding breakout performance by running back Edwin Simmons made the day even brighter.

Arkansas at Little Rock gave the Horns no problems, except that Simmons, star of the OU game the week before, blew out his knee on his first carry and was out for the season. *Long Live the Longhorns* quoted Arkansas head coach Lou Holtz as saying, "Nebraska [ranked number one] is a great team, but Texas is awesome. There's some discrepancy about who's the best team in Texas—the Cowboys or the Longhorns....In all my years of coaching this is the best defensive team I've ever seen."

Texas and SMU were both undefeated in conference play. Number nine SMU came to the game with a talented roster and a 21-game unbeaten streak. Texas had scored only on Jeff Ward's two field goals, so Dodge came off the bench to throw a touchdown pass, pulling Texas ahead. SMU scored again, pulling to within one point of the Horns, but Jerry Gray batted down the attempted conversion pass. A safety made the final score 15–12, Longhorns.

Dodge came off the bench again, this time against Texas Tech, to ignite the Texas offense with two touchdowns. He earned the starting job against Houston, but once again, the offense sputtered, and Ward, the steady freshman kicker, accounted for all of Texas' points. The defense was tenacious and kept Texas in the games, while the offense was stalling out with regularity. The defense was beginning to grumble.

Just before halftime of the A&M game, the Horns used their third quarterback of the season. McIvor entered with the score

13–0 and used his rocket arm to score 45 points in 15 minutes. His four touchdown passes tied the record previously held by Clyde Littlefield and Randy McEachern.

The number two Horns, undefeated in the regular season, dominated Georgia in the Cotton Bowl but ultimately lost to the Bulldogs on a fluke play, a fumbled punt that Georgia recovered. Three plays later Georgia scored, and the extra point gave them a 10–9 win. It was a sickening end to the season; Akers called that loss the most heartbreaking he'd suffered in his career.

Later that evening, Miami stunned number one Nebraska 31–30 in the Orange Bowl.

86 Celebrate Texas Independence Day

Spend five minutes with a Texan and chances are he'll mention that Texas is the only state in the Union that was once its own country. Texans are eager to brag about their unique history and are dead serious about observing March 2—Texas Independence Day. Because the history of Texas and the history of The University are interwoven, celebrating independence from Mexico is serious stuff at UT.

In 1897 a group of University students, desiring to properly celebrate Texas Independence Day, requested a holiday from their studies and classes. UT President George Winston, a former teacher at the University of North Carolina and decidedly not a Texan, refused what he considered a frivolous request. So, a rowdy crowd of law students—led by J.S. "Snaky" Jones, who played end for the Longhorns—marched to the Capitol, appropriated a cannon, and dragged it back to campus. Shots hurtled down University Avenue,

Texas Trivia

Y.A. Tittle was almost a Longhorn. The future Pro Football Hall of Fame quarterback had committed to play for LSU, but the Texas coaches flew him to Austin for a visit. One week in Austin did the trick; he changed his mind and committed to Texas. He settled in with roommates, but the day before Tittle was to enroll in school, the LSU coaches came calling.

They convinced Tittle that he'd never play because the great UT quarterback Bobby Layne was just a sophomore. Since LSU's team was very young, the coaches assured him he could certainly play for the Tigers at once.

Intimidated by Layne's prowess on the field *and* by his wild party life, Tittle told the two coaches he was coming with them. He packed his bags, jumped in the car with the men, and headed to Baton Rouge, Louisiana, without saying a word to his roommates or to coach D.X. Bible.

All-American "Slingin' Sammy" Baugh wanted to attend Texas, too, but head coach Jack Chevigny would not assure Baugh that he could compete in football and baseball. Baugh found a home at Texas Christian University. Chevigny never beat TCU the entire time Baugh was a Horned Frog.

shattering windows in the Main Building. The group of future attorneys was ordered to remove the cannon.

The obedient group did remove the cannon; they moved it to Clark Field and began firing again. Eventually, subscribing to the "if you can't beat 'em, join 'em" theory, Wilson joined the crowd and delivered this now-famous speech:

"I was born in the land of liberty, rocked in the cradle of liberty, nursed on the bottle of liberty, and I've had liberty preached to me all my life, but Texas University students take more liberty than anyone I've ever come in contact with."

In 1900, the Texas Ex-Students Association adopted a resolution stating: "Whenever two ex-students of The University of Texas shall meet on Texas Independence Day, they shall sit and break bread and pay tribute to the institution which made their education possible."

In response to the ROTC's cannonfire commemorating Texas's independence from Mexico, Kappa Sig fraternity members dressed as Mexican soldiers returned fire, starting a tradition that lasted two decades.

Armed with that mandate, the annual celebrations grew more raucous and outlandish each year. There were pushball contests in the '20s, dorm riots in the '30s, and in the '60s alcohol-fueled Kappa Sigs dressed as Mexican soldiers firing cannons from the roof of their fraternity house. The University wisely took over the celebration and made it an official University function that featured the ROTC firing rifles, a short concert by the Longhorn Band, and the raising of the Texas flag.

Issues of safety and ethnic insensitivity put a temporary halt to UT's sponsorship of the March 2 celebration, but finally March 2 observations were revived. Today the gatherings are more sedate and dignified, emphasizing Texas excellence more than Texas independence from Mexico.

Nevertheless, the tradition continues. Across the globe, wherever two ex-Longhorns are gathered together on March 2, you can bet there will be a party…and lots of bragging.

87 The 1990s

The decade started as it should have, with Texas back on top as Southwest Conference champions. Longhorn fans had suffered through three losing seasons since 1986, and "despondent" doesn't begin to describe the mood of the Longhorn faithful. When David McWilliams was hired after Fred Akers was fired in 1986, Longhorns were giddy about the choice. David was a Longhorn; he'd been a captain on the 1963 National Championship team and had coached under both Royal and Akers. He left Texas before the 1986 season to take the head coaching job at Texas Tech, and he won there; in fact, he beat Texas.

Everybody loved McWilliams, and as much as they wanted Texas to win, they wanted *him* to win.

Only it didn't happen, not right off the bat, anyway. But in 1990, Texas beat Penn State in the season opener, and after a one-touchdown loss to Colorado in the second game, Texas never looked back. For the second time in a row, unranked Texas came back in the fourth quarter to beat OU 14–13.

In the eighth game of the season, number three Houston came to Memorial Stadium with Heisman Trophy candidate David Klingler and their run-and-shoot offense. Houston had beaten UT three years in a row, outscoring Texas 173 points to 64. Fans didn't take kindly to being humiliated by "Cougar High" and wanted revenge. They got it in the form of 626 yards of total offense, four Klingler interceptions, a total shutdown of the vaunted Cougar offense, and a

45–24 victory. McWilliams had called on the Texas fans to be loud when Houston was on offense, and the crowd responded as if their lives—and the conference championship—depended on it.

Flying high at number three in the nation with a 10–1 record, Texas was shot down by number four Miami, 46–3, at the Cotton Bowl—where Miami reached a new low in thuggish behavior and a new Cotton Bowl high in penalties, with 130 yards. The Horns went 5–6 in 1991, and after his third losing season, David McWilliams was relieved of his duties.

Texas won the last Southwest Conference championship in 1995 and the first Big 12 championship in 1996 under head coach John Mackovic, but those years were the best years of his erratic career at Texas. Fans were apoplectic in 1994, when Texas lost to Rice for the first time in almost 30 years, and were absolutely speechless in 1997, when UCLA beat Texas at home 66–3.

After that 4–7 season, Mackovic was replaced with North Carolina's Mack Brown, known for turning losing programs into winners. He came from the right part of the country, said all the right things, and schmoozed all the right people. But could he really turn this thing around?

He could and he did.

Great Pep Talk Number 9

Down 35–14 in the 2004 game against Oklahoma State at halftime, Mack Brown borrowed a page from Darrell Royal's book of motivational methods.

He wrote on the chalkboard "42–35." He told the team that's what they could do.

But with Cedric Benson rushing for five touchdowns, Vince Young putting on his best show to date by completing 12 straight passes, and the Texas defense shutting down the Cowboys in the second half, the Horns came back and won the game 56–35. At the time, it was the biggest comeback in UT's history.

And Brown had to apologize to his team for underestimating them.

In 1998, with Ricky Williams back for his senior year and a dynamic winner, redshirt freshman Major Applewhite at quarterback, Texas went 9–3 on the season. On the way to a 38–11 Cotton Bowl victory over Mississippi State, the Longhorns hammered Oklahoma, beat number six A&M, and stunned number seven Nebraska in Lincoln, breaking the Huskers' 47-game home winning streak. The Horns helped Williams break the NCAA rushing record and celebrated his winning the Heisman Trophy.

88 The Impostor

The Horns had just run undefeated through the 1995 Southwest Conference and had gone 10–2–1 for the season. The Conference was being dismantled, scattering teams that had been conference rivals for 81 years, and it was fitting that Texas had won the last championship. UT had been the dominant force in the conference in almost every sport during the SWC's existence.

While the team was in New Orleans to prepare for the upcoming Sugar Bowl contest with Virginia Tech, University of Texas officials were notified that Ron McKelvey, a special-teams player and defensive back who had played in 11 games for Texas, had been "outed" by a Salinas newspaper, *The Californian*. His parents identified his picture in The University of Texas' media guide and claimed to have had no idea that their son, Ron Weaver, was playing for Texas.

Weaver's football eligibility had expired after the 1989 season when he had played at Sacramento State, a Division I-AA program; however, he played at Los Angeles Pierce College in 1993–94 and was enough of a standout player to earn a full scholarship from The University of Texas.

Keeping up with the Joneses

That was the problem that arose in the summer of 1976, when two offensive starters named Johnny Jones were on the field.

Johnny Jones from Hamlin, Texas, was a speedy Longhorn freshman running back in 1975 who wore jersey No. 25.

Johnny Jones from Lampasas, Texas, was already a superstar and gold medalist at the Montreal Olympics when he arrived on campus as a freshman in 1976. He, too, was a running back and wore UT jersey No. 26.

During two-a-days, coaches would write the players' last names on masking tape and slap the tape on the front and back of the helmets to help them identify players. Two Johnny Joneses on the practice field and in the film room was confusing for everyone: the coaches, spotters in the press box, sportswriters, and confusing for the two Joneses themselves.

So Darrell Royal and sports information director Jones Ramsey devised a surefire way to tell the two men apart. Johnny Jones of Lampasas would be "Lam" and Johnny Jones of Hamlin would be "Ham." Simple enough.

Simple until the summer of 1978, when another Jones showed up. A.J. Jones, a running back from Youngstown, Ohio, wore jersey No. 24. He became known as "Jam."

Throughout the 1977 and '78 football seasons, it was their opponents who had trouble keeping up with the Joneses. In the 1978 Sun Bowl, Ham and Jam combined for 211 yards rushing and four touchdowns, helping to break the nation's third-longest scoring streak by defeating Maryland 42–0.

The day before the bowl game was to be played, after UT officials began investigating the charges, Weaver packed his belongings and disappeared without notifying the team. It was initially rumored that McKelvey/Weaver was doing research for a book that would expose scandals in college football, but he dispelled those rumors when he responded, "I am not writing no book. I have a hard enough time in English class."

His teammates were shocked; they described him as a diligent student and a dedicated gym rat. It turned out, in his sister's words: "He loves football and just wanted a second chance to play."

The Horns lost that Sugar Bowl game to Virginia Tech 28–10. Federal prosecutors launched an investigation for fraudulent misrepresentation. Hey, Texas has had a few coaches who could have been found guilty of that. Nevertheless, Weaver pleaded guilty to a federal charge of misusing Social Security numbers and was ordered to pay The University of Texas $5,000, the cost of his scholarship. After the dust settled, the NCAA imposed no sanctions on Texas. Maybe they figured the embarrassment was punishment enough.

89 Take a Tower Tour

Before the invasion of the skyscrapers, the Texas Capitol building and the UT Tower were the most prominent, majestic features of the Austin skyline. Since its opening in 1937, the Tower has been a beacon for The University and for the city. It's always been a tourist attraction, marking the center of the campus, and has served as a directional marker for countless freshmen trying to find their way to class. "Excuse me, how do I get to Batts Hall?" "Just go to the Tower and turn right."

It is a timepiece, pealing every 15 minutes until, on the hour, the time is announced with the corresponding number of gongs. On Mondays, Wednesdays, and Fridays at 12:50 PM, Tom Anderson, the carillonneur who'd played the bells at the top of the tower for 62 years, treated the campus to a short concert on the Kniker Carillon, the largest carillon in Texas. Since his retirement, those duties are handled by the Guild of Student Carillonneurs. The four gold-leafed clock faces, each of which is 14'8" in diameter, are large enough for people to read from almost anywhere on campus.

The Tower was a symbol of and a reason for Texas hubris, The University's attempt to be recognized as a force in academia. John Henry Faulk said, "It's the most ridiculous thing I ever saw. With as much room as there is in Texas, and as many acres of land as The University owns, we have to put up a building like those in New York." He proposed it be knocked down and laid on its side.

The Tower is also a barometer of athletic success, announcing victories with its orange lights. There is a perplexingly complex set of "rules" for lighting the Tower, but generally speaking, the top of the Tower is lit orange for game victories. The entire tower is bathed in orange for a conference championship, and there are few sights more beautiful than seeing the Austin skyline anchored by the Tower, bathed in orange while the windows are lit to form a number "1" on all sides.

Rising out of the Main Building, it is the epicenter of campus activity and student activism. For students attending UT prior to 1974, the top of the tower and its four-sided open viewing deck provided a respite from the frenzy of protests, politics, drum circles, solicitors, and street preachers that was the West Mall.

You'd enter the Main Building underneath the words carved in limestone, "Ye Shall Know the Truth and the Truth Shall Make

Longhorn Lore

The University of Texas was the first state school in the nation to require entrance exams of all its students. After head coach Ed Price led the Longhorn football team to their worst record in school history, a 1–9 season in 1956, the newly toughened academic standards were held partly to blame. Coach Price, a fine gentleman who was loved by his players, was hanged in effigy three times that season. The University president didn't escape the fans' wrath. He, too, was hanged in effigy that season.

Few sights are more beautiful than this: the UT Tower, bathed in orange and lit with the No. 1, signifying another National Championship.

You Free." Take the elevator to the 27th floor and exit into a drab reception area, which contained a desk but no attendant. It was always surprising, after the tragedy of the Charles Whitman shootings in 1966, that security at the top wasn't tighter. A few steps up through the heavy metal door, and there you were, on the top of the world, almost always alone, with the most gorgeous view of God's country you'd ever seen. You really could see forever. The view, the quiet, the solitude made it a perfect place for contemplation, for ratcheting down one's pre-final anxieties. But that was after...and that was before.

Nine troubled students chose the Tower as the place to ease their pain permanently. There was talk of closing the Tower after the Whitman shootings but finally, after the ninth suicide occurred in 1974, the Tower viewing deck was closed to the public.

For 23 years, students could attend and pay for and graduate from UT without ever being allowed access to the boldest symbol on campus. But after countless meetings and engineering studies and yet more meetings, the Tower was enclosed with safety glass and a steel grate and on September 14, 1999, the viewing deck was once again opened to the public.

It's not as easy to gain access to the top of the Tower today. Guided tours are given on a limited basis; advance reservations must be made through the Student Union (www.utexas.edu/tower), but it is worth the extra planning and trouble. The scenery's changed and the city's unrecognizable, but it is still awe-inspiring to stand at the top of the Tower and behold our great University.

90 More Traditions

Hex Rally

The Longhorn faithful were anxious in 1941; Texas was to face the Aggies at Kyle Field, where UT hadn't beaten A&M since 1923. It had been a bittersweet year for Texas. They'd gained the number one ranking and been featured on the cover of *Life Magazine*, only to be tied by conference patsy Baylor. The following week, still reeling from the loss of their perfect season, the Horns lost to TCU. They were desperate to salvage their season by beating A&M at College Station.

A group of students consulted local psychic Madame Augusta Hipple for advice. She prescribed lighting red candles to break any kind of hex. Red candles blazed in the windows of every dormitory, fraternity and sorority house, and business lining the Drag the week leading up to the game. When the Longhorns beat the number two Aggies in College Station, a tradition was born.

Pig Bellmont

Although the "Longhorns" moniker had caught on and stuck, UT's first live mascot was a dog, a tan-and-white bulldog mix, brought to campus as a puppy in 1914 by Theo Bellmont, UT's first athletics director. During a football game, UT center Gus "Pig" Dittmar was standing beside the dog when someone pointed out how bowlegged both of them were, and thereafter the dog was called "Pig." For the next nine years Pig had the run of the campus—attending sporting events and befriending students and faculty members—until his tragic death in a car accident.

Although Pig was much-loved, UT traded up for its next live mascot. The ornery, aggressive longhorn steer was a more apt representation of Texas football.

The Hex Rally is still the main spirit event before the Thanksgiving Day game, even though the Aggies have departed. Seems the Hex worked....

Same Hex. Same Spirit. Different Team. It's a huge nighttime rally on the south steps of the Main Building, attended by the football team, the Longhorn Band, cheerleaders, and all the other spirit groups affiliated with UT. With the backdrop of the giant flag draped from the UT Tower and thousands of red candles being lit as the Band plays "The Eyes of Texas," the atmosphere of the Hex Rally will raise goosebumps on the most sophisticated of orange-bloods.

The Texas Flag

When Texas played Ole Miss in the 1962 Cotton Bowl, the Mississippi band had an enormous Texas flag made as a salute to The University and to the state. The flag was presented to Governor Price Daniel as a gift from Mississippi's governor, Ross Barnett. Governor Daniel, not knowing what to do with the flag, generously presented The Largest Texas Flag in the World to the Longhorn Band.

Vincent DiNino, director of the band, didn't quite know what to do with it either; the band couldn't spare the number of bodies necessary to "run" the flag. DiNino regifted the flag to the athletics department, which was also stumped as to how to make use of it. It was so huge as to be unmanageable.

Athletics passed it along to the service organization Alpha Phi Omega, which has been responsible for it ever since. The flag, previously 153 feet tall and 270 feet wide yards, is now 100 feet by 150 feet and is still the largest Texas flag in the World. APO runs the flag before all home games. Some 52 years later, it is still stirring to see that beautiful flag unfurled over almost the entire football field.

It is galling that a certain school to the north now has a giant state flag that they run before their games. But imitation is the sincerest form of flattery, no?

91 The 2000s (The First Half)

Ten seasons into the new millennium, Texas had compiled a 110–19 record and set impressive benchmarks.

Of course, in 2005 there was the 13–0 National Championship season, which finally sated the fans who'd been starving for 35 years. That team set an NCAA scoring record for most points in a year, scoring 652 and averaging 50.2 points a game.

There have been the heart-stopping, come-from-behind wins that leave the fans asking, "Where was that team in the first half?" The top five biggest comebacks in UT history have occurred since 2001.

In 2001, the Longhorn family almost split up over the Major Applewhite–Chris Simms quarterback controversy. In 1999,

One of the most divisive issues in Texas football history was the question of who should quarterback the Horns in 2000 and 2001. In the eye of the storm, Major Applewhite, No. 11, and Chris Simms, No. 8, handled their quarterback controversy better than many Longhorn fans did.

fan-favorite Applewhite was named the Big 12's co–Offensive Player of the Year. But after he suffered a knee injury at the end of the 2000 season, forcing him to miss spring practice, he lost his starting position to Simms. The Horns went 11–2 and won the south division of the Big 12, despite losing to the Sooners for the second year in a row. After struggling in the Big 12 championship game against Colorado, Simms was replaced by Applewhite, who constructed a thrilling comeback that fell just short of a win. He earned the starting job in the Holiday Bowl, however, and the Horns beat Washington in what was then the biggest comeback in Longhorn history.

With Simms at the helm in 2002, Texas won 11 games for the second year in a row and tied for first place in the south zone of the Big 12. Texas captured its first conference win over Kansas

Priceless Aggie Moment

Texas scored six points while holding the potent 1899 A&M offense scoreless, but the game ended in dispute after Texas was awarded possession of a fumble at the Aggies' 2-yard line. Aggie captain Hall Moseley led his team off the field with 28 minutes to play, and they took their ball and went home.

State and snapped its eight-game home win streak. The Wildcats attempted a field goal on the last play to try to tie the game, but Marcus Tubbs blocked the kick for the Horns and preserved the 17–14 victory.

Texas went back to Nebraska and this time snapped a 26-game home winning streak, thanks to great performances by Simms, who passed for 419 yards; Roy Williams, who set a school record with 13 catches for 161 yards; and Nathan Vasher, whose last-minute interception preserved the Longhorn victory. The Longhorns finished the year with a 35–20 win over LSU in the Cotton Bowl.

Beginning in the 2004 Texas Tech game, Vince Young finally became Vince Young. He had struggled in the first half of the season, but after Mack Brown and Greg Davis showed him video of his best moments as a Longhorn and as a high school star and told him, "That's the guy we want to see," he relaxed and started playing Young's game.

After two wild come-from-behind victories against Oklahoma State and Kansas, a BCS berth was in doubt. It would come down to either Cal or the Longhorns playing in the Rose Bowl. After Texas beat A&M, Brown publicly urged voters in the BCS polls to take a close look at UT. After Cal struggled against Southern Mississippi and the new polls came out, Texas was in.

The 2005 Rose Bowl marked the first time Texas had played Michigan, and it was Texas' first trip to the Rose Bowl. At the end of a wild game that saw five lead changes, Dusty Mangum kicked a wobbly 37-yard field goal for the 38–37 win. Young won the game's Most Valuable Player award and promised the fans in the Rose Bowl and the audience at home, "We'll be back."

One year later, they were back, standing on the podium as victors once again, but this year the trophy they held was a Waterford crystal ball.

92 The 2008 Season

The Longhorns entered the 2008 season ranked number 10 in the coaches' poll. By the time they met Oklahoma on the second Saturday of October, Texas was undefeated through five games and had risen to number five in the country. After they defeated the top-ranked Sooners with a 25–14 second-half surge, the Horns vaulted to the number one spot in the polls. They beat Missouri at DKR-Memorial Stadium, marking the first time since 1977 that Texas had played at home holding down the number one spot. Next, Texas dispatched with undefeated number eight Oklahoma State.

Going to play Texas Tech in Lubbock is always risky, and 2008 was no exception. Tech was sitting at number seven, and in front of a record-setting television audience, the underdogs led Texas almost the entire game. With about a minute and a half left, Texas took the lead and the Longhorn nation finally took a breath. But a last-second touchdown pass from Tech quarterback Graham Harrell to Michael Crabtree beat the Longhorns 39–33.

Texas won out easily and beat Texas A&M 49–9. When the dust settled on the regular season, Texas, OU, and Texas Tech were in a three-way tie for the Big 12 South. Big 12 rules state that in the event of a three-way tie, the team with the highest BCS ranking

Longhorn Lore: Most Memorable Moment

ESPN's most memorable moment of the BCS era: Vince Young, Part II:
Texas trailed undefeated and "the best ever" USC 38–33 with just 26 seconds left and had fourth-and-five from the 8-yard line. With the 2005 BCS title on the line, "Vince Young dropped back to pass but saw nobody open, and immediate sprinted for the right pylon for the title-winning score in the marquee game of the BCS era."

would play in the conference title game. It seemed inconceivable that OU might make it to the title game in light of Texas' solid 45–35 win back in October. Yet when the final BCS standings of the regular season were posted, Oklahoma had passed Texas. After OU beat Missouri in the Big 12 title game, the Sooners were off to play for the 2009 National Championship, where they lost to the University of Florida, 24–14.

Texas ended the year in spectacular fashion, winning its fifth straight bowl game by beating Ohio State in a dramatic back-and-forth 24–21 contest at the Fiesta Bowl in Arizona. Quarterback Colt MCoy earned offensive MVP honors for the third time in three bowl wins, and had 41 completions on 58 tries for 414 yards passing. The Longhorns finished the year 12–1, only the second 12-win season in school history. You'd think that would be reason enough to brag.

But in one of UT athletics' most embarrassing moments, reporters spotted something odd on the wall of the team meeting room after the 2009 Spring Game. One wall lists UT's football accomplishments by year, and under "Big 12 Champions", 1996 and 2005 were listed, followed by "2008*" complete with asterisk. Huh? Three schools tied for the south zone title, but only one school, Oklahoma, won the Big 12 championship. "Shoulda won it" doesn't count in football. No one seemed to know how the asterisked championship got there, but after it was discovered by reporters, it was taken down pretty quickly.

93 The 2009 Season

The 2009 season made up for the heartbreak of the "45–35" year, when OU made it to the National Championship even after losing head-to-head to the Longhorns. The Rose Bowl was back in rotation for the National Championship game, and so was Texas. Colt McCoy, consensus All-American quarterback was back, as was Colt's roommate and fleet-footed receiver Jordan Shipley. McCoy's backup was Garrett Gilbert, ranked the top quarterback in the 2009 recruiting class. Texas had no trouble with its first five contests, winning by a margin of 236–75. The Horns rolled into Dallas holding down the number three spot to face number 20 Oklahoma. Thanks to Texas' stifling defense, the team came away with a 16–13 victory, its fourth over the Sooners in five years. Texas caused five OU turnovers and held the Sooners to 13 points and minus-16 rushing yards.

The rest of the season—up to the Aggie game—was a cakewalk. Fans at DKR–Texas Memorial Stadium witnessed Colt McCoy win his 43rd game to set the NCAA record for career wins by a quarterback. In the first half alone against Kansas, McCoy completed 18 of 22 for 238 yards and two touchdowns.

The Aggie game turned into a quarterback showcase, as A&M QB Jerrod Johnson refused to blink against the number two team in the country. He was 26 of 33, threw for 342 yards and four touchdowns, with one interception. Colt McCoy threw for 304 yards and four touchdowns and logged his first 100-yard rushing game of the season. Coming into the contest, Texas' regular season record was 11–0; A&M's was 6–5. But the Aggies made the Horns earn a victory in a rough game at Kyle Field in College Station. The 49–39 victory gave Texas its second consecutive 12-win season, a first in Longhorn football history.

Texas played number 21 Nebraska in Cowboys Stadium for the Big 12 championship, and once again, the defense came to the rescue. It was a rugged night for Colt McCoy, as he threw three interceptions and was sacked nine times, four of those by defensive monster Ndamukong Suh. The UT offense couldn't make anything happen in the face of Suh and Nebraska's swarming defense. Fortunately, Nebraska's offense had a poor showing as well.

After a 42-yard field goal put the Huskers up 12–10 with just 1:44 left, Texas started its drive at the Texas 40. Facing third-and-13 from Nebraska's 29, McCoy ended up scrambling and scrambling and holding the ball as millions of TV viewers screaming "Throw the ball!" watched in disbelief as a perfect season seemed to go down the drain. McCoy threw the ball out of bounds as time ran out and Nebraska players rushed the field, believing they had upset Texas for the Big 12 championship.

Officials asked to review the final play. Rules state that the clock runs until the ball hits something, and the officials were able to see one second left on the clock as McCoy's pass hit a railing in the stadium. So with one second remaining, kicker Hunter Lawrence, who had never kicked a game-winning field goal, saved the day with a perfect kick. This time, Texas players rushed the field.

In the 2008 season, Michael Crabtree's last-second score broke the Longhorns' hearts. This year, Texas used that final second to be the heartbreaker.

UT was getting pretty familiar with the Rose Bowl. Three trips out west in five years seemed to validate the strength, the success of our program. Texas was in the national championship hunt after winning the Big 12 championship and ending the regular season ranked number two, and Longhorn fans were jacked. Things were lining up just as they had in 2005: Texas had faced the previous national champions (USC) and the current Heisman Trophy winner (Reggie Bush), and look how that turned out. Once again, in 2010, Texas was facing the previous season's national champ

Great Pep Talk Number 10

David McWilliams, tri-captain of the 1963 team and former Longhorn head coach, calls it the best pep talk Coach Royal ever gave.

The Navy head coach, attempting to fire up his own team before the 1964 Cotton Bowl, instead set the stage for Darrell Royal's famous two-word pep talk, which Longhorns still talk about half a century later.

The undefeated Horns were matched with Navy and Heisman Trophy winner Roger Staubach in the '64 New Year's Day classic. Texas had already been named National Champions by the UPI poll before the bowl game, and Navy was a distant second. Navy fans and the Eastern press were all eaten up with that and picked Navy to annihilate Texas.

The pregame introductions were televised, so all the country heard Navy coach Wayne Hardin proclaim: "When the challenger meets the champion and the challenger wins, then there is a new champion."

Coach Royal's response was short but fiery: "We're ready." With chills down their spines, goosebumps on their arms, and fire in their eyes, and armed with the confidence of their coach and the defensive scheme of Mike Campbell, Texas defeated Navy 28–6 to remain undefeated.

(Alabama) and the 2009 Heisman Trophy winner (Mark Ingram). Just the way we like it, right? Besides, in eight meetings, the Tide had never, ever beaten Texas. This was going to be great.

On the first offensive series, with Texas in position to score the game's first touchdown, Alabama's Marcell Dareus popped Colt McCoy and knocked him out of the game with a pinched nerve in his throwing shoulder. True freshman Garrett Gilbert, the backup quarterback, had seen little action during the season, throwing just 26 passes in nine games. Gilbert's inexperience showed, as he missed on nine of his first 10 throws.

Texas scored a field goal on each of its next two drives, but 'Bama turned up the defensive pressure on Gilbert, and the Longhorn defense could not stop 'Bama's running game. Just before halftime, Dareus intercepted Gilbert's shovel pass and returned it for a touchdown, making the score 24–6, Alabama.

The second half saw a couple of Gilbert-to-Shipley touchdowns, along with Texas' defense shutting down Alabama. With six minutes left to play, the Crimson Tide led by just three points, 24–21, and UT was in position to take the lead. Disaster struck again with three Texas turnovers in the last three minutes. When the clock ran out, 'Bama had won 37–21.

94 2010–13

After losing only two games in two years, the way the 2010 season ended was inconceivable to the Longhorn Nation. Texas entered the year ranked fifth in the nation, but the Associated Press couldn't see the internal injuries from which Texas' football program still suffered as a result of the loss in the 2010 BCS championship game.

By the time Texas played its seventh game of the year, the Horns had lost to UCLA, Oklahoma, and Iowa State and had fallen to number 25. Inconceivable.

The following week Texas lost to Baylor and future Heisman Trophy winner Robert Griffin III, 30–22. To *Baylor*. No one seemed to know how to fix the freefall, and each week's press conferences sounded like sessions with Dr. Phil, with talk of feelings, confusion, and anger. UT finished the season by losing to Kansas State, Oklahoma State, and A&M. There *was* a win in there against Florida Atlantic. It was UT's first losing season since 1997, and distraught Texas fans shuffled around with stooped shoulders and blank eyes, looking like zombies from *The Walking Dead*.

When all was said and done, Greg Davis, Mack Brown's longtime offensive coordinator and great friend, was a casualty of the wretched, rancorous season. Will Muschamp, defensive coordinator and head-coach–in–waiting got tired of waiting. He left a boatload of money and a special position—created for him to ensure he wouldn't leave—and accepted the head coaching job at Florida. There would be no bowl game for the Horns. Because Texas had snagged Gilbert, the premier quarterback of the 2009 class, they didn't recruit another quarterback that year. That left only three scholarship quarterbacks on the 2010 roster: Gilbert, a true sophomore with little experience, and Case McCoy and Connor Wood, both with only high school experience. Mack Brown announced "a nationwide search immediately for a new defensive coordinator."

Garrett Gilbert retained his starting position in 2011, but by the second game had been demoted to second string, with Case McCoy and David Ash sharing the starting duties. Connor Wood had transferred to Colorado and won the starting position there, and after Gilbert suffered a shoulder injury, he expressed his desire to transfer to SMU. Texas had two scholarship quarterbacks on the roster, neither with any game day experience.

Mack Brown hired 36-year-old Manny Diaz, considered a rising young star, to be the team's defensive coordinator. He had only one year of coordinator experience at a BCS school, but his defense at Mississippi State had finished third in the SEC in points allowed. Brown brought in Boise State's young offensive coordinator, Bryan Harsin, to be offensive co-coordinator with running backs coach Major Applewhite.

Texas finished the 2011 season with an 8–5 record, certainly more encouraging that the 2010 campaign. Still, there were five conference losses, including a second loss to Baylor and a humiliating 55–17 loss to the Sooners.

The grumbling reached new levels in 2012. West Virginia, in its inaugural season in the Big 12, beat Texas 48–45, Texas still hadn't figured out how to beat Kansas State—it had lost five times

Longhorn Lore
The Longhorns played Tennessee in the first nationally televised New Year's Day game. NBC broadcast the 1953 Cotton Bowl in which Texas defeated Tennessee 16–0.

in a row—and once again, Texas fans poured out of the Cotton Bowl in the third quarter, preferring corn dogs and beer to witnessing another beatdown at the hands of Oklahoma, this one ending 63–21. The season's defensive performance was statistically the worst in Texas football history. The 9–4 record (5–4 in conference play) left us playing number 15 Oregon State in the Alamo Bowl. After defeating the Beavers 31–27, we landed back in the BCS rankings at number 23.

With 19 starters back from 2012, and carrying a number 15 preseason ranking, Brown announced that he thought the team had enough talent to win all its games. It didn't take the Horns long to prove their coach wrong. Harsin had left in the off-season to take the head job at Arkansas State, leaving Major Applewhite and receivers coach Darrell Wyatt sharing the offensive coordinator duties. Brown made no changes on the defensive staff, but Greg Robinson, former defensive coordinator of Texas' 2004 Rose Bowl team, was hired as a "player personnel analyst" who would break down film of upcoming opponents.

In the second game of the 2013 season, Texas traveled to Provo and was mauled by the unranked BYU Cougars 40–21; starting quarterback David Ash was knocked out of the game with head and shoulder injuries, and the defense gave up 679 yards. Diaz was reassigned before the sun rose on Sunday morning, and Greg Robinson stepped into the coordinator's role.

Next up was Ole Miss. Texas had handled the Rebels easily the year before in Oxford in a 66–31 Longhorn win, but 2013 saw the tables turned. Greg Robinson had only had four days to work with the defense, and Case McCoy took over quarterback duties for the injured Ash. After the 44–23 home loss to the Rebels, people cried "the sky is falling" and began debating openly over whether Mack Brown's time here was finished.

Texas then went on a six-game run, confusing the doubters. First Kansas State fell, for the first time in six meetings, then the Horns got by Iowa State by the skin of their teeth. Next up was Oklahoma, and for the first time in memory, tickets to the game were available anywhere, everywhere. Some Texas fans just couldn't face what they believed would be another inevitable shellacking at the hands of the Sooners. Those Longhorns who did go witnessed one of the most surprising and enjoyable upsets in the series, as Texas never trailed in the 36–20 victory. Case McCoy directed a balanced game, with Johnathan Gray and Malcolm Brown both topping 100 yards rushing and McCoy throwing for 190 yards and two touchdowns. Texas scored two non-offensive touchdowns, one on an interception return by Chris Whaley and another on a Daje Johnson punt return. It was a beautiful thing.

A 38–13 loss to Oklahoma State almost popped the balloon, but when OU beat OSU at Bedlam, Texas was right back in the conference championship chase. It all came down to the Baylor game, the last game of the regular season. Win this game and Texas—improbably—would win the Big 12.

The game was tied 3–3 at halftime, but in the second half, the Horns were exposed. The Bears ran 92 plays for 509 yards to UT's 69 plays for 217, they intercepted McCoy twice, and scored 17 unanswered points in the third quarter. The disappointing 30–10 loss spurred even more talk about Brown's possible resignation.

On December 15, 2013, Mack Brown indeed resigned after 16 years as head coach at The University of Texas. Citing a divided fan base as one reason for leaving, Brown said, "I sincerely want what's best for The University of Texas. There are just too many distractions, too many negatives, and the players and assistant coaches shouldn't have to deal with negatives about me.

"I want to be remembered as bringing some joy back to Texas, getting us back on track. The second thing is that I did it with integrity and class."

Brown left Texas with a record of 158 wins, 48 losses, two conference championships, and the 2005 National Championship.

95 And It's Goodbye to A&M

"Let's talk about conference realignment. We have said from day one our goal was to stay in the Big 12, and we are doing that minus two."

So wrote former A&M athletics director Bill Byrne in June of 2010. He continued:

"...we are better off in the] Big 12. Here are some reasons why. First, we are still in the same time zone competing. That means we can get our student-athletes back in class the next day after a road trip. It's one of the reasons our student-athletes were so supportive of us staying in the Big 12. Second, we are receiving the same financial dollars we would have received by going east or west. Plus, our operating costs are reduced. Our estimates said it would cost us an extra million dollars a year in travel to go east or west. Third, by adding another conference game to our regular schedule in football and two more conference games in basketball, we will have more attractive schedules. And, we won't have to pay as many exorbitant fees to get non-conference teams to come play us in Aggieland.

"Throughout this I said we are committed to the Big 12. We never wavered and our future is financially better.

—Former A&M athletics director Bill Byrne
"Let's talk Conference Realignment," AggieAthletics.com
June 16, 2010

One year later:

"This morning, Texas A&M University President R. Bowen Loftin sent a letter to Big 12 Conference Commissioner Dan Beebe, informing him that Texas A&M is submitting an application to join another conference. If the application is accepted, we would leave the Big 12 following this athletic season....

"As President Loftin has repeated over the past several weeks, the goal of our University is to increase the visibility of Texas A&M and our student-athletes, be in a stable and strong conference, and ensure the long-term future of Texas A&M financially.

—Former A&M athletics director Bill Byrne
"Bill Byrne's Weekly Wednesday," AggieAthletics.com
August 31, 2011

On July 1, 2012, Texas A&M got its wish—to get out of the shadow of The University of Texas. After years of lusting after the Southeastern Conference, A&M—and Missouri—officially joined the SEC. The Aggies now compete in the SEC-West against 'Bama, Arkansas, Auburn, LSU, Mississippi State, and Ole Miss. Missouri plays in the SEC-East.

A&M's exit from the Big 12 signals the demise of the 118-year football rivalry with UT, a series Texas dominated 76–37–5. It seems particularly ironic that the tradition-addicted Aggies were the ones to end the longest-running intrastate rivalry in college football.

Texas won't continue to play A&M because, according to former Texas athletics director DeLoss Dodds, "They're the ones who left the conference."

But the reason for not playing the Aggies anymore was best explained by Baylor women's basketball coach Kim Mulkey. When asked at Big 12 media days if she would schedule the Lady Ags in a non-conference game, she remembered that A&M president R. Bowen Loftin compared their leaving the Big 12 to a "loveless marriage" and a divorce.

We're Number One, Again

The University of Texas owns more Big 12 regular season titles than any other Big 12 school, with 45. Baylor's next with 30; 20 of those are for tennis. The evil empire north of the Red River is third, with 22 titles. Nine of those are football titles.

"My feeling is this," Mulkey said. "If a man wants to divorce me and says our relationship has no value to him, and then asks me if he can sleep with me, the answer is 'No'!"

In their last meeting on the football field, in November 2011, the Aggies held the lead for much of the game. A stellar performance by the defense and some explosive offensive plays gave Texas the lead in the third quarter. But with under two minutes remaining in the game, Ryan Tannehill's touchdown pass to receiver Jeff Fuller gave A&M a 25–24 lead. To lose this final game to the Aggies would be disastrous; our Aggie friends would talk about the win throughout eternity, and there would be no "wait til next year" for the Horns.

With 1:42 left in the game, Texas needed to drive 71 yards to position itself for the win. After converting third-and-one to the A&M 48, Case McCoy slipped away from Aggie defenders and ran the ball 25 yards to the Aggies' 23-yard line. Texas called timeout with just three seconds left on the clock. A&M called a timeout of its own in an attempt to freeze the kicker.

In the last meeting between the Aggies and Longhorns, Texas senior Justin Tucker kicked a 40-yard field goal as the clock ran out to give Texas the 27–25 victory over Texas A&M at Kyle Field.

God's in His heaven, all's right with the world.

96 Take Another Number

'Bama doesn't do it. Notre Dame doesn't do it. Michigan changed its mind and doesn't do it anymore. OU doesn't do it. And for 85 years, neither did we.

Earl Campbell's number 20 jersey was retired in 1979, breaking UT's long-standing tradition of not retiring player numbers. In October 2010, Colt McCoy became the sixth player in University football history—joining Campbell, Ricky Williams, Tommy Nobis, Vince Young, and Bobby Layne—to have his jersey retired. Colt was a two-time Heisman finalist, won the Walter Camp Award twice, and the Maxwell Award once, in 2009. He led the Horns to an undefeated season and the National Championship game against Alabama. He is the second-winningest quarterback in NCAA history, is smart, funny, and lives out his faith every day.

The question is not whether Colt—or any of the other guys—is deserving; it's whether UT should play that game at all.

We are The by-gosh University of Texas. We are the second-winningest program in the history of NCAA football. We land one of the nation's top recruiting classes every year. We expect our players to win national awards. We have Heisman Trophy winners, national award winners, three-time All-Americans. In addition to the six players whose jerseys are no longer available, UT has 10 other "national award" winners. If we start retiring all those jerseys, we won't be able to field a team; we'll run out of numbers.

Darrell Royal was opposed to retiring jersey numbers. He told his players, "If you want to celebrate in the end zone, you'd better wait for the other 10 players to get there, 'cause you didn't do it all by yourself." If football is "the ultimate team sport," why retire an individual's jersey? Not one of those fellows "did it by himself."

TRIVIA
Question

Name the five winningest coaches in Longhorn football history.

Trivia answers on page 255.

No jersey number has been so revered—or so feared—as the burnt-orange number 60. Worn by four consensus All-Americans—Johnny Treadwell ('62), Tommy Nobis ('65), Jeff Leiding ('83), and Britt Hager ('90)—number 60 came to represent the best tooth-jarring defenses UT has fielded. The jersey was handed out sparingly, sometimes as an award, occasionally as an incentive. There was a lot of honor and a lot of pressure associated with wearing that jersey. But no more.

Let's take a page from the playbook at Michigan—the winningest program in NCAA football. They have stopped retiring jerseys. They recirculated all previously retired numbers and recognized them as Michigan Football Legends. Current players who wear those numbers honor the legend with a patch on the upper left chest of the jersey.

Sounds like a winner. Texas greats would be honored, and generations of boys could still be inspired by the dream of wearing the burnt-orange jerseys of their heroes.

97 Conference Realignment v.2.0

After A&M and Missouri left the Big 12 for the SEC in 2012, fans of the remaining Big 12 schools dreamed big. Could we get Notre Dame? An overachieving ACC team? Texas smarted from A&M's betrayal as well their glee to be divorcing us. Longhorns couldn't wait to show off the Big 12's trophy bride. With a disappointing thud, the Big 12 announced TCU and West Virginia were the newest members of the conference.

Longhorn Lore
The 1965 Orange Bowl was the first bowl game played at night.
It featured national champion Alabama, with Joe Willie Namath at
quarterback versus the number five Longhorns. The 80,000 fans in
attendance, along with one of the largest television audiences ever for
a college football game, watched Texas beat Alabama 21–17.

Texas has a long, if interrupted, history with TCU. Both
were members of the Southwest Conference and have played one
another off and on since 1897 (TCU was then named Add-Ran
College). The Horned Frogs didn't manage to beat Texas until
1929 in a 15–12 victory.

In the 1930s, '40s, and '50s TCU showcased famous players
(Sammy Baugh, Davey O'Brien, Johnny Vaught) and equally
famous coaches (Matty Bell, Dutch Meyer). By the '60s, TCU
wasn't much of a threat, although it did manage to surprise Texas
now and then. In 1961, they spoiled Texas' undefeated season and
their bid for the national championship, prompting coach Darrell
Royal to compare TCU to a "bunch of cockroaches. It's not what
they eat and tote off, it's what they fall into and mess up that hurts."

By the '70s, TCU football was irrelevant. From 1966 through
1997, TCU spent years in football hell, only achieving five winning
seasons. Texas, A&M, Tech, and Baylor cut and ran to the Big 8 in
1994 to form the Big 12, leaving TCU in their dust.

Dennis Franchione won 71.4 percent of his games from 1998
through 2000, and since the hiring of Gary Patterson in 2000,
TCU's success had been explosive, dominating the Mountain West
Conference. That success, however, hasn't yet translated to the Big
12. Since joining the conference, their league record is 6–12.

When new Big 12 members TCU and West Virginia meet on
the football field, there will be a built-in rivalry. West Virginia has
never won a national championship in football, but the Mountaineers
claim 14 national championships in the sport of riflery.

Upstart TCU snatched the 2010 and 2012 NCAA rifle championships, so you can already see the makings of a bitter feud.

The Mountaineers wear old gold and blue, and their mascot dresses like Daniel Boone, in buckskin, coonskin hat, totin' a long rifle and powder keg. It's easy to see why WVU was attracted to the Big 12. They're eager to set their recruiting footprint in Texas, because as Mountaineer athletics director Oliver Luck said, "West Virginia's high schools produce fewer D-I football recruits than a Pearland High, or a Westlake." The Big 12 sends teams to the National Championship. WVU's travel budget will increase by a million dollars, and they were assessed a $5 million exit fine from the Big East, but they'll still come out ahead with the new TV deal, the SEC-Big 12 Champions Bowl, and the Big 12's greater revenue sharing package.

Texas fans were fed the story that UT wouldn't consider going to the SEC because of their schools' low academic rankings. According to *US News and World Report*'s college rankings, West Virginia's rank is 170 (Texas is number 52). That's 20 spots below Ole Miss, the lowest-ranked college in the SEC. The Mountaineers were a steady presence in the Big East, but their two-year record against Big 12 teams matches that of TCU's 6–12.

98 Nate Boyer

The "old man" bursts through the cloud of smoke into the sunshine to the cheering of 100,000 fans. At age 32, the team's designated flag bearer is a little long in the tooth to be playing college football, but "starting long snapper for the Texas Longhorns" is merely the latest incarnation of Nate Boyer.

From entitled, troubled teen to two attempts at being a college student; to Hollywood for a failed acting career, where he sometimes slept in his car, sometimes slept in the park. He became a part time "nanny" to several autistic boys until he realized that his acting gig wasn't going to work. From Hollywood, he flew 8,500 miles to volunteer in Darfur refugee camps for a month. And when he returned, in looking for his next challenge, he decided to join the U.S. Army. Not just the Army, but the Army's 18X program, the course that leads to becoming a Green Beret. Of the 150 soldiers who started the 18X, only 11 finished with a Green Beret. Nate Boyer earned his in December 2006.

While living on base in southwestern Iraq, Boyer determined that he would become a college football player; he didn't let the fact that he'd never played a down of organized football stand in his way. In his "spare time" between training the Iraqi special forces and fighting a war, Nate studied up on how to be a wide receiver. He watched tutorials on YouTube. He practiced footwork and balance and running routes. On January 7, 2010, Boyer's vision began to come into focus. As he watched Colt McCoy and the Longhorns lose the National Championship game to Alabama, he decided—he who had never played football—that he would play for the Longhorns.

He showed up at Texas' open tryouts the following winter. He tried harder, ran farther, ran faster, than the other experienced players. He showed up each day, turning himself into a kamikaze, until one day, tryouts were over and an equipment manager took Boyer to a closet and told him to pick out cleats and a jersey. He'd made the team. At what position? He didn't have a clue.

He had practiced being a wide receiver, but a teammate advised, "You're not a receiver, you're a safety." But he wasn't exactly a safety either. Former defensive backs coach Duane Akina said, "Nate Boyer had no idea how to play football." He was still all-out effort on every play and every drill. He had the coaches' admiration, but as

No Brag, Just Fact

"Maybe the reason we have the bull's-eye on our chest is that we are all—from the president of The University on down—extremely proud of Texas. We understand that we are supposed to show excellence in our lives. From the fans who never played a sport here to Earl Campbell and Ricky Williams...we're all in that same category." — Keith Moreland, defensive back in 1973–74

a walk-on—a walk-on who'd never played organized football—they all knew he'd never see the field. Being an inspirational bench-sitter wasn't enough for Nate, though. He studied the depth chart and found two seniors at long snapper who would be gone after the next season. Good enough—it was a chance.

Boyer sought advice from a couple of other long snappers, but once again he turned back to You Tube, studying the mechanics of the position. And he practiced, a minimum of 100 snaps a day. By the start of the 2012 season, Boyer was backup long snapper; by the second game of the season, Nate Boyer was the starting long snapper for The University of Texas.

Boyer brought discipline and leadership skills, honed in the Special Forces, to The University of Texas community. He is the 24th Longhorn football player to be named to the Academic All-American team, and in 2012, he received the Disney Spirit Award for being college football's most inspirational figure. A Green Beret Staff Sergeant and a Bronze Star recipient, Boyer was honored with the 2012 inaugural "Armed Services Merit Award", presented by the Football Writers Association to a veteran who used his armed forces experiences to benefit his teammates and coaches. Boyer continues his military career as a Special Forces member of the Texas National Guard. Named the 2012–13 Big 12 Sportsperson of the Year, Boyer is the recipient of the 2013 National Football Foundation Legacy Award, honoring those who have made extraordinary contributions to the NFF or who embody its mission.

99 Things Lost

Things lost when the Aggies left the Big 12:

- The annual Thanksgiving Day clash, the third-longest rivalry in D-1 football and the oldest intrastate rivalry among major college football, established 1894.
- The Hex Rally, started in 1941 when psychic Madame Hipple advised lighting red candles to break the "Kyle Field Hex." Students lit red candles all over campus the week of the game, and it worked. Texas beat number two A&M 23–0, ending the 18-year Kyle Field jinx. The Hex Rally still takes place, but without the Aggies, it's lost much of its mystique.
- The Aggie Torchlight Parade. Now held before the OU game, the parade down Guadalupe Street began in 1916 before the traditional Thanksgiving Day game against the Aggies.
- Recruiting domination in the state of Texas.
- Battle of the Brazos between Baylor and A&M, established 1895.
- The Aggie Parade down Congress Avenue: the spectacle of precision marching and the whooping of thousands of Aggies and the chance to see the Corps up close—guys in full military regalia and embarrassingly bad haircuts.
- The Aggie Supper. For at least 90 years, the Longhorn football team sequestered itself one night the week of the Aggie game to talk about what the game meant and about how to beat the Aggies. It started as a way for the seniors to share with the underclassmen the tradition of—and the urgency of—whipping A&M.

Priceless Aggie Moment
With five minutes remaining in the 1924 game, Texas threw a fourth-down pass that soared over the head of Stookie Allen, the intended receiver. Rather than intercepting the ball, the Aggie defender batted it down—right into the arms of Allen, who scored a Texas touchdown. Final score: 7–0.

The supper evolved, and in its final years, the team gathered in the swanky Centennial Room and ate a catered meal. Former players would attend and share their memories of beating the Aggies. A players-only affair, Bobby Lackey, quarterback in 1957–59 said, "It was the most tear-jerking thing I've ever seen. That was such an emotional evening—if you couldn't get ready to play football then, I don't believe anything else could get you ready to play."

- The State Farm Showdown. Yawn.
- Building on the 76–37–5 lead that Texas had over the Aggies.
- Annoying our little brother. Aggie jokes are just not as much fun now that they've left home.

100 Branding the Horns

- For the eighth straight year, The University of Texas collected more royalties than any university represented by the Collegiate Licensing Company. For the year ending June 2013, no other Big XII school was represented in the top 10. Selling stuff—clothing, video games, flip flops, bottle openers that play "The Eyes of Texas", toilet seats, photos of Earl and Coach Royal—is big business for the

Steve Patterson

The rumor had been floating around the Longhorn Nation for months: DeLoss Dodds, UT's longtime athletics director, would tender his resignation in the fall of 2013. Yet in mid-September, when an online message board reported Dodds' impending resignation, both Dodds and a UT's sports media representative vehemently denied any such plans with this statement: "Three words: Absolutely not true."

Two weeks later, there were just two words: Absolutely true. As soon as the 76-year-old Dodds announced his plans to retire at an October 1 press conference, tongues started wagging and the message boards started exploding. Suppositions were made, leaks were orchestrated, then denied, and finally, "those in the know" were certain that our next athletics director would be Oliver Luck, the athletics director at West Virginia.

Then, one week after he denied being interested in the Texas job, University of Texas president Bill Powers, along with an eight-member advisory committed, offered the job to Steve Patterson, the athletics director at Arizona State. Patterson's one of us; he earned his undergraduate and his law degrees at UT.

He's served as general manager of the NBA champion Houston Rockets, the Houston Aeros hockey team, and was president of the Portland Trail Blazers from 2003 to 2007. His tenure at Arizona State saw him serve as COO for Sun Devil Athletics, managing director of Sun Devil Sports Group, and, for just under two years, athletics director.

Patterson has enormous shoes to fill, of course, but he brings a reputation for bold decision making and for trimming fat from organizations. His business experience and marketing expertise are "musts" in dealing with The Longhorn Empire. The main goal, however, will be to restore Texas' programs to championship levels.

Horns. But what probably put us over the top were all those Longhorn stickers bought by OU fans and displayed upside down.

Thanks, Sooners. We needed the money.

- "The A+ student at bringing in football money is The University of Texas: The Longhorns expanded their football revenue from $25.6 million in 2000–2001 to $103.8

million in 2011–2012. That's a quadruple increase in one decade." So says BusinessWeek.com in its article "The Amazing Growth in College Football Revenues."

- UT's Longhorn logo was named "College Football's Best Official Logo" by Athlon Sports in August 2013. The logo has been in use since DKR promoted its use in 1961. Again, Texas was the only Big 12 school represented in the top 10. The burnt-orange silhouette of a Longhorn steer's head is famous throughout the world.

    Athlon's Matt Taliaferro said, "The Longhorn is classic, simple, unchanging, but also unique and creative. There is nothing more to say."

- *Forbes* magazine recently declared the Longhorns "College Football's Most Valuable Team," based on value to The University, value to the athletic department, value to the conference, and value to the surrounding community.

    Texas football generated a profit of $82 million for its athletic department, $20 million more than any other school in the nation.

    As uber-booster Red McCombs said, "All the money that is not up at the Vatican is at UT."

Trivia Answers:

Page 2

Texans as a species are over-the-top proud of their state's history. Davy Crockett, Stephen F. Austin, and Sam Houston are venerated for their roles in forming first a great nation, then the greatest state in the Union. We take this "hero" stuff seriously.

In 1981, Earl Campbell was enshrined by the Texas legislature as an Official State Hero, joining only Crockett, Austin, and Houston.

Page 28

Four. One to screw it in, three to talk about "how Darrell would have done it."

Page 117

One. And he caught it in the 38–3 blowout of Texas A&M.

Page 191

The Longhorns won 25 championships—19 outright—in football. The Aggies are in second place with 17.

The Horns also led the Southwest Conference in number of championships in the following sports: baseball (69), men's basketball (22; tied with Arkansas), men's cross-country (37), men's golf (39), swimming, and diving (38), outdoor track and field (45), women's basketball (10), men's tennis (20), women's golf (10), women's swimming and diving (14), women's tennis (11), women's indoor track and field (11), women's outdoor track and field (10), and volleyball (13).

Page 246

Name	W–L–T	Career %	Conference %
1. Darrell K Royal	167–47–5	.774%	.797%
2. Mack Brown	158–48	.767%	.748%
3. Fred Akers	86–31–2	.731%	.756%
4. D. X. Bible	63–31–3	.665%	.612%
5. Clyde Littlefield	44–18–6	.691%	.615%

Notes

The author gratefully acknowledges the following sources used in researching and writing this book:

2007 Oklahoma Sooners Football Guide, OU Athletics Department, 2007.

Athlon Sports. Game Day: Texas Football, Triumph Books, 2005.

Banks, Jimmy. The Darrell Royal Story, Shoal Creek Publishers, Austin, Texas, 1973.

Bible, D.X. Championship Football: A guide for Player, Coach, and Fan, Prentice-Hall Inc., New York, 1947.

Cunningham, William H. with Monty Jones. The Texas Way: Money, Power, Politics, and Ambition at The University. Tower Books/UT Press. 2013.

Forsyth, John D. "The Aggies and the Horns," Texas Monthly Press, 1981.

Frantz, Joe. "Forty Acres Follies," Texas Monthly Press, 1983.

Garner, Bryan A. Texas our Texas: Remembrances of The University, Eakin Press, 1984.

Hawthorne, Bobby. Longhorn Football: An Illustrated History, UT Press, 2007.

Jenkins, Dan. I'll Tell You One Thing, Woodford Press, 1999

Jones, Mike, edited by Dan Jenkins. Dance with Who Brung You. Texas College Football Legends Series: Darrell Royal. Epic Sports. 1997.

Little, Bill. Stadium Stories: Texas Longhorns, Globe Pequot Press, 2005.

Little, Bill, and Brown, Mack. One Heartbeat II, BrightSky Press, Albany, Texas, 2006.

Little, Bill, and McEachern, Jenna. What It Means to be a Longhorn, Triumph Books, Chicago, 2007.

McEachern, Jenna. DKR: The Royal Scrapbook. University of Texas Press. 2012.

Maher, John and Bohls, Kirk. Long Live the Longhorns! 100 Years of Texas Football, St. Martin's Press, 1993.

Maher, John. Bleeding Orange: Trouble and Triumph Deep in the Heart of Texas Football, St. Martin's Press, 1991.

Maysel, Lou. Here Come the Texas Longhorns: 1893 – 1979, Stadium Publishing Co., Ft. Worth, 1970.

Maysel, Lou. Here Come the Texas Longhorns: 1970 – 1978, Burnt Orange Publishing, 1978.

Pennington, Richard. Breaking the Ice: The Racial Integration of Southwest Conference Football, McFarland & Co., 1987.

Ramsey, Jones. Memoirs of Jones Ramsey, 1990.

Richardson, Steve. Tales from the Texas Longhorns. Sports Publishing LLC. Chicago. 2005.

Sharpe, Wilton. Longhorn Madness: Great Eras in Texas Football. Cumberland House Publishing, Nashville, 2006.

Steinmark, Freddie. I Play to Win, Little Brown & Co., 1971.

Stratton, W.K. Backyard Brawl: Inside the Blood Feud Between Texas and Texas A&M. Three Rivers Press, New York, 2002.

Switzer, Barry. Bootleggers Boy, W. Morrow Publisher, 1990.

Taliaferro, Tim. "The War for the Trees," The Alcalde. January/February 2008, p. 44. Texas Monthly Custom Publishing.

Texas Ranger, The. Volume 69, No. 1. September 1956, p. 20. Texas Student Publications, Inc. University of Texas.

Mark Wangrin. Horns! A History, Simon & Schuster, 2006.

Digital Media:

Austin American-Statesman.com Online Archives. "The Longhorn Economy, Part I," by Eric Dexheimer. September 30, 2007.

Austin American-Statesman.com Online Archives. "'Peyton Jr.' to Take a Shot at Being this UT's Manning" by Mark Wangrin. September 15, 1998.

Austin Past and Present, an Interactive Digital History. Karen Kocher, producer. Waterloo Press. Copyright Karen Koche r 2001-2006.

www.alcalde.texasexes.org/2012/05/frank-denius-the-knight-in-burnt-orange-armor/ "Frank Denius: the Knight in Burnt-Orange Armor". by Joseph Washington. May 31, 2012.

www.athlonsports.com/college-football/college-footballs-best-and-worst-logos-2013. "College Football's Best and Worst Logos for 2013. by Braden Gall. August 5, 2013.

www.attcottonbowl.com/hall_of_fame. 2008, 2009 AT&T Cotton Bowl Classic.

www.bleacherreport.com/articles/1863840-texas-football-win-or-lose-longhorn-football-reigns-over-the-state-of-texas. "Texas Football: Win or Lose, Longhorn Football Reigns…" by Taylor Gaspar. November 26, 2013.

http://books.google.com/books?id=8Py0twYbZZ0C&pg=PA123&lpg=PA123&dqthe =integr ation+of+univ+of+texas+track+and+field&source. "Integrating the 40 Acres: The Fifty-Year Struggle for Racial Equality at the University of Texas." by Dwonna Goldstone.

www.businessweek.com/articles/2013-09-26/the-amazing-growth-in-college-football-revenues?campaign_id=yhoo. "The Amazing Growth…" Eric Chemi. September 26, 2013.

www.blogs.dallasobserver.com/unfairpark/2012/05/mayor_mike_texas-ou_rivalry_on.php." Texas-OU is Staying at the Cotton Bowl". *Dallas Observer.* by Eric Nicholson. May 11, 2012.

www.espn.go.com/blog/ncfnation/post/_/id/93072/the-10-most-memorable-bcs-moments

www.espn.go.com/college-football/story/_/id/9560094/texas-longhorns-again-top-merchandise-sales-list. "Texas Leads in Merchandise" by Darren Rovell.August 12, 2013.

www.forbes.com/pictures/elfl45fflj/college-footballs-most-valuable-teams/"College Football's Most Valuable Teams" by Chris Smith. December 18, 2013.

www.houstoninformer.com/"No Gaines Fiasco" for Texas Negroes. June 10, 1950.

www.lhab.org. "Mr. D." by Scott Harmon. The Blast. Volume 41, No. 2. Summer 2005.

www.lhb.music.utexas.edu. Longhorn Band "The Showband of the Southwest" History. Copyright 2008 Longhorn Band.

www.mackbrown-texasfootball.com. History, Archives.

www.ncaa.org. Official NCAA Football Records Book. National Collegiate Athletic Association. Indianapolis. 2007.

http://scholar.lib.vt.edu. "Family of Missing Texas Impostor Concerned.*" The Virginian-Pilot.* January 1, 1996. Landmark Communications. 1996.

Texas A&M Athletics online. "Bill Byrne's Wednesday Weekly". August 31, 2011.

www.texasalmanac.com/history/highlights/swc/. "A Look Back at the Southwest Conference." Sam Blair. Texas Almanac. 1998-1999.

www.tshaonline.org/handbook/online. Texas State Historical Association w/ Holt, Rinehart Winston. Updated December, 2007.

www.usatoday.com/story/sports/college/2013/05/07/ncaa-finances-subsidies/2142443/. "Most Division-I Athletic Departments…" by Steve Berkowitz, Jody Upton, Eric Brady. July 1, 2013.

www.utexas.edu/features/2008/chase/

www.utexas.edu/tuition/. 2007 Tuition Policy Advisory Committee Recommendations: Public Forums.